A FAMILY OF KINGS

Also by Theo Aronson

ROYAL VENDETTA

The Crown of Spain 1829–1965

THE GOLDEN BEES

The Story of the Bonapartes

THE COBURGS OF BELGIUM

THE FALL OF THE THIRD NAPOLEON

THE KAISERS

QUEEN VICTORIA AND THE BONAPARTES

GRANDMAMA OF EUROPE

The Crowned Descendants of Queen Victoria

A FAMILY OF KINGS
THE DESCENDANTS OF CHRISTIAN IX OF DENMARK

THEO ARONSON

THISTLE
PUBLISHING

This edition published in 2014 by:

Thistle Publishing
36 Great Smith Street
London
SW1P 3BU

www.thistlepublishing.co.uk

ISBN 13: 978-1-910198-12-4

For
André Bothner

CONTENTS

ILLUSTRATIONS

Between pages 179 *and* 198

Author's Note

This book is not a biography of King Christian IX of Denmark. It is an account of the extraordinary aggrandizement of his house; of its rise from relative obscurity to a position of international importance. Rather than with the King himself, this study deals with those of his children, and grandchildren, who became crowned heads in Europe.

To encompass so large a subject, however, I have found it necessary to set myself certain limits. In the first place, I have confined the study to the period of the dynasty's most spectacular flowering: the half-century before the First World War. After this, the link between the patriarch and his crowned descendants is too tenuous; these various kings and queens could no longer be regarded as Danish royals. Secondly, I have not attempted to write a full-scale biography of each character. At the risk of playing down certain aspects of their lives, I have emphasized their relationships to each other. I have treated them as members of a clan, of the Danish royal family, rather than as monarchs or consorts in their respective countries.

They are dealt with as descendants of King Christian IX first and as sovereigns second. And finally, what I have written is a domestic, rather than a political, study. The focus is on the various courts, not the countries, into which the King's family spread. This is a book about people, not politics; it is biography rather than history.

I have received a great deal of assistance during the writing of this book. My chief thanks are to Det Kongelige Bibliotek, Copenhagen; for this help, I am grateful to Mr Johan Hvidfeldt, Miss Birgitte Hvidt and Mr Erik Ulmer. I must thank also the Danish Ministry of Foreign Affairs in Copenhagen; the British Museum, London; and the Library of Congress, Washington. I am particularly grateful to Miss Myra Conradie who, as always, provided me with a splendid genealogical table (which, unfortunately, I have been obliged to condense) and who lent me a number of books. For information, material, advice and help I am indebted to Miss A. T. Hadley, Mrs E. Nel, Mrs Edna Fitzgerald, Mrs van der Hoven, Mrs Katherine Drake, Mr P. Skovgaard Andersen and Mr Lars Jensen, I am grateful to those many people who have gone out of their way to help me on my various visits to Denmark.

My heartfelt thanks, as always, to Mr Brian Roberts, without whose expert advice and constant encouragement this book would not have been written.

Works which have been of great assistance are *The Letters of Tsar Nicholas and Empress Marie*, edited by E. J. Bing (Ivor Nicholson and Watson, 1937), and *My Fifty Years* by Prince Nicholas of Greece (Hutchinson, 1926). Four recently published books which have proved especially useful and to whose authors I am deeply indebted are *Queen Alexandra* by Georgina Battiscombe (Constable, 1969), *Nicholas and Alexandra* by Robert K. Massie (Gollancz, 1968), *The Last Grand Duchess* by Ian Vorres (Hutchinson, 1964, and by permission of Collins-Knowlton-Wing, New York), and *Haakon, King of Norway* by Maurice Michael (George Allen and Unwin, 1958).

I must also acknowledge the gracious permission of Queen Elizabeth II to republish passages from various printed sources of which the copyright in the original text belongs to Her Majesty.

PROLOGUE
EUROPE'S FATHER-IN-LAW

1

For five days in the spring of 1892, the little city of Copenhagen was *en fête*. The Danish sovereigns, King Christian IX and Queen Louise, were celebrating their Golden Wedding.

From 25 to 29 May, the charming but normally tranquil Danish capital was transformed. Bells pealed, flags fluttered, tapestries billowed, great swags of greenery swayed above the narrow streets. Even the sun came out to set the city's waterways a-sparkle. In the Old Market Square, gilded balls, representing golden apples, bobbed and flashed in the waters of the fountain. The avenue leading from the Amalienborg Palace was said to be 'a vista of garlanded arches'; a gratified firm announced that it had supplied the city with countless tons of greenery. In the Höjbro Plads, looking incongruous amongst the unpretentious houses, rose a triumphal arch—elaborately pillared, massively domed, fulsomely inscribed and hideously festooned. All day, and all night, the crowds surged through the streets. There was so much to see: royal processions, military parades, thumping bands, massed choirs and, not least of all, the wonder of decorations in electric light. Never, in living memory, had the Danish capital presented so animated, so colourful and so splendid a sight.

The celebrations on the day itself—Thursday 26 May—began with the singing of an ode of congratulation by a thousand choristers massed outside the Amalienborg Palace. Onto the balcony in answer to this lustily rendered tribute, came the King and Queen. At seventy-four, King Christian IX was a slender, stiff-backed and luxuriantly bewhiskered figure; the seventy-five-year-old Queen Louise was smaller, frailer but still remarkably pretty. When the great surge of sound from the square below had ended, the King lifted up his baby great-grandson for them all to see. At this typically spontaneous gesture on the part of their old King, the crowd roared with delight.

Later that morning, the royal couple drove in state to a thanksgiving service in the Castle Church. Under that flamboyant arch in the Höjbro Plads their carriage halted and the Burgomaster of Copenhagen read out an address of congratulation. To the Burgomaster's effusions, the King replied, in his simple fashion, that he always regarded the people of Copenhagen as his 'brothers and children'.

The scene in the Castle Church was said to be magnificent: the spring sunlight, slanting through the tall windows, heightened the kaleidoscopic colours of the uniforms, the glitter of arms and the sheen of dresses. The service lasted for an hour. Back at the palace, the royal couple received deputations from the two Houses of the Danish Parliament and that night, having attended a banquet 'of brilliant character', given by their eldest son, Crown Prince Frederick, they went on to a gala performance at the theatre. Not until almost midnight did they drive back, through the tumultuous, dazzlingly lit streets, to their palace.

Their Golden Wedding had been, in the words of one of their many grandsons, 'the celebration of a great day which was to be the crowning event in their richly blessed lives'.

This was not mere rhetoric. The lives of King Christian IX and Queen Louise had indeed been richly blessed. Denmark might be small, poor, unsophisticated and unimportant, but her sovereign enjoyed a position of considerable eminence: his standing in Europe was out of all proportion to that of his country. King Christian IX ranked amongst the Continent's most respected sovereigns.

None of this, it must be admitted, was due to the exercise, or even the existence, of any exceptional qualities on the part of the King. Born an obscure and impoverished princeling, with nothing remarkable about him but his name—Prince Christian of Schleswig-Holstein-Sonderburg-Glücksburg—he had inherited the throne through two fortunate circumstances: the reigning house had run out of direct heirs, and his wife—Princess Louise of Hesse-Cassel—was even closer to the throne than he. Thus when, in 1852, the Great Powers of Europe had to decide on a male heir to the Danish throne, it was he whom they chose.

This elevation had made precious little difference to Prince Christian's way of life. He had lived on a scale hardly better than that of any other army officer. Neither he nor Princess Louise had had a personal fortune; the couple had been forced to manage on little more than his army pay. Their home, grandiloquently named the Yellow Palace, had been no more than a large town house; Bernsdorff, their country place, had been merely lent to them by the King. The result was that their six children—Frederick, Alexandra, William, Dagmar, Thyra and Waldemar— had been raised in the utmost simplicity. The parents had taken a hand in their education, the family had devised their own amusements, the girls had been obliged to make their own clothes. Of luxury, they had known nothing. They might have been royal but their home life had been that of any ordinary Danish bourgeois family. And, as in such families, this home life had been all-important.

Christian had ascended the throne in 1863, at the age of forty-five. Whatever change this accession might have brought to his family's status, it had wrought none in him. King Christian IX remained what he had always been—an upright, conscientious and unaffected man but sadly lacking in flair, intellect or astuteness. He had, pronounced a French minister in Copenhagen, 'but a mediocre intelligence'.

How, then, had this unimportant and unremarkable monarch come to occupy so significant a place on the European scene? Simply by virtue of that age-old formula for dynastic aggrandizement—the judicious marriages of his attractive descendants. Bismarck, who used to refer to Coburg as 'the stud farm of Europe' could just as well have applied his epithet to Denmark. For, as the Coburgs had climbed to power a generation before, so, in the second half of the nineteenth century, did the family of King Christian IX begin its hardly less spectacular expansion.

By 1892, the year in which King Christian and Queen Louise celebrated their Golden Wedding, their descendants were spread throughout the major courts of Europe; in the years ahead they would occupy, or have occupied, no less than nine European thrones—the British, the Russian, the Greek, the Norwegian, the Belgian, the Romanian, the Yugoslav, the Spanish and, of course, the Danish. One of the King's daughters became the Queen of England; another the Empress of Russia; a third married the *de jure* King of Hanover. His eldest son inherited his own throne; his second son became King of the Hellenes; his third son refused the offer of the crown of Bulgaria. One of his grandsons became the King of Norway; one of his great-grandsons became the King of Romania. One great-grand-daughter became Queen of the Belgians, another the Queen of Yugoslavia. A third great-grand-daughter is married to the Prince who has been chosen as the future King of Spain.

The dynasty's rise had been little short of phenomenal. From what were relatively the humblest of beginnings, King Christian IX's family had burgeoned into one of the most notable in Europe. Grander, more powerful and longer established dynasties stood amazed at this flowering of the Danish King's house. Only the family of Queen Victoria—who was, after all, ruler of the mightiest nation on earth—was more widely and influentially spread. Indeed, between them, Queen Victoria and King Christian IX supplied Europe with the majority of its reigning sovereigns. If Queen Victoria was the Grandmother of Europe, then King Christian IX was certainly its Grandfather or, as he was known in his day, its Father-in-law.

2

Yet, for all its splendid ramifications, King Christian IX's family remained remarkably unpretentious. In a way, it had never outgrown those lean years in the Yellow Palace. The Danish royal family, claimed Queen Victoria, 'are wonderfully united—and never breathe a word against each other, and the daughters remain as unspoilt and as completely Children of the Home as when they were unmarried'. And not only did the daughters remain loyal and unspoilt; the sons were hardly less so. Of all the royal families of Europe, none was as unaffected, as cheerful, as easily amused, as high-spirited, as affectionate, as clannish and, it must be admitted, as devoid of cultural or intellectual interests, as the Danish.

The tone was set by the old King. In no way had the brilliant marriages of his children gone to his head. The Danish monarch might have the looks of a *grand seigneur*—he was tall, slim, erect, courtly—but his manner remained modest, kindly and unaffected. He was undemanding in his tastes, abstemious in his habits and unquestioningly religious. Above all, he was a loving patriarch, devoted to his family.

So unimpressed was he by the heights to which his children had risen in the world that he could never even appreciate that they had grown up. His son, the middle-aged King of the Hellenes, would be forced to stand silent while his father reproached him for ordering horses for a drive without first asking permission; his daughter, the future Queen of England, married for over thirty years, would be lectured on how best to handle a husband. That his grandsons would one day be reigning kings and emperors dazzled King Christian not at all. To them, he was known as Apapa: an approachable old gentleman from whom they could wheedle almost any favour and whose sense of humour was hardly different from their own. He would join in their sky-larking and, even in his seventies, race them along the garden paths of his country palaces.

His court was run on the simplest lines. The Danish monarch had neither the taste, the talent nor the money for a show of royal splendour. Nor, in democratically-minded Denmark, where a king was not so far removed from a commoner, would any such show have been appreciated. The Danes were happy enough to have a king provided he remained a citizen king, and Christian IX was certainly that. The occasional state entertaining which took place in the Amalienborg Palace in Copenhagen was on the most modest scale; the atmosphere might be somewhat stiff (the King had old-fashioned manners) but the tone was homely, unsophisticated, provincial.

Queen Louise was no less natural. She did not even have the benefit of her husband's impressive looks, for she was delicately built. She walked with a slight stoop and, by her seventies, often used a wheel-chair. On her grey hair, she always wore a lace cap. Her 'gentle expression,' says one of her grandsons, 'was one of irresistible charm.'

Yet her appearance was deceptive. Queen Louise was made of altogether more forceful stuff than her husband. Although Queen Victoria's opinion that she was 'false, intriguing and not wise', was somewhat too harsh, it was true that Queen Louise was livelier, sharper, more dogmatic than her husband.

Born a member of the wide-ranging Hesse-Cassel family, Queen Louise had influential connections. During the course of a lifetime's visits to the Hesse-Cassel family centre—Schloss Rumpenheim near

Frankfurt—she had kept her ears and eyes open: she was never one for letting slip the opportunity of making use of a well-placed relation or of building up a valuable friendship. If King Christian was in no way responsible for his family's aggrandizement, the same could not be said of Queen Louise. She could not, perhaps, do much, but she did what she could. While her husband ruled Denmark, she ruled the dynasty.

Yet theirs was a happy marriage. Their personalities were complementary and Louise shared her husband's taste for simplicity. No less than he, she was devoted to their family. Queen Louise might have been a little more severe with her children and grandchildren, but she was no less fond of them. And they, in turn, adored her.

'Apapa and Amama were the centre of everything,' wrote their grandson, Prince Nicholas of Greece. 'It was around them that the whole family gathered with love, respect and devotion.'

And gather they certainly did. Nothing gave the members of the Danish royal family more pleasure than those vast reunions which took place, every summer, in one of King Christian's country palaces. Not for the world would the King's sons, daughters or grandchildren have missed these jamborees; 'the entire family of uncles, aunts, cousins and other various relations used to gather there, and at least half a dozen nationalities were represented,' remembers one member of the family. These reunions, claims another, were like being in 'seventh heaven'. Drawn from such distant, and different, places as Athens, London and St Petersburg, these emperors and empresses, kings and queens, princes and princesses, would flock back to lead that homespun family life they all adored.

And this happy Danish household, with its modest beginnings, was to leave its mark throughout the courts of nineteenth and twentieth-century Europe. For not only did the sons and daughters of King Christian IX remain, as Queen Victoria put it, 'Children of the Home', but they carried away from that home—and into other royal families—many of its more admirable characteristics. To often stolid and joyless courts they brought their good looks, their good manners, their simplicity, their frankness, their ease, their unpretentiousness, their lightness of touch, their sense of the ridiculous, their democratic outlook and their strong sense of family. Some of them might have been, at times, artless to the point of childishness, but they were never unkind, never ungenerous, never underhand. That the home lives of so many European royal families were, at certain stages, to be so notable for their cheerfulness, harmony and lack of pomposity, was due to this Danish influence; to the characteristics of the family of Europe's Father-in-law

PART ONE
SPRING

CHAPTER ONE

1

The first step towards the dynasty's aggrandizement had been taken on 10 March 1863. On that date Princess Alexandra, the eldest daughter of Prince Christian (he was not to become King of Denmark until later the same year) married the heir to the British throne.

The most labyrinthine of paths had led to the attainment of this glittering prize. The course of this particular love—whether true or not—had run anything but smooth. On one score only, it appears, had Princess Alexandra been considered eligible: that of her personal attractions. These, fortunately, were considerable.

Born in 1844, the second of Prince Christian's six children, Princess Alexandra (or Alix as she was invariably called) was sixteen at the time that her name was first bandied about as a possible bride for Queen Victoria's eldest son—Albert Edward, Prince of Wales. Even at sixteen, Alix was a beauty: slender, creamy-complexioned, brown-haired, blue-eyed. Her bearing was relaxed and graceful; her manner natural and charming. Despite the fact that her parents had very little money or perhaps because of it, she dressed with a quiet elegance. No more than any of the members of that extrovert family did she have any intellectual or artistic tastes but then, for the particular position for which she was being considered, this hardly mattered. The Prince of Wales—Bertie— was certainly no intellectual or cultural giant.

With these personal attributes, however, Alix's suitability ended. Both Queen Victoria and the Prince Consort were determined that their son should not marry Prince Christian's daughter. There were several reasons for this. The Queen was convinced that 'the German element' was the one to be 'cherished and kept up' in the British royal family; what they were looking for was a German princess. Backing up this preference was the fact that relations between Denmark and the German Confederation— led by Prussia—were severely strained. The quarrel concerned the duchies of Schleswig and Holstein, hitherto ruled by the kings of Denmark. Were Queen Victoria to sanction a marriage between her heir and a Danish princess, she would appear to be siding with Denmark against Prussia—the very last impression she wanted to create.

There were more personal objections as well. To the Queen, the Danish royal family was anathema; 'it would be *too* horrid,' she exclaimed, 'if [Bertie] should become one of *that* family.' It was not that she minded Alix's immediate family circle. What she objected to was the reigning King Frederick VII of Denmark (then in the last years of his dissolute life) and, even more strongly, the relations of Alix's mother, Princess—later Queen—Louise. The very thought of Princess Louise's frivolous, gossiping, mischief-making, anti-Prussian Hesse-Cassel relatives was enough to send shivers down the earnest spines of the Queen and the Prince Consort.

This was all very well but with a Danish princess ruled out, who else was there? No one, it seemed. Or at least, no one with the right qualifications. For what the idle, feckless and irresolute Prince of Wales needed—or rather, what his parents decided he needed—was a princess with 'good looks, health, education, character, intellect, and a good disposition'. But where was such a paragon to be found? Certainly not in the *Almanach de Gotha*, sighed Bertie's elder sister Vicky, Crown Princess of Prussia, to whom the Queen had entrusted the finding of a suitable bride. And even if she were to be uncovered, would the young man accept the choice? Possibly not. Queen Victoria knew what she was doing when she put 'good looks' at the head of her list of necessary qualities, for although Bertie would happily have dispensed with education, character and intellect in a bride, he would never have settled for plainness. Cleverness, 'without some attractions to capture him', agreed Vicky, would be no use at all. Irresolute in some things, Bertie could be surprisingly stubborn in others.

And so, try as they might to avoid it, that serious-minded triumvirate—Victoria, Albert and their daughter Vicky—were drawn back to Prince Christian's beautiful daughter Alix. 'Princess Alexandra is indeed lovely,' sighed the Queen on seeing her photograph for the first time, 'what a pity she is who she is!'

And if, in a photograph, Alix's looks were impressive, in the flesh they were almost overwhelming. The Prussian Crown Princess arranged to meet her at Strelitz and was enchanted. The Queen was subjected to a positive bombardment of adjectives from her enraptured daughter: Alix was lovely, graceful, bewitching, ladylike, aristocratic, simple, natural, unaffected. In the face of this broadside, the Queen's reservations were carried away. The jewel must be secured for the British crown at all costs. Already other suitors were putting out feelers.

In September 1861, the nineteen-year-old Bertie was packed off to the Rhineland where his sister Vicky was to arrange a 'chance' meeting with Princess Alix.

And Alix herself? As yet, she knew nothing of these involved negotiations. Her parents, and more particularly her sharp-witted mother, were all agog at the prospect but they had kept her in complete ignorance. It was thus all unknowing that one day, while on holiday in the Rhineland, Alix accompanied her parents on a visit to Speyer Cathedral. There, as if by chance, they came face to face with the Crown Prince and Princess of Prussia, who 'happened' to have with them the Prince of Wales. In the cool half-light of the Cathedral, the little group of royals stood chatting in hushed voices. While Vicky was being impressed by Prince Christian's gentlemanly bearing and Princess Louise's quick apprehension (she might almost 'hear the grass grow'), Bertie was warming to Alix's good looks and charming manners. There was nothing, it now seemed, to stand in the way of taking the business a step further.

But there was. Bertie, although well enough pleased with Alix, was revealing a strange reluctance to get married. His hesitancy astonished his family. The Prince Consort tried to overcome it by treating the boy to one of his wordy memoranda; Queen Victoria put it down to her son's inability to show enthusiasm for anything; the Crown Princess decided that if the lovely Alexandra (who would have made 'most men fire and flames') was incapable of kindling even one flame in Bertie, no one would succeed in doing so.

Yet someone already had; that was the trouble. During the summer of 1861, while the Prince of Wales had been doing a spell of military training at the Curragh camp near Dublin, he had been introduced to, slept with, and embarked on a liaison with an actress named Nelly Clifden.

The news of this escapade horrified the priggish Prince Consort. He took this far-from-uncommon incident very seriously indeed. Was Bertie about to tread the profligate path of Queen Victoria's notorious uncles? 'You *must* not, you *dare* not be lost,' he wrote in anguish to his son. The only way to avoid this, he reckoned, was an early marriage: plans for the engagement to Princess Alix of Denmark must go ahead.

The Prince Consort, though, would not be the one to forward them. Late that November he travelled to see Bertie at Cambridge in order to discuss more fully the matter of his moral lapse. He returned to Windsor feeling ill and tired. The Prince had contracted typhoid fever and a mere three weeks after his visit to his errant son, he died—on 14 December 1861.

That Bertie's 'fall' had caused her husband's death, the grief-demented Queen Victoria had no doubt. So strong was this conviction that she could not even bear to look at her son. Her antipathy towards him was such, she cried out, that 'I feel daily, hourly, something which is too dreadful to describe'. Would it not be fairer, she now began wondering, to warn Princess Alix's parents about Bertie's true character; to tell Princess Louise about his lapse?

Princess Louise already knew. But to that more worldly woman, the idea of a prince losing his virginity before marriage could have been neither shocking nor novel. It might almost have been more disturbing if he had not lost it. No, the thought of a breach between Queen Victoria and her son was far more alarming than the escapade that had caused it. The Queen's dislike of her son might well extend to his future wife as well.

Whether or not that future wife knew anything about the affair is uncertain. In any case, Alix would probably not have been unduly shocked. Her own father and mother might have led virtuous lives but the same could not be said of her various relations. The twice-divorced Danish King Frederick VII had lived openly with his mistress for years; Princess Louise's Hesse-Cassel relations were reputed to be highly immoral. Like so many women of her day, Alix probably accepted that there was one code of behaviour for men and another for women.

Her reactions towards the proposed marriage are difficult to uncover. 'In those days,' as one British princess was to say, 'girls were kept in ignorance of the marriage plots of their parents.' If, by this stage, Alix was not exactly in ignorance of the plot, it is unlikely that she was kept *au fait* with its various ramifications. In any case, she was no doubt ready enough to fall in with her parents' plans; for a poor and unimportant princess such as she, the prospect of one day becoming the Queen of England must have been heady indeed.

For that the marriage would still take place there was no question. On this Queen Victoria was determined. In death, no less than in life, her husband's wishes were sacrosanct; and Albert had wished for the marriage. The next thing to be done was for the Queen to see Alix for herself. Victoria arranged to spend a few days with her Uncle Leopold, King of the Belgians, at his palace of Laeken, near Brussels. To

Laeken, therefore, were summoned Prince Christian, Princess Louise and Princess Alexandra.

Although Queen Victoria was no more impressed by the parents than she had ever been, she was completely won over by the daughter. For her first meeting with the widowed Queen, Alix had the tact to wear a simple black dress and no jewellery. Her usual vivacity was tempered by a slight shyness in the presence of the intimidating Queen. Victoria was enchanted. 'Alexandra,' she afterwards enthused, 'is lovely, such a beautiful refined profile and quiet ladylike manner.' And during the next few months, Victoria's appreciative comments on Alix's beauty, sweetness and naturalness poured forth in a steady stream.

More penetrating, however, on this question of Alix's qualities, were the remarks of those two dissimilar men—the astute King Leopold of the Belgians and the artless Prince Christian. 'There is something frank and cheerful in Alix's character,' wrote King Leopold, 'which will greatly assist her to take things without being too much overpowered or alarmed by them.' Prince Christian's summing up was even more matter-of-fact. His daughter, he assured Queen Victoria, was 'a good child, not brilliant, but with a will of her own'.

That, precisely, was what the Queen was looking for.

Satisfied that Alix was the right choice, the Queen journeyed on to Coburg to visit the scenes of the late Prince Consort's youth, leaving Bertie to do the actual proposing. This he did, on 9 September 1862. While the royal party were strolling through the gardens at Laeken, King Leopold saw to it that the young people were allowed to fall back behind the others. Bertie said his piece and Alix accepted. That the two young people were well enough pleased about their engagement, one must assume; that Prince Christian was delighted, there is no doubt. 'I don't think I ever saw anybody so much pleased as he was,' reported the Prince of Wales to his mother.

By no means, however, were things plain sailing from now on. As the affair between Bertie and Alix matured, so were relations between Denmark and the German Confederation, on the Schleswig-Holstein question, deteriorating. More than ever was the pro-German Queen Victoria determined that the coming marriage should not take on the appearance of an Anglo-Danish *entente*. Thus when Prince Christian, on the Queen's instructions, brought his daughter to Osborne for yet another inspection, Victoria insisted that he return home immediately, leaving Alix with her. She even made him put up at an hotel in London rather than spend one night under her roof.

Nor would the Queen allow Bertie to visit Copenhagen. For this, the Queen's reasons were as much personal as political. Given what she now called Bertie's 'weak' character, his association with Princess Louise's dissolute relations could lead to Heaven knew what licentiousness.

This same combination of reasons ensured that Princess Alexandra's immediate family circle only was invited to the wedding, set for 10 March 1863. Not for the world would the Queen have asked the disreputable Danish King, Frederick VII. And, having cut down on the Princess's relations, Queen Victoria decided to exclude a few of her own as well: several of her German connections were denied invitations.

Further ill-feeling was caused by her decision that the ceremony be held in St George's Chapel at Windsor and not in some place more easily accessible to the general public. In addition, she decreed that the court would remain in mourning for the Prince Consort, with the members of the royal family being permitted to wear only white, lilac or grey, while the Queen herself would keep to black. Instead of taking part in the ceremony, she would merely watch it from a gallery overlooking the altar.

By none of these restrictions, however, was the brilliance of the occasion substantially dimmed. The bride, hailed in Tennyson's *A Welcome to Alexandra* as the 'Sea-King's daughter from over the sea', had already been given the most vociferous welcome by the British public; the guests at the wedding were no less enthusiastic. The ceremony was all very spectacular: the richly-robed clergy, the blazing jewels, the gleaming satins, the glinting orders, the scarlet of the Beefeaters, the

gold of the trumpeters, the rose-garlanded crino-
lines of the bridesmaids, the bridegroom in Garter
robes and gold collar over general's uniform, and
finally the bride in silver tissue, lavishly trimmed
with lace and garlanded with orange blossom.

To the members of Alexandra's family, so unac-
customed to pageantry on this scale, it must all have
seemed overwhelming: a dream come true, a fairy-
tale come to life.

In Prince Christian of Denmark, standing
there so tall and straight in his uniform, it must
have aroused a tremendous sense of achievement.
With this marriage of his daughter to the heir to
the British throne, his family (it was not yet a reigning dynasty) had been linked to the foremost royal
house in Europe. Yet he could hardly claim that
the *coup* had been of his making; nor was his more
resourceful wife responsible for it. Indeed, there was
almost nothing that they could have done towards
achieving the alliance. If Queen Victoria—and still
more, the Prince Consort—had not favoured it, the
match would have come to nothing. This dynastic
triumph had been the result of the simplest equa-
tion: a good-looking and gracefully-mannered
bride had been needed for the Prince of Wales,
and Prince Christian had happened to be the father
of the most beautiful and charming princess in
Europe. Greatness was being thrust upon the royal
house of Denmark.

2

The second dynastic achievement followed close on the heels of the first. On 30 March 1863, three weeks after Princess Alexandra's marriage, Prince Christian's second son, William, was proclaimed King of the Hellenes.

Until the previous year, and since the establishment of a monarchy in Greece after the War of Independence in 1830, Greece had been ruled by King Otho I, a Bavarian. King Otho had been a well-meaning monarch, but something more than good intentions had been necessary to handle so turbulent, touchy and mercurial a people as the newly independent Greeks. One revolution forced Otho into granting the country a constitution; a second, in 1862, forced him to flee the country.

To fill the now vacant Greek throne was going to be no easy task: not every prince was prepared to face the caprices of Greek politics. This reluctance in no way inhibited the provisional Greek government from staging a plebiscite in which Queen Victoria's second son, Prince Alfred, Duke of Edinburgh, was elected King of the Hellenes by a massive majority. The glad news was proclaimed throughout the country, warships fired 101-gun salutes across the sparkling waters of Piraeus, and Athens was joyously illuminated.

No one, however, had thought of consulting Prince Alfred on the matter. When they did, the

British government politely explained that it would not do: according to an earlier international agreement, which had apparently been overlooked by the ebullient Greeks, no member of the British royal family was eligible for the Greek throne. Prince Alfred could not, therefore, accept their kind invitation.

This was not to say that Britain was not interested in the Greek throne. On the contrary, she was deeply interested. As one of the 'guaranteeing' powers of the Greek state (the others were France and Russia) she was only too anxious to increase her influence in the Aegean. Prince Alfred might not be eligible but she had plenty of other candidates up her sleeve. There was always a Coburg to spare on these occasions or, if he proved unwilling (and this particular one did) might some other German princeling not do? France and Russia, of course, were no less anxious to supply the need; if anything, their list of candidates was even more impressive. The conflict was cleared up only after the French Emperor, Napoleon III (who was always anxious to keep on the right side of Britain) decided to support a British candidate.

That the Greeks would accept a British choice there was little doubt. Prince Alfred's election had been due, not so much to his personal attributes (which were, quite frankly, unremarkable) but to the fact that the British candidate might bring with him the gift of the Ionian Islands, at present occupied by Britain. For these, Greece was more than ready to fall in with Britain's wishes. And these wishes, by now, that the seventeen-year-old Prince William of Denmark become the new Greek King.

Exactly how this unlikely-seeming lad came to be chosen is uncertain. That scurrilous nineteenth-century gossip, William Osgood Field, claimed that it was because the good-looking youngster had 'taken the fancy' of the Parisian hostess Esther Guimon. She commended his candidature to one of the Emperor Napoleon III's ministers who, in turn, commended him to the Emperor.

Princess Alexandra used to tell a different story. One night Prince William, who had stayed on in London after his sister's marriage, was asked by Lord Palmerston and Lord John Russell if he would like to be the King of Greece. The youth, realizing that being a king would mean an end to dreaded examinations, laughingly replied that he would like nothing better. With that, he had been chosen as the official British candidate and the news telegraphed to Athens.

But however William came to be selected, the choice delighted the Greeks. His sister's marriage to the Prince of Wales had enhanced his family's status; this connection, they fondly imagined, would ensure Greece British protection. On 30 March 1863, amidst scenes of great enthusiasm, the Greek National Assembly proclaimed Prince William as George I, King of the Hellenes. Once again, and with more justification this time, the nation rejoiced, the guns roared and the capital was illuminated. A delegation set out at once for Copenhagen to make a formal offer of the crown.

Few could have been more surprised by the turn of events than the new King himself. Only just seventeen, Prince William—or Willie as his family called him—was still a naval cadet: a handsome, smiling, unaffected youngster with his full share of the family ebullience. Until now, it is doubtful that he had ever given Greece, let alone the vacant Greek throne, much thought. His interests were centred on his life at the Naval Academy and on his family. One would not even have described his behaviour as particularly regal; on the contrary, he was noted for his irrepressible spirits. On the Danish royal family's arrival in England for Princess Alexandra's wedding, a grinning Willie was seen to be dodging the blows rained on him with the scroll of welcome which Alexandra—with suitable gravity—had only just accepted from the hands of the mayor of Margate.

And on the very day of his election as King, Willie was involved in one of those practical jokes for which he—and all the rest of his family—had such a weakness. It appears that during the previous morning he had slipped out of his class at the Naval Academy to nail his old professor's galoshes to the floor. The lesson over, the professor had eased his feet into the galoshes and, on trying to step forward, had fallen flat on his face. Furious, the professor had complained to the Commander of the Academy, who was no less furious. The following morning, in full uniform, the irate Commander called on the boy's father, Prince Christian, to make a complaint.

While he was in an ante-room, Prince William appeared.

'I suppose you have come to congratulate me, Captain?' he asked with assumed innocence.

'Congratulate?' spluttered the Commander, launching into a stream of invective.

'Oh, I beg your pardon,' said the wide-eyed Willie. 'You may not have heard that I have been elected King of Greece.'

The Commander had not, and it was with very little difficulty that the youngster was able to convert his call of complaint to one of congratulation.

Later, Willie would protest that he himself had learnt about his election only on the day of its announcement. 'No one had told me a word about it,' would be his unblushing claim; he had read the announcement in the newspaper wrapped around his day's sardine sandwiches.

But for all this, Willie was more than just an amiable buffoon. Like his sister Alexandra he had, in the words of King Leopold, 'something frank and cheerful' in his make-up, which would prevent him from becoming too depressed or alarmed by the difficulties which doubtless lay ahead. That easy, unpretentious, democratic manner and that sunny nature were exactly what was needed in Greece; some stiff-backed, tight-lipped autocrat would not have done at all. The very straight-forwardness of Willie's character was to prove invaluable against the changability of some of the Greek politicians.

If Willie was happy about accepting the Greek throne, his father was not. Prince Christian considered the Greeks too volatile by half; he would refer to the Greek crown as a 'crown of thorns'. Then Willie was so absurdly young, utterly without experience. By nature unambitious and unadventurous, Christian had been thrown into an agony of indecision by his son's election. He kept asking for more time to consider it. Even his wife, the more dynamic Princess Louise, did not favour the proposal. She wrote to Queen Victoria in the hope that the English Queen might scotch the plan; she appealed to her daughter Alix to influence Palmerston and Russell against it.

When nothing seemed likely to prevent Willie's formal acceptance (the Danish King, Frederick VII, was all in favour of it), Prince Christian insisted on certain conditions being thrashed out beforehand. The three protecting powers, Britain, Russia and France, must guarantee his son the sum of £25,000 a year in the event of his dethronement. Prince Christian knew too much about the life of a penniless prince not to wish to safeguard his son against such an eventuality. Nor would the Prince be allowed to go to Greece before Britain had promised to hand over the Ionian Islands. And finally, the goodwill of the royal house of Bavaria, to whose bosom the somewhat bemused King Otho had returned, had to be retained. Not until the last week in May 1863 were these conditions satisfactorily settled.

Even then, Prince Christian was far from happy. When the Marshal of the Court came to discuss details of the ceremony which was to mark the formal acceptance of the throne, he found Prince Christian in a state of deep dejection. 'Do whatever you like,' said the Prince. 'It's all one to me. My sole duty is to obey.'

None the less, the ceremony, held in the Christiansborg Palace on 6 June 1863, was appropriately colourful. Prince William was as delighted to accept the crown as the Greek delegation was to offer it. That accomplished, the new King George I of the Hellenes, looking engaging in his captain's uniform (he had been promoted three days previously) drove beside his father through the beflagged and sunlit streets of the Danish capital.

'People of Greece, rejoice!' trumpeted the Athenian newspaper *Evnomia* on hearing the news. 'Your troubles are at an end and our prayers have been heard! The dangers of Hellas are past, the ground has ceased to tremble, the earthquake has subsided before the edifice of the State was shaken to its foundation. The throne is saved; already the shadow of the Crown spreads over the country...'

This was all very well in its way, but the less effusive Danish royal family let it be known that the new King would be keeping his bags ready packed in the event of his subjects one day deciding that they no longer wanted him.

Late in October 1863, having paid courtesy calls on the crowned heads of the three protecting powers—Queen Victoria, Tsar Alexander II and the Emperor Napoleon III—King George arrived in Greece. The youngster was rapturously welcomed. But how long, it was wondered, could this enthusiasm possibly last? 'The task', wrote the always cautious King Leopold of the Belgians to his niece Queen Victoria, 'will be a very difficult one, especially as a Constitutional Monarchy. A Dictator would be more likely to succeed.'

But unsuspected by his sceptical fellow sovereigns, this unimportant Danish prince was about to embark on a long and ultimately glorious reign.

Once more the prize had fallen, as it were, into the lap of Prince Christian's family. Not through any machinations on the part of Prince Christian nor because of any outstanding qualities in his son had the Greek crown been won. Prince William had been chosen as King of the Hellenes for a variety of reasons: other, less adventurous, princes had declined the offer; the Powers were anxious to get the matter settled speedily; the Greeks wanted a British candidate who would bring then the Ionian Islands; Princess Alexandra's marriage to Queen Victoria's heir had enhanced her brother's standing; no one, other than the Germans (at loggerheads with Denmark over Schleswig-Holstein) actually objected to him. In a way, Prince William was everyone's second, not to say third, choice.

Perhaps the whole business was best summed up by the magazine *Punch* in its cartoon of a band of heavily armed Greek brigands standing guard over a mountain pathway. 'Too bad for him,' one of them is saying to the others. 'The first man who passes, we'll make him King!'

CHAPTER TWO

1

On 15 November 1863, a fortnight after King George's arrival in Greece, his forty-five-year-old father finally ascended the Danish throne as King Christian IX.

The new King, with the cordon of the Order of the Elephant aslant his uniform, stepped onto the balcony of the Amalienborg Palace while, to the great crowd below, the President of the Council announced that 'King Frederick VII is dead. Long live King Christian IX.' The watching French Minister, M. Dotézac, informed his government that 'Christian IX is tall, handsome and elegant and has an admirable presence. His Majesty was warmly applauded and had to show himself twice more.'

That was the Minister's official report. His confidential one, sent later by cipher telegram, told a somewhat different story. The King's reception, he assured Paris, had not been nearly as enthusiastic as it could have been; in fact, it had been 'no more than adequate'. The Danes were anxious to know how the new King was going to measure up to the difficulties which lay ahead. King Christian, continued Dotézac, 'of gentle nature, high principle and mediocre intelligence, was meant to rule only in quiet times'.

And these were not, by any stretch of the imagination, quiet times. King Christian IX's accession inaugurated considerably more than a new reign. It brought the Schleswig-Holstein question to a climax.

The issue was an extremely complicated one. Only three people, runs Lord Palmerston's classic quip, understood it: the Prince Consort, who was dead; a German professor, who had gone mad; and himself, who had forgotten all about it. Reduced to its simplest terms, the quarrel concerned the rival claims of Denmark and the German Confederation to the duchies of Schleswig and Holstein. Denmark was determined to hang on to the duchies, while the German Confederation—led by Bismarck's Prussia— was as determined to wrest them from her.

With King Christian's accession, the long-smouldering feud flared up once more. 'What *is* to happen now?' cried Queen Victoria who, although favouring the German claim, was a little hazy about the rights of the case. But whatever the rights of the matter might have been, it was might that finally counted. Early in 1864 the combined Prussian and Austrian armies marched against Denmark. Despite a spirited defence, the Danes were soundly beaten and the duchies lost. Within a matter of months, King Christian IX was forced into relinquishing almost half his kingdom. It was hardly an auspicious opening to the reign.

The long-term effects of the war were to be more serious still. For Bismarck, it was to be the first step towards the rapid aggrandizement of Prussia. Within two years, the victors—Prussia and Austria—were to be at loggerheads. In a war as ruthlessly contrived as had been the one against Denmark, Prussia thrashed Austria, thereby proving herself the most powerful nation in the German Confederation. Four years later, the combined German armies conquered Napoleon III's France. In January 1871, the German Reich was proclaimed, with King Wilhelm of Prussia taking the title of German Emperor. In seven years, over the bodies of Denmark, Austria and France, Prussia had leapt from a position of relative unimportance to that of leader of the foremost nation on the Continent.

Less tangible, but hardly less significant, was the effect of Prussia's victory over Denmark on the dynasty of King Christian IX. In the minds of his children was implanted an undying hatred of Prussia. To this, with all the simplicity and stubbornness of their natures, they clung throughout their lives. Intensely loyal to their father, their house and their country, these Danish princes and princesses refused to be reconciled to the state which had despoiled the Danish kingdom. King Christian's daughters might have been exceptionally a-political, but their one political tenet was this aversion towards Prussia. It was a tenet which they introduced, with considerable success and not unimportant results, into other royal houses of Europe.

2

If King Christian IX's domain had shrunk, his dynasty was continuing to expand. Indeed, it was the very weakness of his position that was working to his advantage.

The Tsar Alexander II of Russia was on the look-out for an uncontroversial bride for his son and heir, the Tsarevich Nicholas. Who better than one of King Christian IX's attractive daughters? In no way could such an alliance be looked upon as a political marriage, such as a match with a more important princess might be. Matrimonial alliances between two major powers could so often lead to trouble; now that the Schleswig-Holstein question had been settled, the choice of a Danish bride could offend no one.

Furthermore, the ruling houses of Russia and Denmark were already related: amongst other connections, Alexander II's sister had married the brother of Queen Louise of Denmark. In these particular marriage negotiations, in fact, one can see the hand of Queen Louise.

Thus, in the summer of 1864—which had proved so territorially disastrous for Denmark—King Christian was officially approached with a proposal that his second daughter, Dagmar, become engaged to the Grand Duke Nicholas, Heir Apparent to the Russian imperial throne. The King, as considerate a father and unambitious a monarch as ever, accepted only on condition that the Princess be allowed to make up her own mind once she had met the Tsarevich.

Princess Dagmar—or Minny as she was called in the family—turned seventeen that year. If Dagmar was less beautiful than her sister Alexandra, she had a livelier, more engaging face. Her chief attractions were her large, velvety eyes and her wide, flashing smile. Where Alexandra was all grace and elegance, Dagmar was all mobility. Smaller than her sister, she had the same slender figure, the same flair for wearing clothes and what Queen Victoria called the same 'pretty manners'. And although by no means an intellectual, Dagmar had sharper wits and wider interests. That the Tsarevich Nicholas should be attracted to this pert, pretty and sweet-natured girl the minute he set eyes on her is not surprising; there were few unmarried princesses in Europe to equal her.

If Dagmar was exceptional, Nicholas was no less so. Twenty-one at the time, this eldest son of Tsar Alexander II was quite different from his five hulking brothers; he was a slim, handsome, graceful, delicate, gentle and well-read young man, with something of his father's subtle mind and liberal leanings. In short, he was just the sort of romantic figure to appeal to the young and unsophisticated Danish Princess.

And appeal he did. By the time he left Copenhagen, in September 1864, the engagement had been agreed upon. Nicholas and Dagmar would marry in the spring of the following year. For the Danish royal house, it had been another tremendous *coup*. It was no wonder that the London *Times* was beginning to compare King Christian's family with the Coburgs.

But the marriage was not to be. The Tsarevich's delicacy was not confined to his breeding and his features. His cheeks had always shown a suspect flush and that winter he suffered an attack of bronchitis. The doctors advised him to make for a warmer climate and he was packed off to Nice in the South of France. More than a dose of winter sunshine, however, would be needed to save Nicholas. By March 1865 it was clear that he was dying. Accompanied by her mother, Queen Louise, and her eldest brother, Crown Prince Frederick, Dagmar hurried down to the South of France. Here was collected the entire Russian imperial family.

The story goes that the Tsarevich, realizing that he was dying, decided that something must be done about his desolate fiancée. He would bequeath her, along with his rights to the throne, to his brother Alexander. Alexander, he assured the weeping Dagmar, would make her a better husband than he would ever have done. With that, he sent for his brother and, putting Dagmar's tiny hands into Alexander's enormous ones, linked the couple's future. The gesture made, Nicholas died.

It makes a touching story but one suspects that it was invented to mask the indecent haste with which Dagmar was expected to switch her affections.

The man to whom the bewildered Dagmar now found herself bequeathed was a very different type from his dead brother. The Tsarevich Alexander was a giant: a huge, broad-shouldered, slow-moving, heavily jowled creature with nothing of his brother's grace or refinement. His physical prowess was exceptional. The same, alas, could not be said of his mental ability. As Alexander had been only second in line of succession, not much attention had been paid to his education. In any case, his tutors had found the teaching of this ponderous young bull a singularly thankless task. It was not that he was indolent; on the contrary, he was painstaking, conscientious and eager to please. He was just desperately slow. As one of his fellow countrymen put it, Alexander was 'essentially a man of duty and took life seriously with that persistent obstinacy with often carries stupid people further than the clever'.

But for all his gruffness of manner and rigidity of mind, the new Tsarevich—in his family circle— could reveal himself as good-natured and approachable. Properly handled (and the lively Dagmar would soon learn how to handle him) this great shambling Russian bear could be quite human.

What Dagmar's views were on being expected to marry the lumbering Alexander in place of the sensitive Nicholas one does not know. In common with most princesses of her day, she had a strong sense of dynastic obligation. Royal blood entailed royal duties; if a marriage to the Tsarevich would be to the advantage of her house, then marry him she must, whatever he was like. And, in any case, not many princesses, as relatively unimportant and impoverished as Dagmar, were likely to let slip the opportunity of one day becoming Empress of Russia.

With a new wedding date set for 9 November 1866, Dagmar resumed her preparations for her future life. She took instruction in the Orthodox faith, she started to learn Russian, she did what she could towards assembling a wardrobe more suited to one of the most sumptuous courts in Europe. The Assistant Secretary of the American Navy, passing through Copenhagen at this time, was enchanted by the sight of the small, dark-eyed Princess in a blue and white striped crinoline and a pink hat. 'She is possessed of more than ordinary personal beauty,' he enthused. 'She has an oval face, regular in outline, a brilliant complexion, glossy brown hair, and bright intelligent eyes. She conversed with freedom, speaking English fluently and correctly...'

It was no wonder that on her arrival in St Petersburg, in the autumn of 1866, Dagmar was given a tremendous welcome. She stood on the deck of a Danish frigate, a tiny figure dressed all in white and holding a white parasol, while the crowds massed along the great granite quays roared their approval. She might have shocked the watching Russian aristocracy by shaking hands with one of the Danish sailors but this show of familiarity delighted the rest. For this sort of common touch, relative though it might be, Dagmar was always to be very popular amongst the Russian people.

'Rarely,' remembered Princess Catherine Radziwill who, as a young girl, was taken to see Dagmar make her entry into St Petersburg, 'has a foreign princess been greeted with such enthusiasm as [Princess Dagmar] who from the first moment she set foot on Russian soil, succeeded in winning to herself all hearts. Her smile, the delightful way she had of bowing to the crowds assembled to welcome her, laid immediately the foundations of her popularity...'

She might have won the approval of the crowds but she did not yet pass muster with the imperial family. The silk purse of a Russian empress was still to be fashioned out of this sow's ear of a Danish princess, they reckoned. From the moment of her arrival until her wedding day, Dagmar was subjected to a rigorous course of training for her new position. It was almost as though, with that shaking of the Danish sailor's hand, she had said goodbye to the informality of her past life.

The scale of these preparations must have exceeded the girl's wildest imaginings. In the first place there was the overwhelming splendour of St Petersburg itself—a vast, elegant, formally planned city of enormous squares, sweeping boulevards, grandiose buildings and immense waterways, a giant Venice of the North. Beside its grandeur, Copenhagen must have seemed like little more than a country town. Then there were the palaces, all of them gorgeous but none more so than the one in which Dagmar found herself housed: the Winter Palace. With its magnificent *enfilade* of state rooms, gleaming with marble, porphyry and malachite and glittering with gold, glass and crystal, it was breathtaking. Within these cathedral-like galleries, the girl was introduced to the most formal, exacting and lavish ceremonial in the world. She was driven in colourful processions through the streets. She was taken to the Cathedral, in the massive fortress of St Peter and St Paul, to lay a wreath on the white marble tomb of her first fiancé. She was received into the Orthodox Church. Her name and title were changed from Princess Dagmar to the Grand Duchess Marie Feodorovna.

The ceremonies on the wedding day itself—9 November 1866—were almost overwhelming in their magnificence. There was the formal dressing of the bride in the Malachite Room of the Winter Palace by the ladies of the imperial family, when Dagmar, in a dress of silver tissue, a train of silver brocade lined with ermine, and sparkling with jewels, had the special diamond nuptial crown placed on her head by her future mother-in-law, the Tsaritsa. Then, as a 21-gun salute thundered out over St Petersburg, the giant Tsarevich, in the blue and silver uniform of his Cossack regiment, led her through a succession of crowded galleries to the Palace Church. Here the richly robed and mitred priests performed the wedding ceremony. Four young princes—among them Dagmar's brother, Crown Prince Frederick of Denmark—took turns in holding the massive gold crowns above the heads of the bride and groom during the long and elaborate ceremony.

Absent from the proceedings were the bride's parents, King Christian and Queen Louise. The impecunious Danish sovereigns would not even have been able to afford the tips, let alone the other expenses, of a visit to St Petersburg. The Tsar, who could have paid their expenses without blinking, had decided against doing so: with Dagmar having brought no dowry, Alexander II felt that he had done enough for the Danish royal family.

At five o'clock, 'at tables groaning under the weight of the Imperial gold and silver plate', the company sat down to a state banquet. While more salutes thundered out across the snow-blanketed city, various toasts were drunk: to the Tsar and Tsaritsa, to the bridal couple, to the King and Queen of Denmark, 'to the clergy and all faithful subjects'. At eight there was a ball in the White Throne Room. The imperial party and their royal guests, watched by the glitteringly dressed company, opened the ball with a polonaise.

Not until late that night could the exhausted young couple leave for what was henceforth to be their own palace. Yet even this move was hedged about with protocol. Escorted by Cossacks, preceded by six gilt coaches, surrounded by mounted aides-de-camp and running footmen, the bride and groom were obliged to drive with the Tsar and Tsaritsa in a great golden coach drawn by eight richly caparisoned horses. In the entrance hall of their new home, they were welcomed by the Grand Duke Constantine and his wife, who duly blessed them with a holy image of the Saviour and presented them with the traditional round loaf of rye bread and a cellar of salt. The bride was then formally disrobed by the Empress and the other ladies of the family.

Only after the Tsar's carriage procession had rolled away into the bitterly cold night did the little Danish Princess find herself, for the first time in her life, quite alone with her bear-like husband.

3

King Christian IX's eldest son, Crown Prince Frederick, had been born on 3 June 1843. He had been known, throughout his childhood, as 'Freddie with the pretty little face'. Until his father had been chosen as heir to the Danish throne in 1852, it was assumed that this asset would be all that the youngster was going to need. However, with the family's sudden elevation to prominence, the spotlight was turned on to the ten-year-old boy who would one day succeed his father as King. Freddie was whisked out of his public school and put in charge of a private tutor, Professor Petersen, who was assisted, it was claimed, 'by masters of the first eminence in their various departments'. At fifteen he was bundled into uniform and three years later commissioned as a second lieutenant in the infantry.

In October 1863, when Prince Frederick was twenty, he was sent to Oxford for a year's study, but the accession of his father the following month put paid to any such project. Freddie returned home to take up his duties as Crown Prince. These, for the most part, consisted of journeys in connection with his family's manifold marital activities. Crown Prince Frederick of Denmark was forever accompanying a brother or a sister on their march to the altar. This dynastic expansion afforded him pleasurable opportunities for travel: to his sister Alix in London, his sister Dagmar in St Petersburg, his brother George in Athens. By his mid-twenties, Crown Prince Frederick had developed into an affable, assured and elegant young man—hat dashingly tilted, moustache jauntily waxed, clothes beautifully cut. He might not have been especially intelligent but he was frank and cheerful; very much the child of King Christian and Queen Louise.

'The Crown Prince Frederick is now twenty-three,' reported the French Minister in Copenhagen to his government. 'Without yet possessing his father's *grand air*, he looks admirably distinguished.'

The question of a suitable bride for this debonair young Prince was was one to which his family, and particularly his ambitious mother, was giving considerable thought. With Alix and Dagmar having married so well, Queen Louise saw no reason why Freddie could not fly equally high. Queen Victoria still had two marriageable daughters on the market: Princess Helena and Princess Louise. Surely Freddie could land one of them?

He could not. On this point, as on so many others, Queen Victoria knew her own mind perfectly. What the English Queen wanted for her daughters were tame German princelings who would be willing to make their homes in England, not heirs to foreign thrones who would take her daughters away. As it was, the Schleswig-Holstein business had caused enough trouble in the family; another Danish alliance could only aggravate things. Nor was Queen Victoria prepared to forgive or forget the treatment of an earlier British royal bride—her great-aunt, Queen Caroline Mathilda—at the hands of the Danes. The poor young woman had been tricked, by her jealous step-mother-in-law, into signing a confession of adultery and was then banished from court. Queen Victoria considered this treatment deplorable.

Thus, in an unequivocal note to the British Minister at Copenhagen, the Queen made it clear that she would never consent to a marriage of any of her daughters to the Crown Prince of Denmark. 'Kindly, but in a manner to preclude the possibility of a mistake', her minister was to make the Queen's views known to the Danish King.

Thwarted, Queen Louise was obliged to lower her sights.

Not much, however. In July 1868, at the age of twenty-five, Freddie became engaged to the seventeen-year-old Princess Louise, only child of King Charles XV of Sweden.

Princess Louise's second and third names—Josephine Eugenie—bore witness to her romantic ancestry. For the Swedish royal house had been founded by that Napoleonic campaigner, Jean Baptiste Bernadotte. Bernadotte's wife, whom Napoleon himself had once considered marrying, had been a silk merchant's daughter named Désirée Clary. To strengthen still further the Napoleonic flavour of the dynasty, Bernadotte's son, King Oscar I of Sweden and Norway, had married the daughter of Napoleon's adopted son, Eugène de Beauharnais. Indeed, flashing brightest amongst the Swedish royal jewels were those that had once belonged to Napoleon's Empress, Josephine. It was with good reason then, that the names of the Swedish King's only daughter should have so Napoleonic a ring.

There, alas, all such colourful associations ended. Of the panache of the Bonaparte, or rather, the Beauharnais, family, Princess Louise had not a trace. She was a plain, shy, stiffly-mannered girl: serious-minded without being intellectual, good natured without being animated. Even at seventeen, she showed signs of the piety that was to develop into a positive bigotry. Despite her expensive clothes and her elaborately dressed hair, she looked frumpish. Compared with her fiancé's stylish and vivacious sisters, Princess Louise was as dull as ditchwater.

But she was very rich. Her mother had been Princess Louise of the Netherlands and from her had come the Princess's considerable fortune. To the impoverished Danish royal house, Louise would be—in the strict sense of the word—a most valuable acquisition. There were pretty faces enough amongst King Christian IX's children (including the Crown Prince's own); what was needed were some more tangible assets.

The couple were married in Stockholm on 28 July 1869. With this being a wedding that King Christian IX could afford to attend, he took all available members of his family over to Sweden for the occasion. It was certainly well worth it. The water city was looking its sparkling best; the flags of Sweden and Denmark were joyously fluttering; guns thudded out in gratifying salute from the ships of various nations; the crowds were suitably enthusiastic; the presents (including, the bride was no doubt pleased to see, a 'magnificent Bible') poured in. After a short honeymoon at the Castle of Haga, the Crown Prince and Princess—with the rest of the Danish royal family still in tow—arrived in Copenhagen. 'So genuine, so hearty, so universal was the joy with which Prince Frederick and his bride were received,' noted one enraptured correspondent, 'that it reminded us Englishmen of the reception given to the Prince and Princess of Wales on their bridal entry into London.'

Through a rain of flowers, flung from the balconies and windows by ecstatic Danish matrons, the couple drove from the quayside to the Christiansborg Palace. They were immediately plunged into a round of banquets, balls and receptions. So astonished, for some reason, was one British observer at the dignified behaviour of the Danish guests at these royal festivities that he was moved to claim that 'ladies and gentlemen in a West-End drawing room could not have behaved themselves with more propriety and decorum'.

Although, when set against the spectactular matches made by his sisters Alix and Dagmar, Frederick's marriage might have seemed a pretty conventional, almost run-of-the-mill affair, it was extremely popular in Denmark, It heralded, no one doubted, a period of closer understanding between Denmark and Sweden; it went some way towards making up for Sweden's notable lack of support for Denmark during the Schleswig-Holstein war. Surely, with this marriage, a new era of Scandinavian solidarity (for the Swedish King ruled Norway) was about to dawn.

The celebrations over, Prince Frederick and Princess Louise set up home in the Crown Prince's official residence: one of the buildings making up that elegant set of palaces known as the Amalienborg. In the summer they moved out to Charlottenhund, a roomy, simple, white-washed palace set on a wooded ridge above the shores of the Öresund. From its beach was a splendid view of the ships plying the Sound and of the fort of Middelgrund.

Although, as one writer (appreciative of the bride's considerable fortune) has put it, 'the couple were able to live better than the inadequate revenue allotted to the Crown Prince would otherwise have allowed', their style of life was comparatively modest. Frederick, like all his family, never hankered after the grandiose and Lousie would have considered anything too luxurious or ostentatious as positively sinful. And if, with the passing years, Freddie found his wife a little too priggish and their entertainments a little too solemn, there was nothing to stop him from looking for more frivolous company elsewhere. Nineteenth-century husbands, and princes in particular, were not expected to account for their every move. Freddie, like his sister Alix's husband Bertie, had an eye for a pretty face; in fact, the two young men would sometimes compare notes: about a 'Miss Hannah' here, or a 'Miss Ida' there, or 'that little very nice girl' in the perfume shop somewhere else.

But to one of his marital obligations Prince Frederick applied himself assiduously. Within a year of marriage, Louise bore him a son and heir (the future King Christian X of Denmark) and, during the following twenty years, she presented him with seven more children. If, a generation before, the Danish throne had been in danger of running out of heirs, that particular bogey had now been well and truly laid. Indeed, from now on, not only the Danish, but several other European thrones, would be kept plentifully supplied with Danish or part-Danish heirs.

CHAPTER THREE

1

Alexandra, like her sister Dagmar, had quickly established herself as a great favourite with the public. With her mother-in-law, Queen Victoria, living a life of the utmost seclusion, this hitherto unimportant Danish princess was immediately pitched into the position of the leading figure in fashionable society. She played the role admirably. Strikingly beautiful, transcendentally smart and socially accomplished, Alix none the less remained sweet-natured, approachable and modest. Wherever she went, she inspired loyalty and affection. Even her formidable mother-in-law had very few complaints. 'Alix,' wrote Queen Victoria on one occasion, 'is really a dear, excellent, right-minded soul whom one must dearly love and respect.' She might be a little too lacking in seriousness for the Queen's taste, but Victoria could not deny her daughter-in-law's essential goodness of heart.

On the face of it, Princess Alexandra had everything she could possibly wish for. She was married to a genial and attractive young man. She had, for the first time in her life, enough money to satisfy her every desire. Her homes—Marlborough House in London and Sandringham in Norfolk—were sumptuously and comfortably furnished. She led an active and varied social life. In January 1864, her first son was born. Christened Albert Victor, he was to be known in the family as Eddy. During the following five years, she bore four more healthy children—George, Louise, Victoria and Maud. She was devoted to her children, and they to her. All in all, the Princess of Wales should have been radiantly happy.

But she was not. The trouble lay in her relationship with her husband. Bertie's and Alix's marriage was not really satisfactory and, with each passing year, it became increasingly less so.

The fact was that Alix was married to one of the most difficult of men in one of the most difficult of positions. To the world, the Prince of Wales might appear as an easy, gregarious, well-mannered and warm-hearted *bon viveur*; a man who lived, as his disapproving mother only too frequently pointed out, purely for pleasure. To those who knew him more intimately, however, Bertie was not nearly as resolved a personality as he seemed. He was moody, restless, quickly bored and easily depressed. Lacking in application, nothing could hold his interest long; without mental resources, he could not bear to be alone; very conscious of his royal dignity, he was easily affronted. It needed very little to make him lose his temper.

Altogether, the Prince of Wales was not an easy man to live with.

The main trouble, of course, was that he did not have enough to do. For this, Queen Victoria was entirely responsible. In the first place, she had a very poor opinion of her son's abilities; in the second, she was determined that no one should play the political role that her husband had once done. Considering Bertie to be irresponsible, immature and indiscreet, the Queen refused to involve him in the workings of the monarchy. She neither confided in him nor consulted him. He must see nothing, she would tell her ministers, of 'a very *confidential* nature'. Only the social and ceremonial duties of the monarchy would she entrust to him, and these he carried out with great style. But about the more serious business of government, the Prince of Wales was kept in almost complete ignorance.

Denied any active employment, Bertie devoted himself to the way of life which he anyway preferred: racing, gambling, shooting, travelling, dressing up, eating out and devising practical jokes. He surrounded himself with hordes of people—financiers, men about town, actresses. He lived, as his mother once complained, 'in a whirl of amusements', forever involved in yet another scandal or embarked upon yet another liaison.

Life with so restless, mercurial and licentious a man could have been no bed of roses. Alix's lot was not an easy one. She frequently felt neglected and humiliated. Yet she seldom complained. Indeed, towards her husband's much discussed infidelities, Alexandra was remarkably tolerant. She always behaved graciously towards such of his mistresses as she met; jealousy, she reckoned, was a worse sin than licentiousness. 'She has behaved so beautifully, so splendidly, but it was a hard trial for her;' wrote Queen Victoria to Alix's mother, Queen Louise, after another of Bertie's frequent lapses, 'she is so simple, so honourable, and, as we say, so right-minded.'

For his wife's understanding attitude, Bertie was always grateful. In his way, he was very fond of Alix and treated her with courtesy and chivalry. 'After all,' she is reported to have said after this death, 'he always loved me the best.'

Bertie's infidelities, however, were not the only reason why the couple were gradually drifting apart. They had so few interests in common. Both might have been unintellectual, immature, fond of clothes and free with money, but each preferred a different way of life. He adored the flash and glitter of society; she lived for her home and family. He was a man of the world; she, for all her social accomplishments and breathtaking chic, was essentially a domestic creature. In a way, Alexandra had never really outgrown the cosy, simple, clannish atmosphere of her Danish childhood.

Nor were all the failings on Bertie's side. Alix, despite her sweetness of nature, had serious defects of character; defects which she could ill afford as the wife of a man like Bertie. Where he was one of the most methodical of people, she was haphazard, unpunctual, badly organized; she had the sort of scatter-brained charm which could be maddening to live with. And while a clever, or at least a sharp-witted, woman might have held Bertie's interest, Alix's lack of brain made her boring. In public she was smiling, gracious, easy, and a joy to look at, but she never shone in private conversation.

To Alix's various mental, and temperamental, shortcomings, was added a physical one. She had inherited from her mother, Queen Louise, a disease known as otosclerosis, which was making her increasingly deaf. With each passing year, she was less able to follow conversation. As a result, she tended to avoid people whose voices she found difficult to hear; this cut her off, more and more, not only from that company in which her husband so delighted, but from her husband himself. It cut her off too, from any opportunity of hearing others' opinions. Alix had never been much of a reader; now she could no longer learn by listening to intelligent conversation. Always rather childlike, she became increasingly so. Her deafness considerably strengthened that barrier between herself and the realities of life.

And as Bertie's lack of occupation encouraged him to lead an ever more frenetic social life, so did Alix's deafness force her away from that life towards those things which she liked best—her children, her horses, her dogs and her homes. It was within the family circle that she was happiest; here her emotions were most deeply involved. Her five children were being raised in the most indulgent fashion. For one thing, the Prince of Wales was determined that they would never be subjected to as joyless and rigorous a course of training as he had had to undergo; for another, the Princess of Wales would have been temperamentally incapable of instituting any such course. On the contrary, she was anxious that they should have as extended and as carefree a childhood as possible.

The result was that the Wales children were being brought up, not only with what Queen Victoria approvingly called 'great simplicity and an absence of all pride', but with a lack of discipline of which the Queen could not possibly approve. Of the serious-mindedness that had characterized the royal nursery of a generation before, there was no trace. It was in this that Alexandra's Danish influence made itself most strongly felt. The Wales children ran, if not exactly wild, certainly very free. They were a happy, high-spirited lot, having inherited, to the full, their mother's taste for knock-about humour and her distaste for study.

As Alix adored her own parents, so did her children adore her. To them she was 'darling Motherdear': a gay, spontaneous, impractical and warm-hearted companion, hardly more grown-up than themselves. It was as though mother and children were living in a world of make-believe, of eternal youth.

2

Another *milieu,* of course, in which Princess Alexandra felt eminently at home was that of her Danish family. Years of living in England never weakened her affection for her relations or her native land. 'Saxon and Norman and Dane are we, But all of us Danes in our welcome to thee,' Tennyson had written in his *A Welcome to Alexandra.* And Danish, in almost every way, Alexandra had remained. Any reference to Denmark delighted her. Once, at an agricultural show, when butter-making was being demonstrated to her, she was quick to claim that the best butter came from Denmark. 'No,' countered her guide with great gallantry, 'our best princesses come from Denmark.' To which the Prince of Wales, with a flash of unusual wit, added, 'Now you're buttering her Royal Highness up.'

The weeks which Alexandra managed to spend in Denmark were always the highlight of her year. Amongst the naïve pleasures of her father's houshold, she could recapture the security, the domesticity and the lightheartedness of her girlhood. The way of life which the Prince of Wales found so tedious was all enchantment to her. Princess Alexandra enjoyed being back in her Danish home, claims her husband's secretary, 'much more than anything else.'

And if Alix was not seeing her relations in Copenhagen, she would be seeing them elsewhere. King Christian and Queen Louise would come to London;

Alexandra would visit her brother, King George, in Greece; her sister Dagmar, now Grand Duchess Marie Feodorovna, with her husband, the massive Tsarevich Alexander, stayed with her at Marlborough House; she and Bertie visited them in St Petersburg. And, of course, there were always those family jamborees at Rumpenheim, the Hesse-Cassel home near Frankfurt.

All this flocking together Queen Victoria watched with a baleful eye. There were few things she approved of less than these Danish family gatherings. Each time Princess Alexandra announced her intention of visiting Denmark, the Queen made objections. If Alix insisted on taking her children with her, the Queen would object more strongly still. It was quite wrong, she would maintain, for the Princess to absent herself from England for such long periods. But Alexandra, who could be stubborn about most things, was most stubborn about this. In the end, she usually got her way.

It was not, in fact, the absences from England that Queen Victoria was so concerned about; it was what she considered to be the pernicious anti-Prussian influence of the Danish court. Only on the condition that it was not to be a political union had Victoria given her consent to her son's marriage to Alexandra of Denmark; by now her apprehensions seem to have been justified. Alix remained violently anti-Prussian. Having very little appreciation of the nature of the Prussian state, her antipathy was simply a matter of personal prejudice. She stuck to it, however, with all the tenacity of a shallow mind.

Once, when Alix was returning home from a holiday in Copenhagen, she saw the Prussian flag hoisted on her yacht at Kiel. She demanded that it be taken down immediately. It was explained that, as they were in Prussian waters, the flag must be flown. That mattered to her not in the least. 'I shall not move one step until that flag is hauled down,' she declared. It was.

And on another occasion, when Kaiser Wilhelm I asked one of her daughters what she would like as a birthday present, Princess Alexandra was heard to whisper, 'The head of Bismarck.'

Nothing would induce her to visit Prussia. Only after considerable coercion and several dangerously insulting delays did she once consent to receive the Prussian King at Wiesbaden. At this her mother, Queen Louise, who happened to be there at the time, hastily packed her bags and, together with her son, King George of the Hellenes and her youngest daughter, Princess Thyra, quit Wiesbaden for the security of Rumpenheim. Queen Victoria was furious at her daughter-in-law's undiplomatic behaviour. 'If only she understood her duties better!' she exclaimed.

Worse still, in the Queen's opinion, was the fact that Alix, in her contempt for Prussia, was influencing Bertie. Neglectful of his wife in some spheres, the Prince of Wales supported her in this. Her anguish at the time of the war between Denmark and Prussia was to have a lasting effect on him. In a very short while, his anti-Prussianism was hardly less virulent than hers. That a Danish wife should make him pro-Danish during the war over Schleswig-Holstein was understandable; but that he should be pro-Austrian during the Austro-Prussian War of 1866, and pro-French during the Franco-Prussian War of 1870, considerably alarmed his Germanophile mother.

Indeed, during the Franco-Prussian War this rivalry between the pro- and anti-Prussian factions of the British royal family was particularly violent. On one side was the Queen herself, her daughter Vicky, and Vicky's husband, Crown Prince Frederick of Prussia; on the other were Alix and Bertie. At a dinner at the French Embassy on the eve of war, the Prince of Wales expressed the hope that Austria might join France in defeating Prussia. His partisan remarks were forwarded to Berlin. From here the Crown Princess dashed off a furious letter of complaint to her mother.

'The King [of Prussia] and everyone are horrified at Bertie's speech...' she reported. That the blame lay with Alix, neither Vicky nor her mother had any doubt. Thus when, a few weeks later, the French Emperor surrendered to the Germans at Sedan, the Crown Princess's tone was triumphant. 'What will Bertie and Alix say to all these marvellous events?' she crowed.

Whenever Alix could discourage the further Prussianization of the British royal family, she did so. A proposed marriage between her brother-in-law,

Prince Arthur and her younger sister, Princess Thyra, had her full approval; when Prince Arthur married a Prussian princess instead, Alexandra was very disappointed.

Another of her wishes, however, was realized. When Dagmar visited her from St Petersburg in 1873, the two sisters did what they could to bring about a match between yet another of Alix's brothers-in-law, Prince Alfred, Duke of Edinburgh, to Dagmar's sister-in-law—the Tsar's daughter—the Grand Duchess Marie. This unusual union, between the matter-of-fact British and colourful Russian royal houses, was celebrated with great pomp in the Winter Palace Church, in St Petersburg, in 1874. The Danish sisters no doubt assumed, in their artless fashion, that the marriage would bring the two countries closer together, at the expense of Germany.

And gradually, Alix's anti-Prussianism began making its mark. That the British royal family should become progressively less enamoured of Germany during the half-century that followed the Danish war, was due to a great many causes. But one of them, undoubtedly, was the influence of the Princess of Wales.

3

Of all the royal households of Europe, none more closely resembled the Danish than that of

King Christian IX's second son, King George I of the Hellenes. The rocky, dusty, sun-baked Aegean Peninsula might have been a far cry from the moist green meadows, billowing trees and grey waterways of Denmark, but the same unpretentious air characterized the royal houses of both countries. This was due, not only to the personality of young King George, but to the nature of the Greek people. Poor, proud and independent, they would never have tolerated an extravagant or pompous court; by his simplicity and his informality, the King struck exactly the right note.

It would have been almost impossible, in fact, for King George to have struck any other sort of note. On his arrival in Greece, in October 1863, George found himself in one of the poorest, most ill-organized and unstable countries in Europe. The mists of romance with which the Great Powers had clothed the Greeks during their War of Independence against Turkey had long since evaporated. They were now looked upon as a semi-civilized, turbulent and untrustworthy race. Amongst the nations of Europe, their country counted for almost nothing. Athens was hardly more than an untidy sprawl of houses, roads were no more than tracks, the mountains swarmed with brigands. Since the revolution which had overthrown King Otho, the governmental machinery had practically ground to a halt. Government posts were filled with rapacious adventurers; the country was deeply in debt. The new King had to rely solely on the army; the very army which had just overthrown the last King.

'It was impossible,' wrote Sir Horace Rumbold, the British Minister in Athens, 'not to feel compassion for the boy-King whose lot was cast among so turbulent and fickle a race as the Greeks...I can well remember how strongly that impression came home to me and others the day on which the youthful sovereign took the oath to the Constitution in the National Assembly. The sight of this slight, delicate stripling, standing alone amidst a crowd of callous, unscrupulous politicians, many of whom had been steeped to the lips in treason, and swearing to observe the most unworkable of charters, from which nearly every safeguard...had been studiously eliminated, was indeed painful and saddening.'

Such problems, which to a more experienced man might have seemed like mountains, were treated as molehills by the ebullient young monarch. Bursting with self-confidence and high spirits, King George applied himself to his task. 'His truthfulness and straightforwardness, united to a considerable firmness of character and high personal courage, at once assured to him an exceptional position with his subjects,' claims Rumbold.

King George certainly needed qualities beyond his years. Indeed, it is extraordinary with what aplomb this Danish boy, just out of the schoolroom, handled the complications of his new position. There is a story that on one occasion, in the course of a cabinet meeting, the King crossed to a map on the wall to illustrate a point. When he resumed his seat, the boy noticed that his watch, which he had left lying on the table, had disappeared. Looking around the assembled, and admittedly brigandly-faced, ministers, he said, 'Will whoever has my watch please return it?'

No one moved. Loath to believe that the watch had been stolen, George said, 'Well, gentlemen, I'm not accustomed to this type of joke. I'd like to have my watch back.'

Still no one moved. More firmly, the King announced that he would put out the light and count up to sixty. 'If I find the watch again on the table, the incident will be closed,' he said.

He turned down the light, counted loudly to sixty and then turned the light up again.

This time his silver inkstand had vanished.

The story is probably apocryphal but that it should be told at all is not without significance.

If the material with which the King had to form a cabinet was not promising, that with which he was obliged to form a court was hardly more so. Where his sister Alexandra had gone to the most assured court in Europe and his sister Dagmar to the most magnificent, George had been faced with the most ramshackle one.

The palace, built for King Otho in the heart of the city (a plan to build the palace on the Acropolis itself had been mercifully scotched by Otho's Hellenistic father, King Ludwig I of Bavaria) was in a sorry state. The building—a simple, stuccoed, pillared and pedimented block—was not unimpressive but it was barely habitable. It boasted only one bathroom to its three hundred and sixty-five rooms; and even that was never used, for the sound reason that the taps released only a trickle of water, black with the corpses of cockroaches. In the winter, the cold was unbearable. Porcelain stoves did little to alleviate it. 'The wind whistled down the corridors and curled like a lash in and out of the lofty *salons*,' complains one inmate. Although some of the reception rooms had a certain grandeur, the private apartments, decorated in what the previous Bavarian occupants had fondly imagined was the 'ancient Greek style,' were hideous.

And, in addition to all these shortcomings, the entire palace had been ransacked since Otho's departure: doors had been smashed, fittings ripped out and furniture stolen. The evidence of such vandalism could hardly have been a welcoming or reassuring sight for the young King. For several years, George could only occupy part of the barrack-like building.

Accommodation, though, was merely one of the problems. The King was obliged to organize his own staff as well. Out of the band of unpolished functionaries who had been assigned to him, he had to fashion aides-de-camp and court officials; to train his own butlers, footmen and grooms. At the age of eighteen, George was expected to set the tone of the court. It is hardly surprising that he was not always successful. The King, says Rumbold, was 'still boyish in many ways and with a flow of animal spirits that

made it sometimes difficult for his daily companions
to maintain the respectful reserve and gravity due to
his royal station.'

Nevertheless, King George had the good sense
to identify himself with his new country as much as
possible. He quickly learnt the language (although
he always spoke it with a slightly guttural accent) and
cultivated a drooping, typically Greek moustache. For
the first four years of his reign, he never left his kingdom. By ship, by carriage, by mule and on foot, he visited every part of the country. Everywhere—in dusty,
close-packed towns or scattered mountain villages—
this tall, slender young man with the twinkling blue
eyes and the easy laugh was made welcome. Lest he be
accused, as had King Otho, of being influenced by the
advisers he had brought with him, King George soon
dismissed his Danish counsellor, Count Sponeck.
Although he remained a Protestant, George always
paid proper respect to the Greek Orthodox Church;
he worshipped privately, in the chapel adjoining his
apartment in the palace. (This same chapel, shared,
during the previous reign, by the Catholic King Otho
and Protestant Queen Amalia, had been systemati-
cally blessed and unblessed on Sundays.)

The framing of a new constitution caused endless
discussion; discussion dear to the hearts of the gar-
rulous Greek politicians but irritating in the extreme
to the unaffected young King. Only by forcing the
issue could George get them to come to a decision.
The resulting constitution was very liberal for its day.

None the less, the King was not responsible to parliament: he could appoint and dismiss ministers and dissolve the assembly. King George was wise enough, however, to involve himself as little as possible in domestic politics. During times of crisis (and in the early years ministerial crises came thick and fast) he would intervene personally but for the most part he left the politicians to get on with things. He never identified himself with any party.

His admirable regard for the constitution was not shared by all his ministers. Old political habits died very hard. Once, before an election, the Prime Minister Voulgaris—who apparently remained as loyal to traditional Greek political methods as he did to traditional Greek dress—told the King that the leader of the opposition must be prevented from coming to power. Surely, answered George in his artless fashion, that depended on the elections: if the electorate wanted Voulgaris's rival, they would vote for him.

'Oh, I don't mean that at all,' explained the Prime Minister patiently. 'We must do away with him.'

It was all very different from the workings of the Danish political system.

4

Having, during the first four years of his reign, established his kingdom, George began thinking in terms of establishing a dynasty. As his ministers only too frequently reminded him, it was essential that he marry and start a family. He was hardly less anxious himself. A strictly brought-up young man, the King was said to have a 'holy horror of vice'. The British Minister writes of being 'both touched and amused one evening by [the King's] confiding in me his determination to marry as early as possible in order to be placed at once out of reach of the many risks and temptations to which he knew he was certain to be exposed.' In time, King George was to show considerably less anxiety to stay out of reach of those 'risks and temptations'.

The place to find a bride would be Russia. Although George remained a Protestant, it was essential that his children be Greek Orthodox; only in Russia would he be able to find a suitably illustrious Orthodox wife. Rendering the prospect still more feasible was the fact that in 1866, George's sister Dagmar married the Tsarevich. With one sister the future Queen of England and another the future Tsaritsa of Russia, George need hardly set out cap in hand. In the spring of 1867, the twenty-one-year-old King George of the Hellenes went to Russia in search of a bride.

He was not long in finding one. The Tsar's younger brother, the Grand Duke Constantine, had a fifteen-year-old daughter named Olga. One look at this fair, plump and pretty Grand Duchess Olga seems to have been enough for George: by the time he left Russia they were engaged. Some six months later, in October 1867, amidst scenes of customary splendour, they were married in the Winter Palace in St Petersburg. To represent the bridegroom's parents (who could no more afford this wedding than they had been able to afford their daughter Dagmar's) came George's brother, the ubiquitous Crown Prince Frederick of Denmark.

On their return to Greece, the newly married couple were given a tremendous welcome. The young Queen had tactfully chosen a dress in the Greek national colours, blue and white, for her entry into Athens. Her gesture delighted the crowds. 'Her shy youth and beauty' is said to have conquered the 'impressionable hearts' of her new subjects. The roaring crowds would probably have been more touched still had they known that, in her luggage, their sixteen-year-old Queen had packed all her dolls.

Queen Olga did not long nurse her dolls. Almost nine months to the day after their wedding, she gave birth to a son. He was named Constantine. In the years that followed, seven children—five boys and two girls—grew up in the royal nursery. Whatever else the Greek kingdom might lack, it, like the Danish, would not lack heirs. And King George's descendants were always to remain royals of both Greece and Denmark.

The marriage of King George and Queen Olga was an extremely happy one. Both little more than children at the time of their wedding, they developed a deep respect for each other. Despite the fact that she came from one of the most formal and lavish courts in Europe, Olga very quickly adapted herself to her husband's unpretentious ways. A warmhearted, sensible and energetic woman, Queen Olga had very little time for the meaningless formalities and enforced idleness that characterized the life of so many royals.

'No one could have had a simpler home life than ours,' wrote one of her sons. 'The rigid etiquette that made life a burden to most royal children of our generation was never enforced by my parents. We were not allowed to be conscious of our rank except through the responsibilities it entailed and, consequently, it was not regarded by any of us as a matter for congratulation.'

Like the children of his sister the Princess of Wales, King George's children were brought up lovingly and naturally. The rooms of the palace in Athens resounded to the noise of the royal children at play. They roller-skated through the ballrooms, they cycled along the corridors (with the King, on occasion, in the lead), they played hide-and-seek in the state apartments. In one respect, however, the Greek royal children differed from their English cousins: they were better educated. Of the advantages of a good education, both King George and Queen Olga were convinced. In this, they could be martinets in a way which would have been quite beyond the Prince and Princess of Wales.

To provide for his growing family a still more relaxed and informal atmosphere, King George bought himself a 40,000-acre property some fifteen miles north of Athens. The estate, named Tatoi, consisted of little more than a couple of shooting boxes set in a wild and rocky pine forest. From its heights, one could get a wonderful view of the shimmering Aegean across the plain of Attica. The family loved it. Once a suitable villa had been built, they spent as much time there as possible. 'Tatoi,' says one of the princes, 'was a refuge, a haunt of freedom...'

But what King George wanted of Tatoi most of all was to give it as Danish a character as possible. A Danish forestry expert named Münter was brought out and, acting as forester, surveyor and engineer, soon turned the estate into a model property. More trees were planted, good roads were laid out, Danish agricultural methods were introduced. Barns, stables and a dairy were built; herds of Danish and Swiss cows were imported; Rhenish wine-growers produced a 'King's wine'—Château Décélie. Before many years had passed, one Danish visitor could profess himself astonished at the fact that the home farm at Tatoi was hardly different from a farm in Denmark.

'With the sound of cow bells, deep bellowing and plaintive bleating, the flocks and herds leave their sheds and pens for distant pastures, with rough-haired, long-backed wolf hounds to keep them in the path. From the dairy comes the hum of the separator and the sharp clink of milk pails. The commanding voice of Miss Petersen, the Danish dairy-woman, is muffled by the whirring wings of a thousand doves, as they fly over roofs and trees.'

But if, in private life, King George could live like a Dane, in public he was all Greek. His country's problems, and its aspirations, were his. The arrival of his first son, Constantine, considerably strengthened this identification with Greece. To his superstitious subjects, the birth, and the name, of the boy were matters of great significance. The Prince had been born on Greek soil; as a member of the Orthodox faith, he would one day be their first national king. Then the name—Constantine—was that of the last sovereign who had reigned over all the Hellenes: Constantine XI had been the last Emporer of Byzantium. Would the Greeks, under this new Constantine, know once again the glories of those far-off days?

For this—the regeneration and unification of all the Greek peoples—was a great national ideal. Along with all his other obligations, King George had inherited this 'Great Idea': the dream of a new Byzantium. For centuries the Greeks had been living under Turkish domination; the Greek War of Independence, which had ended successfully in 1830 (and which had so fired romantic imaginations) was looked upon merely as a first step towards the realization of the 'Great Idea'. A second step had been taken with King George's accession, when his acceptance of the throne had brought with it the Ionian Islands. But with millions of Greeks still living under

Turkish rule, Greece laid claim to the island of Crete, to Thessaly and Epirus on its northern borders and, most fervently of all, to Constantinople. Once again this marvellously domed and minareted city on the shores of the Bosphorus must become the capital of a great Hellenic Empire.

'For every Greek,' wrote one of the King's sons, 'there lingers deep in his soul the haunting yearning for the "city" of his ancestors, where stands the undying glory of St Sophia, the "Basilica" of his dreams, which "Time and years will once again make his".'

At times of great national enthusiasm, the Greek crowds would take up the cry, '*Ke stin poli*'—to the city. Constantinople must be taken from the Turks and Mass celebrated under the vast dome of St Sophia.

And, as King of the Hellenes, George—and his dynasty—was committed to this great Hellenic dream.

For the young, inexperienced Danish prince, it was a daunting legacy. But already King George had taken steps towards its realization. Russia was the traditional enemy of the Turks and by now George was doubly linked to the powerful Russian Empire: his wife was the niece of the Tsar and his sister Dagmar would one day be the Tsaritsa. Surely, in some future struggle with the Turks, these dynastic alliances would stand him in good stead?

CHAPTER FOUR

1

It would have been all but impossible for Dagmar—now the Grand Duchess Marie Feodorovna—to have introduced her Danish family's unaffected ways into the Russian court. Even if the private life of the imperial family could be relatively natural, its public life was highly artificial.

As Tsar of all the Russias, the Supreme Autocrat, the Father of his People, Dagmar's father-in-law was the central figure in a set-piece of almost oriental magnificence; he was the sun about which his gigantic Empire revolved. As such, Alexander II was obliged to conduct his public appearances along carefully pre-scribed lines. The court was run with all the precision of a military review or a classical ballet; everything was formal, theatrical, larger than life. There was very little occasion for a spontaneous gesture, a relaxed movement or a humorous quip. And although Tsar Alexander II was a humane, well-intentioned man, with an unpretentious private manner, he was very conscious of his status. The great achievement of his reign—the liberation of the serfs—had earned him the title of the Tsar-Liberator, but to the majority of his subjects, Alexander II remained a remote and God-like figure.

Into the intricacies of this life, Dagmar was initiated by her mother-in-law, the Empress Marie Alexandrovna. Naturally gracious and observant, Dagmar quickly learnt how to deport herself as a future Tsaritsa. There was little doubt that she would make an excellent one. If not exactly beautiful, Dagmar was one of those women who could give an illusion of beauty: she was small, vivacious, elegant, graceful. Like her sister Alexandra, Princess of Wales, she had the ability to inspire affection. She had, says Lord Frederic Hamilton, 'a large measure of her [sister's] subtle and indescribable charm of manner.'

Where Dagmar differed from Alexandra was that she had a stronger taste for social life: she loved dancing, parties, conversation. Her horizons were wider, her intelligence sharper, her way of life more methodical. Dagmar was altogether a better organized, more resourceful woman.

Like Alexandra, though, Dagmar had the field very much to herself. For just as Queen Victoria shunned public life, so, despite her social accomplishments, did Dagmar's mother-in-law, the Tsaritsa. Not very happily married and often ill, the Empress Marie Alexandrovna absented herself for long periods from the court, preferring to spend her time with her family in Germany.

Thus, Dagmar was very quickly recognized as the leading female figure at the imperial court. The crowds, with whom she was so popular, had ample opportunity to catch glimpses of her, for she and Alexander lived in the Anitchkov Palace which stood on the Nevsky Prospect—that great, busy thoroughfare running through the heart of St Petersburg. On those extrardinarily light summer nights, passers-by could watch their splendid coach, escorted by cossacks, turn out of the palace, and through its windows they could see the hulking form of the Tsarevich with, beside him, the tiny figure of his smiling, dark-eyed wife, glittering with diamonds.

Despite the ease with which Dagmar slipped into her brilliant new role, she remained, at heart, an unspoilt Danish princess. She might have moved into the most indolent, decadent and extravagant society in Europe, but she retained always something of the practical, honest-to-goodness qualities of her Danish upbringing. Revelling in the luxuries of her new life, Dagmar never let them become necessities. The Anitchkov Palace was comfortably rather than elegantly furnished. As in her sister Alix's homes, the rooms were a jumble of plush-covered furniture, looped lace curtains, antimacassars, potted palms, gilt screens, framed photographs and assorted *objets*. For Dagmar, the chief delight was the garden behind the palace, for here she could be assured of some out-of-doors privacy. By the standards of Russian society, she was an exceptionally efficient housewife, interesting herself in such things as the linen store, the servants' rooms and—astonishing to a race who loved living in overheated, hermetically sealed houses—the circulation of fresh air. The lessons learnt in the Yellow Palace, Copenhagen, were not being forgotten in the Anitchkov Palace, St Petersburg.

Unlike Bertie and Alix, Alexander and Dagmar were almost ideally suited. The success of the marriage was due as much to Alexander's personality as to Dagmar's tact and good sense. The Tsarevich was as unlike the urbane, gregarious, luxury-loving Prince of Wales as it was possible to be. 'The massive build,' says Constantine Pobedonostsev, who had been Alexander's tutor, 'the slow *tempo*, the enormous strength, the upward scowl which does duty as a glance, the side gait, awkward bearing and bovine butting of the head, suggested "bullock" as a term of endearment...' And, hand in hand with the Tsarevich's gaucherie, went a dislike of society, a taste for domesticity and a marital faithfulness. The Tsarevich was never happier than when sitting at home with his wife. For her sake, he would tolerate those small, gay gatherings for which she had a penchant, but he much preferred a quiet life. Thus Alexander's uxoriousness, combined with Dagmar's Danish efficiency, ensured that the Antichkov Palace remained, in all that sea of imperial pomp and splendour, an island of almost bourgeois cosiness and respectability.

The couple had five children: Nicholas, born in May 1868, and then, during the following fifteen years, came George, Xenia, Michael and Olga. With each passing year, the love between husband and wife seemed to deepen. The Tsarevich was devoted to his lively little wife and she knew exactly how to handle him. Never hectoringly, but with feminine subtlety, she encouraged him to prepare himself for his future role: to read, to observe, to extend his interests. And, as both a conscientious man and an adoring husband, Alexander did as she said.

There were times, though, when his conscientiousness came into conflict with his devotion. One evening, despite the fact that he was feeling ill, he decided to go on studying. Dagmar promptly ordered him to bed. Not wanting to disobey her, Alexander undressed, lay down beside her and pretended to sleep. As soon as he was certain that she was asleep, he quietly rose, dressed again and tip-toed back to his study.

If Dagmar was responsible for encouraging her husband to prepare himself for his future position, the actual preparation was being done by a far more forceful character: Alexander's old tutor and now his mentor, Pobedonostsev. The Procurator of the Holy Synod, Pobedonostsev was an arch-reactionary. Indeed, his nickname was 'The Great Inquisitor'. A firm believer in the virtues of Autocracy, Orthodoxy and Nationalism, Pobedonostsev had very little difficulty in convincing his bull-headed pupil of the desirability of clinging to these principles. Thus, while the reigning Tsar was gradually, if somewhat haltingly, liberalizing the régime, the future Tsar was being led along a very different path.

How much Dagmar influenced her husband's political thinking is difficult to say. She was not greatly interested in politics, nor was she a particularly clever woman. 'Adore her,' wrote Princess Catherine Radziwill, 'as an exceptionally graceful creature, but do not look for grave intellectual faculties.' Dagmar might have been raised in a more liberal atmosphere than her husband but she never questioned Pobedonostsev's teachings; she very quickly adopted the conventional view of the Russian aristocracy towards the country's complex problems. Like Alix, Dagmar's political opinions were more a matter of personal prejudice than anything else and, again like Alix, her most firmly held prejudice was against Prussia. In this, she certainly was prepared to use her influence. It would not have been difficult to implant a similar antipathy in her husband's uncomplicated mind. A man like Alexander would have been far more receptive to the ideas of his adored wife than to the more reasoned arguments of statesmen.

Despite the fact that his father, Tsar Alexander II, was friendly with Prussia, the Tsarevich became increasingly anti-Prussian and ultimately anti-German. This feeling was considerably strengthened during the couple's visit to Denmark. At the court of his father-in-law, King Christian IX, Alexander would have been exposed to the most virulent anti-German sentiments. 'The source of the Germanophobia of Alexander III...' wrote Vladimir Poliakoff in later years, 'is to be sought as much in the work-basket of Queen Louise and in the table talk at Bernsdorff, as in political influences or national alliances.'

Before many years had passed, Dagmar had encouraged Alexander to turn against Prussia no less successfully than Alix had encouraged Bertie. The sisters might not know much about international affairs but, in the event of some future European war, they wanted to be together on the side that was fighting against Germany. To these daughters of Europe's Father-in-law, it was as simple as that.

2

The fact that his patriarchy was spreading to the furthest corners of Europe was not a source of unmixed satisfaction to the patriarch himself. King Christian IX was a devoted father, never happier than when his children, and grandchildren, were gathered about him. His dynasty might have come a long way from its modest beginnings but he sadly missed its members. And they, in turn, missed not only him, but each other. To be together and, more particularly, to be together in their native Denmark, was regarded as one of life's greatest joys by the members of King Christian IX's family.

There thus developed, during the late 1860s, that tradition of Danish family gatherings, when all, or almost all, the members of the clan came together to spend a few weeks with King Christian and Queen Louise. In time, these great assemblies were to become an established part of the royal European scene. For almost forty years, each summer, King Christian IX would preside over this coming together of his vast, widespread and increasingly illustrious family.

If the gathering were a small one (and not all the family could come every year) it would take place at Bernsdorff, that charming country palace set in its leafy park not far from Copenhagen. Indeed, through its magnificent elms, one could glimpse the copper-coloured domes and spires of that elegant little city. But if the entire family were present (and in addition to his six children, King Christian was to have thirty-six grandchildren; their combined suites would number over three hundred) they would assemble at the larger and grander palace of Fredensborg, some twenty miles from the capital. Set in its vast park, with its views over the lake of Esrom to the hills beyond, Fredensborg spelt enchantment for the family. Fredensborg 'evokes all the best years of our childhood and youth,' remembered one of the princes in his sad and exiled old age, 'the days when no trouble was great enough to upset the glorious happiness of our lives.'

Gathered together, the family formed, in the words of one of the grandchildren, a regular 'Tower of Babel'. Between the lot of them, they spoke no less than seven languages. It was as well that amongst the family's very few cerebral accomplishments was an ability to learn languages. 'This gift of tongues,' says one of the Greek princes, 'came in very handy.'

Once reunited for those weeks in the summer, the adults put aside all cares of state; the children were released from the schoolroom. Everyone lived *en famille*. Queens and princesses shared sitting-rooms; heirs to thrones were packed into little cottages in the grounds. Slips of paper, bearing such illustrious titles as 'The Tsarevich of Russia' or 'The King of Greece' were casually pinned on to doors along the corridors. Breakfast and luncheon were taken informally, without servants. Like any good *bourgeois* housewife, Queen Louise would seat herself at the middle of the table and serve the food from chafing-dishes set before her, while the guests fetched their own plates and cutlery from side tables. Some minor princess was quite likely to find herself being attended to by the Prince of Wales or the Crown Prince of Denmark. The food was equally unsophisticated. Favourite with the children was *øllebrød*: a concoction of black bread boiled with black beer, served steaming hot in a soup plate lined with brown sugar, the whole topped with cream. It never seemed to taste right, admitted a Greek prince, 'out of Denmark'.

The days would be spent in innocent amusements. Indeed, the entire family seemed to live in an atmosphere of permanent adolescence. They rode horses, they devised practical jokes and, when cycling became the craze, they pedalled away for hours. They went picnicking and boating and walking. They played hilarious games of croquet. Occasionally the children might be packed off to some museum but in general there was precious little in the way of serious-minded pursuits. Anyone attempting to do anything as sedentary as writing a letter or reading a book would be mercilessly teased. Even the Princess of Wales, who was becoming increasingly deaf, complained of not being able to concentrate on her letters because of the obligatory racket raised by the others the minute she sat down.

Their boisterousness was exceptional. 'The noise they all made, and the wild romps they had were simply indescribable...' a visiting German princess wrote from Fredensborg. Full-grown princes pick-a-backed each other, flung one another about and 'seemed happier and to enjoy themselves more thoroughly than children of five or six'.

Nor was this hilarity, this naïve, knock-about humour, confined to the princes. To the hysterical delight of his grandchildren, King Christian would accidentally inhale the palmful of pepper which he had been planning to blow in the direction of a particularly long-nosed lady-in-waiting. The giant Tsarevich Alexander—Uncle Sacha to his adoring nephews—would turn a hand-hose on to the top-hatted figure of the King of Sweden. A monkey, tugging at the bright red cherries on Dagmar's hat, would reduce her watching relations to paroxysms of 'uncontrollable mirth'. The Prince of Wales's secretary, opening a wrong door, once came across a middle-aged princess doing the cancan. Even at the sick-bed of an aged relation, Dagmar and Alexandra were so tickled by the sight of one of their nephews with a trick candlestick protruding like a horn from his forehead, that they were forced to flee the room in consternation.

In the evenings, things took on a slightly more formal flavour. Before dinner, the family would assemble in one room, the guests and household in another. King Christian IX was the most punctual of men but not even he could scold his daughter, Alexandra, Princess of Wales, into being on time for this family assembly. Once they had all gathered together, the King led them, in strict order of precedence, into the other room to greet their guests. There would follow what the British royal family always referred to as *cercle-ing*: that slow round of the company with a word or two for each of those present. At this, the less inhibited Danish royalties were far more accomplished than the often inarticulate members of Queen Victoria's family.

Dinner, at which the food was reported to be 'heavy, not to say indifferent', lasted an hour and a half and would be followed by simple parlour games or a little light music, with Queen Louise and her three daughters—Alexandra, Dagmar and Thyra— thumping out eight-handed arrangements on two pianos. The card game, Loo, might be played for 'very small points', always provided that the bear-like Tsarevich Alexander had not treated the company to his particular parlour piece of tearing a pack of cards in half.

At nine o'clock there would be a further spread of homely fare: tea, sandwiches, sour milk and more *øllebrød*. It was very countrified. The Prince of Wales who, if no more intellectual than the rest of them, was certainly more worldly, found it all extremely tedious. For his mother's fears that he would fall into temptation at the Danish court, there were, alas, no grounds whatsoever. There was only one more boring place on earth than Fredensborg, Bertie used to say, and that was Bernsdorff.

3

Although these Danish family gatherings looked artless enough, there were those who suspected that they were not quite as innocent as they seemed. Berlin was particuarly suspicious. And indeed, every now and then would come fresh evidence of the family's anti-Prussian manoeuvrings. The marriage of King Christian's third daughter, Princess Thyra, seemed just such an instance.

Born in 1853, Princess Thyra of Denmark was the gentlest of King Christian's daughters. Boasting neither her sister Alexandra's marvellous beauty nor her sister Dagmar's vivacity, she was none the less an attractive young woman, with a crown of blonde hair and what one witness calls the 'most beautiful large, dark blue eyes with a wonderful expression of truthfulness and goodness in them'. Her amiability seems to have been her most notable characteristic. Queen Louise used to say that of her three daughters, Thyra had the sweetest nature, and one of her nephews speaks of her 'gentleness of manner, her kindness of heart and wonderful unselfishness'.

That this jewel should find as splendid a setting as had her sisters seemed to Queen Louise inevitable. There was certainly no lack of possible suitors. King William III of the Netherlands put out feelers; but not even the prospect of the Dutch crown could compensate for the fact that the widowed King was thirty-six years older than the Princess. Thyra refused him. Instead, William III married the eighteen-year-old Princess Emma of Waldeck-Pyrmont and, with his three sons by Ins first wife all having predeceased him, fathered the future Queen Wilhelmina of the Netherlands.

There was talk of a match with Queen Victoria's third son, Prince Arthur (Thyra had been 'half-promised' said Queen Victoria) and with the exiled Prince Imperial of France. But these proposals came to nothing. Instead, Princess Thyra seemed destined for the future once predicted for her by a gypsy on the beach at Klampenborg: that she would be 'a queen who will never wear a crown'.

The crownless King whom Thyra was to marry was Prince Ernest Augustus of Hanover. She had first met him in 1872, when she was nineteen and he twenty-seven. What Prince Ernest lacked in position he lacked also, alas, in looks. He was an extremely plain young man: tall, narrow-shouldered, long-necked, balding, myopic, with, as one of Princess Thyra's nephews put it, 'practically no nose worth mentioning'. One was forced to admit, wrote Princess Alexandra on one occasion, 'poor dear Ernest is the *ugliest* man there ever was made!!!'— Ugly, and with not even the prospect of a throne to compensate for it. For Prince Ernest Augustus's father was the last reigning King of Hanover, the blind King George V, whose own father had been the Duke of Cumberland—one of the more wicked of Queen Victoria's wicked uncles. Because of its refusal to join Prussia during the Austro-Prussian War of 1866, Hanover had been annexed by the victorious Prussians and its status as an independent kingdom abolished. Not only did the Hanoverian King lose his title, but his considerable personal fortune was sequestrated by the Prussians. It was a situation which neither the old King nor his son was prepared to accept. Ernest still considered himself to be the Crown Prince of Hanover and to have every right to be his father's financial, as well as his dynastic, heir.

Bismarck, who had a tendency to over-estimate, or at least over-emphasize, the danger of royal opposition, always kept an eye on Prince Ernest. When the Prince fell in love with Princess Thyra of Denmark (and she, to the astonishment of all, with him) the German Chancellor took fright. Might the Prince's marriage into the Danish royal family not enhance his standing as a rallying point for anti-Prussian opinion? Would not Prince Ernest, so unresigned to his change of status, become increasingly defiant once he was being backed up by the Danish court, a court that was becoming yearly more influential?

To Bismarck's apprehensions were added those of the Danish government. Not wanting to antagonize the powerful German Chancellor, King Christian's ministers advised against the match. And the King, as a constitutional monarch and a circumspect man, followed their advice.

So, for half a dozen years after the first meeting between Thyra and her gangling Prince, matters rested.

In 1878 old King George V of Hanover died, in exile in Paris. His son now assumed the title of the Duke of Cumberland, for the very good reason that the title of King of Hanover no longer existed. This was a fact, however, which Ernest refused to admit. To anyone who cared to listen, and to a great many who did not, he announced that he was now the King of Hanover. And, as long as he continued to do so, Prussia (or 'the robber' as Princess Alexandra robustly referred to it) hung on to his late father's confiscated fortune.

To complicate matters still further, the old King had left his financial affairs in the hands of Queen

Victoria; she was, after all, his first, and certainly most illustrious, cousin. But the Queen found herself powerless to do anything about getting this sequestrated property returned to Ernest before he gave up his claim to the throne. The more he asserted this claim, the more he antagonized Queen Victoria.

'The Queen...' reported Victoria's private secretary, Henry Ponsonby, to his wife, 'writes a letter saying the Duke of Cumberland is a fool and I say it is perfect, and then I write a letter saying he is a damned fool and she says it is admirable.'

And all the while, despite his lack of looks, fortune or kingdom, Princess Thyra remained determined to marry the Duke of Cumberland. In her determination, she was being backed up by the Prince and Princess of Wales. To show his sympathy with the Duke's cause, Bertie walked side by side with Ernest behind the King of Hanover's coffin at his funeral in Paris. His gesture appalled Bismarck. Alexandra, in the meantime, was working in a more clandestine fashion. She was forever trying to arrange secret meetings between the lovers; but with Prussia, the Danish government and—most formidable of all—Queen Victoria, opposing the match, she had to move cautiously.

Prince Ernest, too, was suspicious of Alix's enthusiasm. Might Princess Alexandra not be acting in Queen Victoria's interests? Might marriage to Princess Thyra not entail acceptance of Queen

Victoria's demand that he give up his claim to the throne?

But Alexandra persisted. In the autumn of 1878 she organized a secret meeting at Frankfurt. With Thyra and Ernest once again in each other's company, all obstacles to the proposed match seemed to melt away. They agreed to marry later that year. The announcement, contrary to all expectations, caused no more than a ripple of disapproval. Queen Victoria, having apparently given up her struggle for the return of Ernest's property, contented herself with saying that he and Thyra would make 'a very plain couple, though very amiable and good'.

If Ernest was still without his fortune (he would have to wait sixteen years for that), he had at least retained his claim to the throne and married the woman of his choice. And King Christian IX had the satisfaction of becoming the father-in-law of yet another, albeit *de jure*, monarch.

CHAPTER FIVE

1

The political worth of the Danish family ties, in which King Christian's children placed such hopes, were put to the test during the Russo-Turkish War of 1877–8. To a greater or lesser degree, three of them—Dagmar, George and Alexandra—were involved in this climax of the complicated and ever-festering 'Eastern Question'.

With Dagmar tending to see political issues purely in terms of family connections, her concern, at the outbreak of the war, was as much for Greece as for Russia. Her brother George was King of the Hellenes; the Greeks and Turks were enemies; might this war between Russia and Turkey not benefit her brother's kingdom?

These were George's thoughts exactly. Surely this was the opportunity to put his close family ties with Russia to good use. If Greece were to come to Russia's aid in her fight against the Turks in Bulgaria, might she not win for herself some Turkish-held territory: Epirus, Thessaly, perhaps even Macedonia? (The fact that Russia had its eye no less firmly on

Constantinople than did Greece was conveniently ignored for the moment.)

For a while, it seemed as though George's hopes would be realized. Tsar Alexander II asked Greece to join Russia. Both George and Dagmar were delighted. But not for long. The alliance was not allowed to materialize. Britain and France who, together with Russia, were Greece's guaranteeing powers, would not hear of it. King George was obliged to remain neutral. Not for the last time in his life was he to appreciate that, in some cases, family relationships counted for very little.

Disappointed, Dagmar none the less busied herself with the Russian war effort. With the Tsarevich away in command of the 12th and 13th Army Corps, she set about organizing hospitals and medical supplies. As always, she proved extremely efficient and hard-working. Yet she found time to miss her rough-hewn and inarticulate husband. There is a story of how late one night the Tsarevich, exhausted after a day's campaigning, returned to his little wooden cottage to sleep. By the light of a solitary candle, he saw a figure dressed in a nurse's uniform come towards him. Puritan that he was, Alexander was about to order her away when he suddenly realized that it was his wife. She had journeyed to the front, in secret, to see him.

Alexander did not shine as a commander. He had neither the taste, nor the talent, for fighting. 'His unaccountable movements and wild manoeuvres,' says one of his biographers dryly, 'did not exhibit any-thing like an inborn genius for the art of war.' The Tsarevich came back from the front with an unshake-able aversion to war. Two things, it was afterwards said, Alexander had no wish to break: the seventh commandment and the peace of Europe.

Nor was he alone in his disillusionment. Although, technically, Russia won the war, she lost the peace. At the Congress of Berlin, held in 1878 to decide the peace terms, Russian prestige suffered considerably. Tsar Alexander II, hitherto the darling of the nation, suddenly lost much of his popularity. And amongst those who protested against his 'capitulation' to the Powers at the Congress was the Tsarevich. Goaded on by his mentor Pobedonostsev, Alexander threw his weight behind the vociferous and ultra-rightist Nationalists. He became more chauvinistic than ever.

If Dagmar's husband's country had emerged badly from the Congress, her brother George's country had, after all, made some gains. From the decaying body of the Ottoman Empire, Greece was given Thessaly and a sliver of Epirus. This time, family ties had counted for something, for it was Britain—in the person of the Prime Minister Benjamin Disraeli—who had achieved these gains. He had achieved them, Disraeli claimed in his flamboyant fashion, because of his devotion to King George's other sister, the Princess of Wales. He knew how passionately Alexandra was concerned with the problems of her brother George; in the spring of 1877 Alix had returned from a visit to Athens determined to do whatever she could to further the Greek cause. 'I did something yesterday for Greece,' announced Disraeli. 'It was very difficult but it was by no means to be despised. It was all done for Her Royal Highness's sake. I thought of Marlborough House all the time…'

So there were more ways than one, it seemed, in which the children of King Christian IX could get what they wanted.

These family ties again came into play during the annual gathering of the family at Bernsdorff in the autumn of 1879. With the Russo-Turkish War having worsened the always uneasy relationship between Britain and Russia, Queen Victoria warned the Prince and Princess of Wales against going to Denmark: the Tsarevich and his wife were to be there and a meeting between the heirs to the Russian and British thrones would not be prudent.

But Bertie, who usually avoided these tedious Danish holidays, was determined to go. Even more determined was Alix. Not for the world was she going to miss an opportunity of seeing her Russian sister and brother-in-law. 'I shall, of course, avoid politics as much as possible,' explained Bertie to his mother, 'but as [the Tsarevich] married dear Alix's sister, who I am very fond of, I am most anxious that our relations should not be strained.'

To Bernsdorff, therefore, they went and the family reunion was the usual success. Although the Tsarevich and the Prince had very little in common, they set out, for the sake of their wives, to be civil to one another. They entertained each other on their respective yachts, *Dirjava* and *Osborne*, they went cruising to Helsingborg, they sat listening while their wives exchanged gossip. On leaving Denmark, both couples travelled on to Paris where there was more hob-nobbing. To prove to Europe that, as far as they were concerned, the Anglo-Russian quarrel had been patched up, the Tsarevich and the Prince together called on President Grévy.

Their gesture did nothing, of course, towards alleviating the bitterness between their two countries but it was not entirely insignificant. Some twenty-five years hence, as King Edward VII, Bertie was to sign an Anglo-Russian convention. Such an agreement, which would have been unthinkable in 1879, was to be hailed as 'the triumph of King Edward's policy'.

2

By the year 1880, Dagmar and Alexander had been married for fourteen years. She turned thirty-three that year, he, thirty-five. Although their married life in no way resembled that of Alix and Bertie, their public position was in some ways not dissimilar. The Tsarevich had no more to do with the government of the country than had the Prince of Wales. Neither heir had any say in affairs of state. But whereas Bertie's lack of involvement was at his mother's express wish, Alexander's was due to a divergence of outlook between his father and himself. The Tsarevich, unlike the Prince of Wales, was allowed to attend ministerial meetings but, with what E. M. Almedingen calls his 'policeman's mind' and 'inquisitor's approach', Alexander was out of sympathy with the Tsar's enlightened ideals. Like many of his countrymen, the Tsarevich considered his father's achievements—the freeing of the serfs, the reform of the judiciary, the army and the navy, the re-introduction of local government—to have been both misguided and unsuccessful. At council meetings he sat silent and disapproving. In turn, the Tsar felt that he could not afford to shift some of his many administrative burdens on to his son's shoulders.

This lack of sympathy between father and son worsened during the late 1870s when Alexander II installed his long-standing mistress, Catherine Dolgoruka, and their three children, in the Winter Palace. Both Alexander and Dagmar were appalled. The Tsarevich was devoted to his mother, the ailing Empress, and, as a model of marital fidelity himself, had no understanding of what he considered to be his father's licentiousness. The young couple were more appalled still when, a matter of weeks after the Empress's death, in 1880, the Tsar married his mistress. He had every intention, it appears, of having her crowned Empress.

Dagmar was particularly upset by her father-in-law's tasteless impropriety. The married life of her parents, King Christian and Queen Louise, had always been above reproach; where, among her other relations, there was any infidelity, it was always conducted with circumspection. Dagmar simply could not reconcile herself to this flaunting of the cool, blonde Catherine Dolgoruka, now known as Princess Yurievskaya. On the rare occasions that they met, Dagmar could not bring herself to be polite to the Tsar's wife.

Even at the risk of defying the Tsar himself Dagmar made no attempt to disguise her hostility. One Sunday morning, after service in the Palace church, the members of the Tsar's family prepared, as usual, to pass before him to take their leave. Usually, on these occasions, his new wife stepped tactfully back, but this time Alexander II kept her by his side. He was determined that she be treated with proper respect. First to approach the Tsar, as leading Grand Duchess, was Dagmar. 'Come, my dear,' said the Emperor, 'say how do you do to the Princess.' With head held high, Dagmar made her curtsy to the Tsar and, without so much as a glance at his wife, moved on and out of the room.

By this time, however, Tsar Alexander II was having to face opposition infinitely more unnerving than that of his family. Despite his well-intentioned reforms, revolutionary movements were spreading throughout the Empire. Acts of terrorism were becoming more and more frequent; there was a political murder every other week. Particularly violent

were the Nihilists. On several occasions the Tsar had
narrowly escaped assassination at their hands. Yet
he refused to take precautions or, for that matter,
to yield to the entreaties of the reactionaries (the
Tsarevich amongst them) to revert to a less liberal
régime. On the contrary, by the opening of the year
1881, he was preparing to grant the country a form of
constitution. A manifesto, granting limited representative government, was drawn up and, on 12 March
1881, it was presented to the Tsar for his signature.
Described as the 'crowning touch' of the Tsar's 'great
reforms', it was to be made public two days later, on
Monday 14 March.

On the Sunday before the proposed publication
of the manifesto, the Emperor attended a parade
at the Michael Riding School. With him was the
Tsarevich. When the parade was over, the Tsarevich
returned directly home to his wife but his father
stopped on his way back to the Winter Palace to pay a
short call on one of his cousins.

Alexander and Dagmar were just going in to luncheon when they heard an explosion. Imagining that
it was the sound of a gun being fired in salute, they
continued on. Minutes later came another, more
violent explosion. Realizing that something was
wrong, Alexander sent someone to find out what it
was. Within seconds an equerry came galloping pell-
mell into the courtyard. Closely followed by Dagmar,
Alexander rushed downstairs. They were told that
the Tsar had been wounded by a bomb. Flinging

themselves into a one-horse sledge, husband and wife made a dash for the Winter Palace. There they found the Tsar, hideously wounded, unconscious and obviously dying.

They learnt that as Alexander II had been driving back to the Palace along the quay of the Catherine Canal, a bomb had been flung beneath his swiftly-moving carriage. From the explosion which followed, Alexander II had emerged unhurt. He had hurried back to see to his wounded cossacks and, on returning to his damaged carriage, had come face to face with a stranger. The man had lifted his hands above his head and flung yet another bomb at the startled Tsar. There had been no escaping that time. Twenty people had been wounded, the Tsar worst of all. His bleeding and mutilated body had been rushed back to the Palace and laid out on a couch. He never regained consciousness. Soon after three o'clock that afternoon he died.

Alexander and Dagmar were now Emperor and Empress.

The manifesto, lying on Alexander II's desk, was never published. Pobedonostsev had very little difficulty in making use of the general outcry against the Nihilists to dissuade the new Tsar, Alexander III, from granting any such representative government. The proposed constitution, which might well have strengthened the bond between Tsar and people was, to all intents and purposes, buried with its originator. Two months after his father's assassination,

Alexander III issued a decree by which his subjects were left in no doubt as to the fashion in which he planned to reign. 'In the midst of our great sorrow,' ran the uncompromisingly autocratic clauses, 'the voice of God commands us to discharge courageously the affairs of government, trusting in God's Providence, with faith in the strength and justice of Autocratic power which we have been called upon to confirm and preserve for the public good...'

Present in St Petersburg for the funeral of Alexander II were the Prince and Princess of Wales. Dagmar, now the Empress Marie Feodorovna, was delighted to welcome her sister. With the Russian capital still in a state of ferment, she needed all the support she could get. Amid the strain, gloom and horror of those days—for the new Tsar and his family were living in an atmosphere of great danger—the presence of the warm-hearted and lively Princess Alexandra was a great comfort. While their husbands were engaged in the elaborate and seemingly endless ceremonies connected with the burial of a Tsar, Dagmar and Alix endeavoured to cheer each other up. That they had some measure of success is evident from an account, given by Lord Frederic Hamilton, of a ceremony held in the Anitchkov Palace a week after the funeral.

The Prince of Wales had been commanded by Queen Victoria to invest Alexander III with the Order of the Garter. Because of court mourning, it had been decided that the investiture would be private, with no one attending other than the Tsar and Tsaritsa, the Prince and Princess of Wales and their staff, the Grand Master and Grand Mistress of the Russian court and the members of the British Embassy. 'This, as it turned out,' says Lord Frederic Hamilton, 'was very fortunate.' As the five members of the staff came pacing solemnly in, each carrying in their arms an item of the insignia on a red velvet cushion, 'a perfectly audible feminine voice' exclaimed, in English, 'Oh my dear! Do look at them. They look exactly like a row of wet nurses carrying babies!' At this, the Empress and the Princess 'exploded with laughter'. Those family spirits, it seems, remained irrepressible.

The Tsar, catching sight of one of the staff hugging his cushion in a particularly maternal fashion, also succumbed; while his face remained under control, his massive frame began quivering like a jelly.

'Never, I imagine, since its institution in 1349', says Lord Frederic Hamilton, 'has the Order of the Garter been conferred amid such general hilarity... The general public never heard of it, nor, I trust, did Queen Victoria.'

With the Tsar hardly cold in his grave, one indeed trusts that she did not. Such royal Danish carryings-on would not have amused the Queen.

PART TWO
SUMMER

CHAPTER SIX

1

Imperceptibly almost, King Christian IX was developing into one of Europe's leading sovereigns. By the 1880s he was in his sixties. As gentle, as unambitious, as unpretentious as he had ever been, he was generally regarded as a man of sound judgement and regal bearing. With a reluctance to assert his authority successfully masking his somewhat rigid and autocratic cast of mind, King Christian was looked upon as being wiser and more democratic than he actually was. To many, he seemed the *beau idéal* of a nineteenth-century constitutional sovereign: a sage, respected and courtly monarch, holding himself high above the hurly-burly of everyday politics.

But chiefly, of course, it was to his position as a patriach, as the head of a nineteenth-century dynasty rivalled only by the Coburgs, that King Christian IX owed his growing eminence. The rise of his house had been astonishing. What other living monarch could boast so many brilliantly placed descendants? Who, a generation ago, would have imagined that the mere fact that the children of the King of little

Denmark were coming to spend a holiday with him would be looked upon as an occasion of such international importance?

Yet, to his credit, King Christian IX took it all in his stride. He always thought of his descendants, no matter how highly placed, as people first, royalty second. The more children and grandchildren he and Queen Louise could gather about them, the happier they were. A year which brought together all their descendants, and not only the more important ones, was always a special year.

Such a year was 1883. By that time the King and Queen had thirty-one descendants—six children and twenty-five grandchildren. There were the Tsar and Tsaritsa with their five children; the Prince and Princess of Wales with their five; the King and Queen of Greece with six children; the Crown Prince and Princess of Denmark with six; the Duke and Duchess of Cumberland with three; and King Christian's youngest son, the still unmarried Prince Waldemar.

Gathered together at Fredensborg, these illustrious royals formed as unaffected a group as one could imagine. More than one observer felt obliged to comment on their particular blend of majesty and ingenuousness. 'The singularly domestic character of this remarkable assemblage,' reported the visiting Mr Gladstone pompously to Queen Victoria, 'and the affectionate intimacy which appeared to pervade it, made an impression upon him no less deep than the demeanour of all its members, which was so kindly and so simple…'

Of the simplicity, or charm, of King Christian's descendants, Queen Victoria needed no reminding. 'The King and Queen of Denmark are most fortunate in their children!' she once told her daughter Vicky, the German Crown Princess. 'All so good, so amiable, and the children again so nice.'

But, for all this, they remained royalty, and their comings and goings were not without a certain brilliance. The young Roma Lister, spending that season in Copenhagen, was deeply impressed by the appearance of the members of the family at a ball at the British Legation. 'When the royalties arrived,' she comments (and well she might) 'the room seemed full of them.' There was the gentlemanly old King Christian, with his silver whiskers and his hair combed carefully forward across his balding head. He was reputed to be a 'wonderful dancer', and despite the fact that he had had a fall while dancing at the American Legation the night before, he insisted on partnering the terrified Miss Lister.

Hardly less unnerving was her encounter with Queen Louise. The Queen had a certain sharpness which belied her small, frail and pretty appearance. She subjected the girl to a 'catechism' of questions; the answers to which the Queen, being very deaf, could not really follow. Most impressive of them all was Tsar Alexander III, 'a very giant of a man', towering over his little, dark-eyed Danish wife. Yet despite his appearance of being what Roma Lister some-what breathlessly calls 'a living irresistible force that would never turn aside from what he willed to do', Alexander proved surprisingly amiable.

The loveliest in the room was Alexandra, Princess of Wales. Already, at not quite forty, Alexandra had perfected the appearance that was to remain almost unchanged for the rest of her life. Her narrow head was topped by a crown of elaborately dressed brown hair; her complexion had the colour and smoothness of cream; to hide a girlhood scar, her neck was encir-cled by a jewelled 'dog-collar'; her figure was that of a girl; she dressed with a bandbox elegance and perfec-tion. She already walked with the famous 'Alexandra limp', an affliction caused by a stiff knee and con-verted by her into a movement of extraordinary grace.

As Roma Lister moved away from greeting the Prince and Princess of Wales (this was another of the years in which Bertie subjected himself to the bore-dom of a Danish holiday) their eldest son Eddy asked his mother to dance. They seemed, according to the girl, 'more like brother and sister than mother and son.' As the couple waltzed about the room, general dancing stopped and the other dancers drew back to look in admiration at the dark, sleepy-eyed young man and his slender, beautiful and perennially youth-ful mother.

Sir Algernon West, visiting Copenhagen in the company of Gladstone that autumn, was no less enchanted by this royal galaxy. The British Prime

Minister had invited the royals to luncheon aboard the *Pembroke Castle* in which he was cruising; their arrival, 'in great state barges from the Russian and Danish yachts' was a wonderful sight. Sir Algernon, too, found the Tsar the most impressive personality. The bear-like figure had not been on board for more than three minutes before he went off with an engineer to examine every part of the ship; he was particularly interested in the engines. He would rather be King of Denmark, Alexander afterwards admitted to his host, than Tsar of All the Russias.

After luncheon, at which there were numberless toasts—to the King and Queen of Denmark, the Emperor and Empress of Russia, the King and Queen of the Hellenes, the Prince and Princess of Wales and, of course, Queen Victoria—Princess Alexandra suggested a little entertainment. Alfred Tennyson, who was also on board, should be asked to read one of his poems. She was told that this would prove impossible: 'one could lead a horse to water, but ten could not make him drink.'

'Oh, but I can,' answered Alexandra promptly.

And she did. With forty royals crowded about him in a small cabin on the deck, and with his great 'wide-awake' hat on his head, Tennyson read a couple of poems. When Dagmar afterwards congratulated him, the short-sighted Tennyson, mistaking her for one of the maids-of-honour, patted her on the shoulder. 'Thank you my dear,' muttered the poet condescendingly to the Empress of All the Russias.

'Between two and three,' reported Gladstone to Queen Victoria, 'the illustrious party left the *Pembroke Castle*, and in the midst of an animated scene, went on board the King of Denmark's yacht, which steamed towards Elsinore.'

Another place in which the royals were often to be seen was the theatre; the Danish family had a passion for play-going. The royal box at the Theatre Royal in Copenhagen was seldom empty. It was here, during the family gathering of 1880, that they first saw the fascinating Sarah Bernhardt. With King Christian and Queen Louise, King George and Queen Olga and Princess Alexandra in the box, the Divine Sarah played first *Adrienne Lecouvreur* and then *Frou-frou*. They were enthralled: the royal ladies flung their bouquets on to the stage, the King presented the actress with the Danish Order of Merit (the fact that it was diamond-encrusted made it all the more acceptable), the royal yacht was placed at her disposal so that she could pay a pilgrimage to Hamlet's tomb at Elsinore.

After her last performance in Copenhagen, Sarah Bernhardt attended a supper in her honour. When the German Minister proposed a toast to 'the country that has given us such great art. To France!', the actress, eyes blazing, leapt to her feet to give her reply. Sarah, like so many of her compatriots, had not forgotten the annexation of Alsace and Lorraine by the Germans after the Franco-Prussian War. 'Yes, to France, Mr Prussian Ambassador,' she cried out, 'but to France in her entirety!'

The news of this exchange could have brought nothing but satisfaction to the family of King Christian IX.

With the Princess of Wales, Sarah formed a lasting friendship. The actress declared herself as blinded by the Princess's beauty as was Alexandra by Sarah's talent. After that meeting in Copenhagen, Princess Alexandra always made a point of seeing Sarah Bernhardt, either on stage or in private. And what Princess Alexandra preferred to discuss above all, Sarah used to say, was 'her beloved Denmark'.

2

If King Christian's present status, as Europe's Father-in-law, seemed impressive, his future status—as Europe's Grandfather—promised to be even more so. By this autumn of 1883, no less than four of his grandsons were the heirs—apparent or presumptive—to European thrones. The eldest of these was Prince Eddy; the second was the Tsarevich Nicholas; the third, Crown Prince Constantine of Greece; the fourth, Prince Christian, son of the Crown Prince of Denmark.

The three youngest, all under fifteen, were as yet unremarkable boys. The Tsarevich was described as 'having a thorough Tartar-looking face, but a jolly boy'; Crown Prince Constantine was considered to be particularly engaging; Prince Christian was showing signs of one day being 'a giant'. But, at this stage, they simply formed part of that host of grandchildren who racketed around the grounds of Fredensborg. They contributed to what Mr Gladstone called 'the unrestrained and unbounded happiness of the royal children...who appeared like a single family reared under a single roof.'

Of them all, it was Prince Eddy, heir to the British throne, who seemed assured of the most brilliant future; who would one day occupy what Queen Victoria used to call 'the greatest position there is'. However, it was not this that set Eddy apart from his cousins. He was different from them in every way. Not only was he older—he turned nineteen that year—but he was quieter. He lacked the boisterousness, the initiative and the sparkle of his Greek or Russian or Danish cousins. It was not that he was more intellectual than the rest of them (on the contrary, he was even less so); his whole being was permeated by an extraordinary lassitude.

He had always been that way. Even in infancy, this eldest son of Princess Alexandra had shown signs of being subnormal. He was not exactly an imbecile; merely slow-witted. As a boy he had been listless, slow to react and utterly unable to concentrate his attention on anything for long. In the Wales household, where the boy's parents were hardly more acute (and where his mother was determined to keep the children as child-like as possible for as long as possible) Eddy's shortcomings had not been too apparent.

However, on being sent as a cadet to the training ship *Britannia*, in the company of his younger and brighter brother, Prince George, his lethargy became more and more noticeable. While Prince George acquitted himself very well, Prince Eddy improved not at all. His tutors could do nothing with him. 'He hardly knows the meaning of the words *to read*,' complained one of them.

Even his mother became increasingly perturbed. Alexandra admitted herself '*dreadfully* distressed' with the reports of his lack of progress. The only hope, she imagined, lay in keeping him in the company of his brother George for as long as possible; some of George's liveliness was bound to rub off on Eddy. Thus, when their time on the *Britannia* was over, the two boys were packed off on an extended cruise aboard H.M.S. *Bacchante*. As far as Eddy was concerned, it made not the slightest difference.

Yet apart from what Princess Alexandra airily referred to as his 'dawdly' qualities, Eddy was a pleasant enough young man. He was gentle, well-mannered, eager to give pleasure and utterly without arrogance. 'Kind' and 'dear' were the adjectives his family most frequently used when referring to him and, like so many of King Christian's descendants, he was essentially good-hearted.

The only pity of it all was that this languid and slow-thinking young man would one day become the King of England.

Missing from the family gathering that autumn was the eighteen-year-old Prince George. As Prince Eddy could not be kept sailing around the world indefinitely, it had been decided that he should go up to Cambridge later that year while Prince George joined H.M.S. *Canada* for a cruise in North American waters. For Alexandra the parting had, as always, been heartbreaking. She adored her second son, as he did her. Of his brother Eddy's negative qualities, George had none. He was a lively, intelligent and hard-working youngster. His character had formed early; those years in the navy had inculcated him with a strong sense of duty. George was steady, straightforward and conscientious.

But, like so many of the Danish family, Prince George was young for his years. To read the letters between his mother and himself—with their endearments and diminutives and whimsy—is scarcely to believe that she was the almost middle-aged future Queen of England and he an adult naval officer. She would refer to herself as his 'silly old Motherdear'; he as her 'little Georgie'.

The same childishness marked Prince George's three sisters—Louise, Victoria and Maud—the eldest of whom was already sixteen. All three girls had suffered from a happy-go-lucky education which tended to make them tongue-tied in public and boisterous in private. Unfortunately, none of them had inherited their mother's marvellous beauty. All three were pale, narrow-skulled and bulbous-eyed. Dressed identically, as little adults, and with their hair tending to rat's-tails, it was difficult to tell the girls apart. Not without reason did Queen Victoria pronounce the Wales children to be a 'puny breed'.

3

There was nothing puny about their Greek cousins—the children of King George of the Hellenes. By now George and Olga had four boys and two girls, with ages ranging from one to fifteen. For even this easy-going family, these weeks in Denmark were a relaxation; a release from all the responsibilities of their position. 'When I am there,' King George I used to say, 'I feel as if I were still a little boy.' He might be a king of twenty years' standing, almost forty years old, tall, assured and shrewd, but once back home, George became simply another son of the house. 'The old King's ascendancy and authority remained so great,' wrote one of George's contemporaries, 'that his children, were they emperors or kings, dared not go into Copenhagen without first asking his leave.'

Prince Christopher of Greece tells the story of how once, after breakfast at Fredensborg, he sat down to play King Christian's mechanical piano. Annoyed at his son's brash behaviour, King George ordered him to stop. At this the old King intervened. 'The child shall do as he likes,' he said. 'Go ahead and play.' King George was obliged to give in while young Christopher, with burning cheeks, played on.

Indeed, under King Christian's benevolent eye, the Greek children got away with a great deal. The King, says one of the princes, 'not only encouraged us in our escapades but joined in them himself.' Their aunts—Alexandra, Dagmar and Thyra—were hardly less indulgent. For all their chic, they would allow themselves to be bundled up into comic clothes, hustled into undignified positions and caught out in embarrassing situations. The exuberance with which the Greek princes disported themselves—riding, cycling, running or simply playing about—astonished more restrained guests. 'Tino and Georgie are as strong as two young Hercules! I only wonder no arms and legs were broken,' reported the serious-minded German Crown Princess to Queen Victoria. Queen Louise's furniture must, she imagined, be exceptionally strong: 'one sofa, I believe, had to have the springs renewed at different times...'

No one escaped their teasing. The autocratic Tsar of Russia was once solemnly handed a document informing him that he was 'too corpulent to take part in the excursions and activities' of their cycling club. Their Uncle Waldemar was urgently summoned to one of their rooms to look at two strange men tucked up together in bed—two men who turned out to be the heavily disguised and hysterically giggling figures of the Empress of Russia and the Princess of Wales.

Chief butt of their jokes was their homely Uncle Ernest, Duke of Cumberland, the husband of Princess Thyra. Ernest and Thyra lived at Gmunden, in Austria, in a style so unpretentious that even the simplicity of King Christian's court was too much for Ernest. Only under protest would he attend these family gatherings. He hated travelling, he hated social life and, most of all, he hated wearing formal clothes. For most of the time at Fredensborg, Ernest lived in his Tyrolean shooting outfit—a short green jacket with no collar, leather shorts revealing his bony knees, and heavy hob-nailed boots on his huge feet. Forced to wear evening dress for dinner, he would sit stiff and uncomfortable until the moment that he could hurry away to change into his beloved shooting outfit. Perhaps it was as well that the Duke of Cumberland never realized his claim to the throne of Hanover. And as well, too, that Princess Thyra was so long-suffering and sweet-natured.

Each afternoon King George, with one or two of his sons, would walk over to see his brother, Crown Prince Frederick of Denmark, who lived with his family at Charlottenlund, overlooking the sea. To the boys, Uncle Freddie seemed 'rather pedantic' but, in fact, he was an unaffected man, not unlike their own father. Like their father, too, Crown Prince Frederick was a stylish figure—jauntily moustached, slender and well-dressed. For the suberb cut of their clothes, the men of the family were no less renowned than their sisters.

Very much odd-man-out in this family circle was
Prince Frederick's wife, Crown Princess Louise. To her
Greek nephews, she was known as 'Aunt Swan'; not
because of any particular grace or majesty of bearing
but because of her 'austere and somewhat forbidding'
presence. Sir Frederick Ponsonby described this tall,
raw-boned princess as one of the ugliest women he had
ever seen, while a French Minister once claimed that it
was simply 'not permissible to be so ugly'.

Unlike the rest of the family, whose Protestantism
was of an unquestioning and unobtrusive variety,
Crown Princess Louise was a bigot. She tried to have
as little as possible to do with even Copenhagen's
unworldly society and was quite out of sympathy with
her husband's frivolous relations. Set against her
elegant sisters-in-law, Louise looked a frump. 'She is
a good soul,' wrote one visiting British princess, 'but
a little queer in the head and very difficult to get on
with as she is so stiff.'

One of the queernesses in Louise's head took
the form of second sight; she claimed that she was
psychic. She was always seeing accidents before they
happened or knowing about deaths before they
occurred. It was small wonder that the others found
her so incompatible.

None of this meant, though, that Louise was content to play second fiddle to her more graceful and
spectacularly married sisters-in-law. She was very conscious of her position as future Queen of Denmark.
The Tsarevich, reporting home on the occasion of

the twenty-fifth anniversary of King Christian's accession, claimed that at times his Aunt Swan was impossible. 'She positively seemed to think that the Jubilee and the congratulations were arranged especially for her. When Apapa and Amama appeared before the people on the balcony she tried to get right in front so as to be in full view and that she would be able to bow to the right and left...'

By this time, Frederick and Louise had six children. Their eldest son, the future King Christian X of Denmark, the German Crown Princess described as 'a bright boy and very nice'.

'The long summer days passed lazily and happily in Denmark,' remembered one of King George's sons. 'One never realizes until it's all too late how absolutely happy one's childhood can be!' Once, at Fredensborg, when Prince Christopher cried out that he wished he were grown up, his mother, the sensible Queen Olga, rebuked him. 'Remember these years,' she said quietly, 'you will always think back on them as the happiest of your life.'

4

To none of the members of the family, however, were these holidays more valuable than to the Emperor and Empress of Russia. The contrast between their lives in St Petersburg and Copenhagen could hardly have been more pronounced.

Ever since his accession to the throne on the assassination of his father, Alexander III had been living in something like a state of siege. For greater security he made his home at Gatchina—a vast, battlemented, barrack-like castle some fifty miles from St Petersburg. Here he was as closely guarded as a prisoner. Troops of cavalry patrolled every road leading to Gatchina. Outside its high walls were established a chain of posts with sentries on constant duty. No one could enter the great gates without a permit; every visitor was checked and double-checked. Within the walls were yet more soldiers.

Both for reasons of security and in tune with Alexander's simple tastes, the family lived, not in the gloomy state apartments, but in a series of even gloomier little rooms on the first floor. Hideously furnished, these rooms were dark, stuffy and depressing. The ceilings were so low that the Tsar could reach up and touch them. There was not even room for the Tsaritsa's grand piano.

One of the richest men in the world, Alexander III was obsessed with cutting down expenses. He curtailed official entertaining, he economized on food and wine, he saw to it that no lights were left burning unnecessarily. In a very short time he had reduced his civil list by almost two million pounds. When Dagmar once paid twelve thousand pounds for a sable coat, he was appalled. His one extravagance was the superbly fashioned Easter eggs, ordered each year from the master jeweller, Peter Carl Fabergé.

When the family were obliged to visit St Petersburg, they lived in their old home, the Anitchkov Palace. Even during the brilliant winter season, the Tsar appeared in public as little as possible. Those sumptuous balls, banquets and receptions, which had always been such a feature of the Winter Palace during the previous reign, were cut down to a minimum. If Alexander wanted to visit a private house, it would be searched from roof to cellar before he set foot in it. At the theatre, the audience would be thick with detectives. When he travelled by train, every inch of the track would be inspected, picketed and ceaselessly patrolled. He simply passed, it was said, 'through a line of guardian troops.'

At home, the Tsar lived the simplest of lives. Rising at seven each morning, Alexander would wash himself in cold water, put on peasants' clothes, make himself a pot of coffee and sit down to work. This consisted, for the most part, in granting audiences to his ministers and in the reading and signing of an enormous pile of edicts, ukases, laws and reports, in the margins of which he would often scrawl such undiplomatic comments as 'What a beast he is!' Extremely conscientious, the Tsar was often described as 'the busiest man in the Empire.'

He was also, unfortunately, one of the most stupid. 'With an intellectual outfit scarcely equal to the task of ruling a hundred of his fellow men,' writes one of his critics, 'Alexander had been saddled with the responsibility of ruling a hundred millions of them.'

Always unenlightened, the restricted life which he felt obliged to lead made him increasingly so. All his faults, all his limitations were intensified. He became more suspicious, more distrustful, more obstinate, more tenacious. He could never change his mind or modify his views. No fresh thought entered his head. He developed into a compulsive worker, obsessed by detail; his life was rigidly organized. He made no friends, he took no one into his confidence, he heeded no advice. 'This is my will,' were the words with which he invariably countered any argument.

It is hardly surprising that Gatchina—so forbidding, so closely guarded, so cut off from the life of the country or from any liberal thought—should come to known as 'the citadel of Autocracy'.

One person only could influence him and that, of course, was Dagmar. Yet she was simply not interested enough in his official life to try and change or moderate his thinking in any way. Nor, in all frankness, would she have been capable of doing so: she was only slightly more intelligent and far-seeing than he. An intensely feminine woman, she always adapted her thinking to his. She identified herself with everything that he did; she was his most loyal supporter. His continuing Germanophobia, which she had implanted, always gratified her. He had a new Russian uniform designed, eliminating all Prussian details; he had anyone with a German name dropped from the government; he forbade the speaking of German at court. More virulent still was his anti-Semitism. This deeply ingrained prejudice Dagmar not only tolerated but adopted. She learnt to hate the Jews. It was they, she was quick to argue, who were undermining the loyalty of Russians to their Tsar. The ease, indeed the eagerness, with which her brother-in-law, the Prince of Wales, associated with Jews was something which she could never understand.

For all her warmth and soft-heartedness, Dagmar seems never to have given the horrors of the reign—the intolerance, the persecutions and the repressions—a thought. They were simply not her business.

What she considered to be her duties, she did superbly. Alexander could not have wished for a more accomplished Empress. Her social gifts were of inestimable value to him. By her good looks, her elegance, her charm and her animation, she made up for his gaucherie, his gruffness and his lack of aplomb. While he shambled about like a bear, she conducted herself with all the grace of a born empress. That the court of Tsar Alexander III could still be notable for its splendour was in no small measure due to the Tsaritsa.

As a wife, Dagmar was even more successful. Here, too, she adapted herself to his ways. Uncomplainingly she lived in those poky rooms at Gatchina; because he abhorred social life, she—who loved dancing—went to fewer balls; she even tried, with very little success, to be more solemn. Both were devoted parents. Alexander III was seldom happier than when in the company of his children. He would take them for walks in the woods, teaching them how to shovel snow, fell trees, build fires and recognize animals tracks. However late he might come home at night, he always made a point of leaning over his children's cots to kiss them in their sleep and to cross himself over them. They loved to see him demonstrate his strength. For their benefit, and in spite of his wife's express wishes, he would bend horseshoes or solid silver plates as though they were so much cardboard. Once, with an eye kept firmly on the study door lest the Tsaritsa enter, he delighted his youngest daughter Olga by first bending, and then straightening out, an iron poker.

Like her sister Alexandra, Dagmar was a loving mother. She was especially protective towards her two eldest sons, Nicholas and George: Nicholas, because he was small and diffident and somewhat in awe of his gigantic father; and George because his health was delicate. A quick-witted and amusing boy, George was allowed to get away with anything, even with tripping up a particularly pompous footman and sending him, with a trayful of tea things, sprawling across the floor.

But the Empress was not normally so indulgent. She had a strong sense of dignity. Indeed, her youngest daughter Olga always found her somewhat intimidating.

None the less, for the first time in many years, the home life of the imperial family was notable for its happiness. Although their Greek cousins might consider things at Gatchina to be ridiculously formal ('I shall never forget seeing the American dentist working busily at Olga's mouth with his tail coat carefully pinned back, his sleeves tucked over his wrists, and an imposing row of orders glistening on his breast', remembered one of them), the children were sensibly and lovingly raised. Into all of them Dagmar instilled her particularly Danish belief that family life was all-important; it was a belief that was to be passionately adhered to by her eldest son, the future Nicholas II.

None of this is to say that the imperial children lived in either luxury or idleness. On the contrary, they slept on camp beds with hard pillows, bathed in cold water and ate porridge and black bread for breakfast. Meals were taken *en famille*, with the children being served after the guests. Often this meant that by the time they had been served, they could only take a couple of bites before the plates were whisked away. The result was that the children sometimes went hungry. So hungry was the Tsarevich Nicholas on one occasion that he opened the hollow gold cross, given to him at his baptism, and ate the beeswax with which it was filled. Remorse quickly followed appeasement, for in the beeswax had been embedded a tiny fragment of the True Cross. It had none the less tasted, Nicholas afterwards admitted, 'immorally good'.

The children were kept at their lessons for the better part of the day. The Tsarevich's studies were often interrupted by the sound of his brother George's merciless ragging of his tutors in the room next door. Indeed, whenever George cracked a particularly good joke, Nicholas would dutifully note it down and file it away. Years later, when he was Tsar, Nicholas could be heard laughing to himself in his study as he re-read his brother's boyhood jokes. Because of his lungs, George was later sent away to live in the Caucasus; he was to die, in 1899, at the age of twenty-seven.

One of Nicholas's tutors was that arch-reactionary who had been responsible for the moulding of the Tsar's mind—Constantine Pobedonostsev. In the Tsarevich, Pobedonostsev was finding an equally responsive pupil. No less than his father, Nicholas came to believe in his tutor's conception of Holy Russia: a state comprising Church, Tsar and People. Any talk of reform was not only dangerous, but positively sacrilegious.

Not until two years after his accession was the Tsar crowned. The coronation scenes in Moscow, in May 1883, were magnificent. 'The blaze of gold and silver,' wrote one enraptured eye-witness, 'the richness of the various uniforms, the sparkling of the gems, the clouds of floating incense, the assembled beauty, valour, rank and station of all Russia and of all the chief States and countries of the world, all this made the scene at once most impressive and memorable...'

Another observer proved rather less lyrical. 'The Empress stands the great fatigue wonderfully, but in slippers, as her feet now refuse to fit any properly sized shoe,' reported Everard Primrose with fine British irreverence. 'It must be no joke to carry five yards of ermine and some lbs of diamonds during several hours—while metallic popes drone and shuffle and wave candles and fling incense and bellow..."

But Dagmar looked lovely. Indeed, one of the day's most memorable sights was that of the Empress at the moment of her crowning. With the spring sunshine streaming through the windows, Dagmar, in a gown of shimmering silver, knelt before the Tsar. Taking the massive crown from his own head, Alexander held it for a moment on his wife's brow. He replaced it and set a smaller crown, topped by a huge sapphire, on her head, 'At that moment,' wrote one observer, 'the Empress raised her beautiful, expressive eyes towards his face, and one could see that between the two there passed one of those fugitive minutes of intense emotion which occur but once in a human life, and which are sufficent to fill up the rest of it, with its remembered joy.'

Gracefully, Dagmar rose to her feet and then, instead of presenting her cheek for a formal kiss, she suddenly reached up, flung her arms about her husband's neck and kissed him tenderly.

5

Set against the splendours, restrictions and dangers of the family's life in Russia, the holidays in

Denmark were like being in another world. The setting out on this annual jaunt was a massive operation.
Over twenty railway trucks would be used to transport
the luggage to St Petersburg; from there it would be
carried on barges to Kronstadt where the imperial
yacht would be anchored. More than a hundred people, plus pets, would accompany the family. Even a
cow would be taken on board, as the Empress insisted
on fresh milk being supplied during the three-day
voyage.

Once arrived in Copenhagen ('dear, calm
Copenhagen' as the Tsarevich called it) Alexander
III would always announce that he was 'out of prison'.
In truth, he behaved with less restraint than any of
them. 'He loved getting into mischief,' wrote one of
his daughters. 'He'd lead us into muddy ponds to
look for tadpoles, and into orchards to steal Apapa's
apples. Once he stumbled on a hose and turned it on
the King of Sweden, whom we all disliked. My father
joined us in all the games and made us late for meals,
and nobody seemed to mind. I remember that courtiers sometimes came with despatches, but there was
no telephone to St Petersburg, and the three weeks in
Denmark meant such a refreshment to him. I always
felt that the boy had never really died in the man.'

All the Tsar's more admirable characteristics—his
honesty, his sincerity, his kind-heartedness, his naturalness, his sense of fun—would come to the surface
in Denmark. Of the adults, he was far and away the
most popular among his nieces and nephews. 'Uncle

Sacha was, to us, an unending delight,' says Prince Nicholas of Greece. 'All his pomp and dignity he left in Russia, and when with us he was just a schoolboy up to all kinds of pranks.'

With remarkable skill he would carve his mono-gram—a great A, with three bars below and a crown above—on the bark of a beech tree. With one jerk he would rip a pack of cards to shreds. Musically, he was very talented. One by one he would take up the instruments left by the band on his yacht and play the Russian National Anthem on each of them. Often he would simply play in the band while the others danced.

Music, of an altogether different nature, he would make as well. To the hysterical delight of the children, he would conceal a 'little instrument' under the tails of his evening coat; whenever some self-important official was paying him ceremonial reverence, the Tsar would manipulate the instrument 'to give out a very fair imitation of certain natural noises'.

The Empress was hardly less of a favourite. She joined in their larks almost as readily. A dedicated cigarette-smoker, Dagmar was anxious that no one, other than the family, should know of her habit. Her nephews were thus always amused to see her, talking politely to some unexpected caller, while from behind her back rose a cloud of cigarette smoke.

Remarkable chiefly for her gaiety, Dagmar was none the less a figure of considerable presence.

'Although she was small,' wrote her nephew, Prince Christopher of Greece, 'she could enter a room so majestically that everyone would stop talking and turn to look at her.'

Even the youngest of Dagmar's children would be conscious of the sense of freedom in Denmark. 'It was freedom in the true sense of the word,' remembered her daughter Olga. 'No member of the Okhrana was there to guard us from dangers which did not exist. Nana and I drove into Copenhagen, left the carriage somewhere on the outskirts, and wandered about on foot, and went into shops. I shall never forget the thrill of walking down a street for the first time, of seeing something that I liked in a shop window and knowing that I could go in and buy anything I pleased! It was more than fun! It was an education! At home, not a drive could be taken unless it involved most elaborate security measures. In Copenhagen we felt we were just human beings...'

They loved mingling with their cousins. One could tell them apart, claims Olga blandly, by their smell. The English cousins smelt of fog and smoke; the Danish of damp, newly-washed linen; they themselves of well-polished leather. On the smell of the Greek cousins, she has no comment.

Few sights impressed the younger children more than that of the great family sitting down to dinner. Creeping out of their bedrooms, they would slip along the corridors to gaze over the railings of the rotunda at the 'splendid sight of Europe's assembled royalty'—the men in dark evening clothes, the women in glittering jewels and gleaming dresses. All about, the air would be pungent with the delectable smell of roast pheasant.

Dinner over, this sophisticated-looking company was quite likely to set off, with all the enthusiasm of schoolchildren, on a ghost hunt. The particular ghost was Waldemar Atterdag. Legend had it that old King Waldemar had so loved his Castle of Gurre that he had once blasphemously cried out that God could keep His Heaven, if he could keep his Castle of Gurre. The understandably offended God had promptly damned Waldemar to ride eternally in death between Gurre and Vordingborg. On certain black nights, it was whispered, the dead King could be seen galloping his horse through the countryside. So, led by the irrepressible King George of the Hellenes, a great caravan of carriages would set out from Fredensborg, to spend half the night in the hopes of catching a glimpse of the ghostly royal ancestor.

But, inevitably, this glorious holiday would come to an end. And by no members of the family would the last of these carefree days be more dreaded than by Alexander and Dagmar. The parting at the close of this gathering of 1883 seems to have been particularly emotional. Princess Alexandra wrote to tell her son, Prince George, of 'that *awful* moment of tearing ourselves away from one another, not knowing *where* and *how* our next meeting may be. Poor little[Dagmar], I can see her now, standing on the top of the steps in utter despair, her eyes streaming over with tears, and trying to hold me as long as she could. Poor Sacha too felt the parting very much and cried dreadfully.'

CHAPTER SEVEN

1

On the face of it, King George of the Hellenes should have been reigning over the most united country in Europe. No basic principles divided the Greek people. They were all satisfied with the constitution, they all practised the same religion, they were all interested in the internal development of the country, they all lived for the day when their fellow Greeks would be freed from Turkish domination. And they were all well enough pleased with their King.

Yet Greek political life was chaotic. There were no large, clearly defined political parties; parliament was made up of numberless bickering factions, forever coalescing or breaking up. No party ever survived the fall or death of its leader. Few programmes, once agreed upon, were carried out. During the first twenty-five years of his reign, King George presided over no less than forty-two governments. It was enough to disillusion even as buoyant, as patient and as realistic a man as he.

But he never despaired. Nor did he ever succumb to the temptation to take a firmer line with the politicians, to assume more power himself. At the risk of being accused of not involving himself enough in the day-to-day workings of the government, King George remained aloof from this political squabbling. More than most of his fellow sovereigns, he appreciated the dangers of a king playing the autocrat. Years later, when the egocentric Kaiser Wilhelm II made a particularly ranting speech in which he extolled the 'divine right of kings' and the use of the 'royal mailed fist', George was highly amused.

'Well, Captain,' he asked of a companion as he put down the newspaper report of the Kaiser's harangue, 'what is *your* opinion of this speech?'

'I have heard of better speeches, your Majesty,' answered the man tactfully.

'Yes,' smiled George, 'but have you ever heard of any worse?'

Towards the social and ceremonial aspects of his position, the King's attitude was equally correct. Although he had very little taste for state entertaining, he forced himself to preside over balls, receptions and banquets. The Greek court might be one of the least brilliant in Europe, yet entertainment at the palace in Athens was not without a certain formality, At nine o'clock, on the occasion of a court ball, the guests would be shepherded into two lines—men on the one side, women on the other, in the Greek fashion—and the double doors would be thrown open to admit the royal family. The tall, flamboyantly moustachioed King George and the plumply pretty Queen Olga would move slowly down the line, saying a few words to each guest. 'Unfortunately,' complains one of the royal children, 'this ceremony was not limited to the King and Queen. Any of the family present were expected to follow them and make an independent progress behind. One had to cudgel one's brains thinking up suitable phrases for these unnatural conversations...'

This 'source of anguish' over, the ball would be opened with a state quadrille: the King dancing with the doyenne, and the Queen with the doyen, of the diplomatic corps.

But even on occasions as formal as this, there was a somewhat happy-go-lucky, almost amateur air about it all. The essentially democratic spirit of the Greek people was always in evidence. At one court ball, Crown Prince Constantine was presented to the wife of a naval officer whose face seemed worryingly familiar; only afterwards did he remember that she was the daughter of his valet and an exnursery maid. As the wife of a naval officer the girl had every right to be presented. On another occasion, a visitor hired a carriage to take him to a ball at the palace that evening. 'Do you mind going rather early,' asked the cabby, 'because I'm going to the Court ball myself and shall have to go home and change?'

No king in Europe was more accessible to the public. 'The royal family of Greece,' announced one gratified American matron, 'is the easiest royal family to become acquainted with.' To be granted an audience with the King, one had merely to sign one's name in a book. One stipulation only was made: that the visiting ladies wear evening dresses and the gentlemen dress clothes and white ties. The local population would thus often be diverted by the sight of a foreign couple emerging from their hotel, in scorching sunlight, to cross the 'small, stony desert' in front of the palace; the wife in tight satin and a mantilla, the husband in a dress suit (shining green in the strong sun), pumps and a straw hat. King George would receive them in a room 'with a purple Victorian wallpaper sprinkled with gilt stars' and, during the entire audience, would stand rocking back and forth on his heels. As the movement was said to be 'as infectious as yawning', the strongest self-control would have to be exercised lest all three found themselves rocking together in unison.

It was as easy to see the King outside the palace as in it. Like so many monarchs, George was an indefatigable walker and almost every day he would stroll through the streets of his capital attended only by an aide or one of his sons. 'Here comes Constantine' or 'Here comes Nicholas' the townspeople would shout to each other as the princes walked by. Often, on a Sunday afternoon, the tram which ran between Athens and the shore of Phalerum would stop outside the palace to pick up the King and his family. If they were slow in crossing from the palace to the tramstop, the driver would impatiently sound his whistle and the family would come scrambling aboard. 'This royal simplicity pleased the Greeks': writes one visitor, 'that was what a king should be.'

King George's Danish relations loved this informal atmosphere. To them all, Athens, no less than Copenhagen, was a holiday home. While, according to one observer, 'all the Greeks thought they had come to render homage to the land of Hellenic culture', these assorted royals came to exchange family gossip and indulge in family larks. A young Englishman, sitting in a rose-covered arbour in the royal garden in Athens was once astonished by the sight of the King of the Hellenes kicking the remains of a hat down the garden path. Behind him, protesting shrilly, scrambled his sister, the Princess of Wales. 'I beg you not to, George,' she shrieked, 'it is my hat: so rude of you.' Catching sight of the Englishman, the unabashed monarch justified himself. His sister's hat, he explained, was so ugly that he had pulled it off and kicked it. 'It was my hat and it was so rude of him,' protested Alexandra, 'and now I can never wear it any more.'

Brother and sister were both nearing fifty at the time.

It was no wonder that the visiting E. F. Benson could describe Greece as a 'toy kingdom'. The whole effect, he says, was inimitable. 'Athens, with its high-born princes, and its national pride, and its army dressed in Albanian costume (embroidered jacket, fustanella, like a ballet skirt, fez, white gaiters, red shoes with tassels on the toes like the seed of dandelions), its fleet of three small cruisers, its national assembly of bawling Levantines, and its boot-blacks called Agamemnon and Thucydides, was precisely like...some Gilbertian realm of light opera.'

Was it not pure operetta, he asks, when that Greek fleet of three cruisers was ordered to sail from its base to Piraeus to welcome the King's nephew, the Tsarevich Nicholas, and it was discovered that there were not enough stokers to enable all three ships to move together? So two ships sailed to Piraeus and, as soon as they were safely anchored there, a party of stokers was rushed back to the base to bring up the third cruiser. By the time the Tsarevich arrived, the entire Greek navy of three ships was there to welcome him.

Nowhere, of course, was this sense of *opéra bouffe* more pronounced than in the picturesque dress of the King's bodyguard—the *Evzoni*. Their behaviour, it seems, could be equally bizarre. On one occasion, when these 'lusty and well-formed' young men in their ballet skirts, tasselled caps and pompommed shoes were drawn up for a review in honour of the King's birthday, a horse suddenly bolted and galloped towards them. As one, this 'flower of the Greek army' broke and scattered to seek protection behind the orange trees and public lavatories of the nearby gardens. Not until the runaway horse had been caught by a bootblack did the men feel it safe to emerge and reform for the march past, 'Long live the bootblack!' trumpeted a headline in that evening's newspaper.

One is not altogether surprised to hear that a Greek king once asked someone to find out if *all* the members of his bodyguard were what he called pansies.

2

It was away from even these easy-going formalities that King George was at his happiest. He loved nothing better than to tramp about the home farm at Tatoi inspecting his cows, pigs and poultry. Proudly he would conduct visitors over the estate, delighting in the shade of the pines and the glimpses of the red deer and wild boar. He was not a keen shot and only very reluctantly would he give his sons permission to shoot. In 1886 he laid the foundation stone of a new house on the estate: a vast, rambling edifice in what was happily called 'the English cottage style', but which, in fact, looked like a large Victorian suburban villa.

The Russian-born Queen Olga loved Tatoi. It was the one place, she used to say, where she never felt homesick. Each year, her birthday was celebrated there with a party for all the tenants on the estate. Around a tablecloth spread on the ground beneath the trees, the workers would gather to eat roast mutton and drink wine. The feasting over, the rustics would dance 'in a kind of chain' to the music of hornpipe, whistle and drum. On to their sweating foreheads, the King, following an old custom, would press a sovereign; it would remain there, as though glued. Long after the family had gone to bed, they would still hear the sound of revelry floating through the pine-scented night air.

A more exotic setting for the court was the palace—called, inevitably, 'Mon Repos'—on the island of Corfu. Here, the somewhat homely atmosphere of Tatoi was exchanged for the almost subtropical delights of this Mediterranean paradise: the spiky palms, the balmy air, the scent of wistaria and orange blossom. Of all her brother George's homes, Alexandra loved the Corfu palace best. She never visited Greece without spending a few days on the island. Impeccably dressed in white serge or tussore silk, in boaters or panama hats, the members of the Greek and British royal families would stroll along the balustraded terraces or take tea in the shade of the striped awnings. Corfu had previously been occupied by the British and a member of the British royal party was once gratified to note the remains of this occupation, 'which even the want of care and slovenliness of the Greeks had been unable to destroy.'

Only by getting away from the country altogether, however, could King George escape the caprices of Greek politics. He loved travelling abroad. Not for the world would he have missed his annual holiday in Denmark. Although he usually stayed at Fredensborg or Bernsdorff, his own palace in Copenhagen—King George's Palace—was always kept in readiness for him. With his slender build, his swinging stride and his silk hat sharply tilted, he was an unmistakable figure in the streets of the city. Often he would be seen walking with his three sisters—Alexandra, Dagmar and Thyra—all with arms linked.

On his way to and from Denmark, George always spent some time in France. Like his brother-in-law, the Prince of Wales, he adored the French. King George of the Hellenes was, says the Frenchman Xavier Paoli (whose duty it was to ensure his safety in France) the most Parisian of foreign royals. 'His Parisianism shows itself not only in the elegant ease with which he speaks our language: it is to be seen in his turn of mind, which is essentially that of the man-about-town, and in his figure, which is slender and strong, tall and graceful, like that of one of our cavalry officers. The quick shrewdness that lurks behind his fair, military moustache is also peculiarly French; and the touch of fun which is emphasized by a constant twitching of the eyes and lips, and which finds an outlet in felicitous phrases and unexpected sallies, is just of the sort that makes people say of *us* that we are the most satirical people on the face of the earth.'

If, in Denmark, George was always made to feel like a boy again, in France he felt like a young man. In Paris, he stayed at the Hotel Bristol. The afternoons he would spend on the boulevards; at night, after an excellent dinner, he would go to the gaming rooms or the theatre. Like the Prince of Wales, he had an eye for actresses: 'no sovereign that I know of,' says Paoli tactfully, 'aroused more affectionate curiosity in female circles than King George'.

Nor was this 'affectionate curiosity' confined to either actresses or Paris. King George was no less the object of female attention at his favourite spa, Aix-les-Bains. If, to the townspeople of Aix, he was known as 'Monsieur le Roi', to the scores of pretty laundresses, past whose open-air wash-houses the King would stroll on his way to the baths, he was greeted as 'Monsieur Georges'. It was not only to hear this cheerful greeting, however, that the King made such a point of passing those public laundries each day. As was customary, these buxom peasant girls wore the scantiest of clothing as they thumped away at their washing. What the disapproving called this 'show of undraped bust and limbs' was a heart-warming sight to the hat-doffing monarch.

The municipal council, however, assumed otherwise. At one stage, fearing that the King might be offended by this unashamed display of female flesh, the Mayor ordered the girls to dress with more circumspection. Reluctantly, the orders were carried out. Only on being reassured, by the disappointed King George, that the local customs were in no way to be tampered with for his benefit, did the Mayor retract his orders.

The following morning, to delighted shouts of 'Vive Monsieur Georges!' the King was once more able to pass along a line of gratifyingly exposed 'busts and limbs'.

But King George's holidays were not all play. These jaunts abroad gave him an opportunity for discussions with various foreign statesmen, diplomats and politicians. 'I am my own ambassador,' he used to say, and he never lost an opportunity of furthering his country's cause. In this, he was greatly helped by his family connections. He might be only the King of Greece, but with one brother-in-law the Tsar of Russia and another the future King of England (and, in time, his eldest son was to marry Kaiser Wilhelm II's sister) King George's hand was considerably strengthened. If, by that stage, royal family connections did not count for nearly as much as some imagined, they still counted for something; and there were few monarchs better connected than he.

In October 1888, the Greeks celebrated the twenty-fifth anniversary of King George's reign with an orgy of flag-waving, flower-throwing, fireworks and national dancing. As much as anything, the Greeks were showing their appreciation of the lustre bestowed on the Greek kingdom by virtue of their sovereign's position in Europe's family of kings.

3

For all his bonhomie, King George of the Hellenes was a strict disciplinarian. His life was well organized; his day ran like clockwork. It was this orderliness which made it so difficult for him to reconcile himself to the impulsive, irregular, slap-happy ways of his subjects. If only, he would sigh, some Danish efficiency or an Anglo-Saxon system of education could be introduced into Greece. To instil some of this sense of discipline into his heir—Crown Prince Constantine—the King fought down the family antipathy towards Prussia and sent his eldest son to Germany to study political economy at the University of Leipzig. From Leipzig Constantine went on to Heidelberg (where tutors were vainly trying to teach his cousin, the apathetic Prince Eddy of Wales, some German) and then to Hanover, where he served in a Guards regiment.

Crown Prince Constantine's German associations did not, though, end with this period of study. While he was in Germany he met, and fell in love with, a daughter of the German Crown Prince. This consorting with what the Danish royal family always considered to be the enemy was not quite as traitorous as it might seem: the German Crown Prince and Princess were hardly typically Prussian. Crown Prince Frederick was a humane, enlightened and well-intentioned man, and the Crown Princess was Queen Victoria's passionately liberal daughter, Vicky. Throughout their married lives, the couple had been in outspoken opposition to Bismarck. By his engagement to their third daughter, Princess Sophie, Crown

Prince Constantine could not really be accused of sanctioning Bismarck's sins.

Constantine and Sophie made an attractive couple. Known as Tino to his family, the Greek Crown Prince was a tall, well-built and good-natured young man; the German Crown Princess was able to assure Queen Victoria that he was 'very nice and charming and well brought up'. Sophie, who was known, more archly, as Sossie, was small, slim-waisted and plump-cheeked, with her fair hair frizzed in imitation of that model for all late nineteenth-century princesses—Alexandra, Princess of Wales.

However, between falling in love with, and marrying, Constantine, Sophie had to live through a particularly harrowing period. Her father, Crown Prince Frederick, developed cancer of the throat. The disease was discovered at the very time when his father, the ninety-year-old Kaiser Wilhelm I, was finally showing signs of coming to the end of his long life. Indeed, at one stage it was wondered which of the two—the father or the son—would die first. It was the old Kaiser who died, in March 1888, and his mortally ill son succeeded him as Kaiser Frederick III. He reigned for just over three months. On his death, Frederick was succeeded by his eldest son, Kaiser Wilhelm II.

With the accession of this bombastic and auto-cratically-minded sovereign, all Frederick's and Vicky's hopes of setting the German Reich along a more enlightened road vanished. Wilhelm II reigned as Bismarck had taught him to reign. The militant Germany of Kaiser Wilhelm II was simply a more powerful version of the Prussia which the Danish royal family had first learnt to hate twenty-five years before.

Not until several months after her husband's death could the heart-broken Vicky, now known as the Empress Frederick, turn her attention to the affairs of her daughter Sophie. In the autumn of 1889, the Empress took Sophie to Copenhagen. At Fredensborg were gathered King Christian IX's family for their annual holiday and among them, of course, was King George of Greece and his brood. Constantine was now twenty-one and Sophie eighteen.

This was apparently the Empress Frederick's first experience of the Danish royal family *en masse*, on holiday. For a woman of her serious nature and intellectual interests, their behaviour was little short of astounding. But the cheerful atmosphere of Fredensborg did the Empress and her daughter the world of good. She found King Christian 'charming as always', Queen Louise 'most kind and amiable' (but a shade too pro-Russian for Vicky's German tastes), Princess Alexandra 'the flower of the flock' and the Greek princes unbelievably high-spirited. But she assured Queen Victoria that Tino 'was the finest of young men, and also the most intelligent'. Her only reservations about the match between Tino and Sophie were their youth and the precariousness of the Greek throne.

In fact, the Greek throne was to outlast the German.

The couple were married in Athens on 27 October 1889. The occasion brought together that host of inter-related royalty which Queen Victoria always referred to as 'the Royal Mob'. It was not every day that a wedding could unite five ruling houses— those of Greece, Germany, Denmark, Britain and Russia. The Danish contingent was headed by King Christian and Queen Louise; the British by the Prince and Princess of Wales; the Russian by Dagmar's son, the Tsarevich Nicholas. The Empress Frederick was there with all her children including, of course, Kaiser Wilhelm II, who brought with him the largest suite of all.

This influx of royal guests sorely strained the resources of King George's court. Although every spare room in the palace had been cleaned out and spruced up, there was still not enough accommodation for all. Appeals went out to private citizens to take in the odd princeling or, at least, a couple of equerries. Nor were there enough carriages. The King borrowed where he could; he was even obliged to hire ordinary cabs and, by dressing the cabbies in hastily run-up blue court liveries, hope that they would pass for royal coachmen. Even the bride drove to her wedding in a second-hand coach which King George had bought cheaply from the pretender to the French throne, once that prince had given up all hope of his line ever being restored.

Although, as one of Constantine's brothers put it, there were 'none of the gorgeous ceremonies prevailing at other Courts', the wedding was a suitably spectacular affair. Ablaze with jewels and orders, the royals drove in their borrowed carriages through the sunlit streets to the new Orthodox cathedral. Tino's best men were his brothers George and Nicholas and his Russian cousin Nicholas; Sophie's bridesmen were her brother Henry and her British cousins, Eddy and George. The Tsarevich complained to his mother that all these bridal attendants were 'half dead from the heat'.

To the Protestant members of the family, the ceremony seemed very theatrical—the hundreds of flickering candles, the incense, the jewel-studded icons, the bearded and mitred bishops, the crowns held high above the bridal couple. As Princess Sophie had not yet been converted to Orthodoxy, this sumptuous ceremony was followed by a simpler one, in King George's private chapel in the palace.

After a gala luncheon, the bride changed from her lavishly embroidered gown into a dress of white and gold and, with her husband beside her, drove to the little rented villa which was to be their first home. They were wildly acclaimed. 'There arose from all the people massed on the square and from those packed on the balconies and windows all around a roar of applause which echoed and reechoed,' wrote one eyewitness. For this excitable, patriotic and suspicious Greek crowd saw, in the marriage, yet another step towards the realization of their country's destiny. On his birth, Crown Prince Constantine had been hailed as the successor to the last Emperor of Byzantium. By taking as his bride a princess by the name of Sophie, he was starting to fulfil an old prophecy: when a Constantine shared his throne with a Sophie (for was not her name synonymous with that of St Sophia in Constantinople?) Greece would once again know greatness. The 'Great Idea' would become a reality; all Greeks would live—free and united—in a new Byzantium.

CHAPTER EIGHT

1

Try as she might, Princess Alexandra could not always turn a blind eye to her husband's infidelities. Forgiving she might be, but she was not superhuman. Although she could ignore his discreet affairs, his more publicized ones caused her considerable distress. Yet Bertie made no attempt to mend his ways. For the Prince of Wales, the company of pretty women, in or out of bed, was essential. His sexual appetite, like all his appetites, was voracious. His liaisons ranged from one-night affairs conducted in an aura of champagne suppers, cigar smoke and curtained alcoves, to full-blown amours with officially established mistresses.

He had merely to glimpse a pretty face from his box at the theatre for a message to be sent down during the *entr'acte*. Only occasionally would he be disappointed in the answer; as was the case when one beauty in question turned out to be the young Prince Felix Youssoupoff dressed as a woman. There were brief infatuations, like the American débutante Miss Chamberlayne (whom the Princess of

140

Wales inevitably nicknamed 'Miss Chamberpots') and Lady Aylesford to whom, imprudent as always, the Prince wrote some compromising letters. Even in unworldly Copenhagen, Bertie managed to find obliging feminine company. On one occasion his assistant private secretary was saddled with the unenviable task of explaining to one of 'the great beauties of Copenhagen' that the reason why his master could not visit her was because he was busily engaged with 'a rival beauty'. But Bertie's best known, and most talked about, liaisons were with celebrated beauties, such as the actress Lillie Langtry and the spirited Frances Brooke, afterwards Lady Warwick.

It was his embroilment with Lady Brooke that caused the normally long-suffering Princess Alexandra some of her most painful moments. During the early 1890s the Prince was already involved in one scandal—the Tranby Croft affair. This episode opened at a house party at Tranby Croft in Yorkshire. One of Bertie's fellow guests was accused of cheating at baccarat. The accusation led to a lawsuit in which the guest claimed damages for slander and to which the Prince was called as a witness. Throughout these unsavoury proceedings, Alexandra gave her husband her unqualified support. In the Lady Brooke affair however, she did not prove nearly so sympathetic. This latest of the Prince's mistresses, having once written a highly indiscreet letter to a previous lover, coerced Bertie into demanding its return. The previous lover was incensed. He insulted the Prince to his face whereupon the prince, no less incensed, imposed a social boycott on him. In no time the affair was made public.

Alexandra, who had never befriended Lady Brooke to the extent that she had Lillie Langtry, was greatly put out by this public scandal. Things came to a head in the autumn of 1891 during the Princess's annual Danish holiday. She promptly cancelled her return to England. Instead, she set off for Livadia in the Crimea. Alexander and Dagmar were about to celebrate their silver wedding; very pointedly, the Princess chose to be with this happily married couple rather than with her husband who was about to celebrate an anniversary of his own—his fiftieth birthday. The significance of Alexandra's absence was not wasted on the British public.

The Princess's domestic problems were not, alas, confined to her errant husband. More worrying, in fact, was the question of her eldest son, Prince Eddy. Even to the doting Alexandra, it had become obvious that something would have to be done about the young man.

In May 1890, the twenty-six-year-old Prince was created Duke of Clarence and Avondale by his grandmother, Queen Victoria. It would have needed considerably more than this impressive double title, however, to give some sort of shape to the future King of England. For Prince Eddy had remained unquestionably slow-witted. One had only to catch a glimpse of him to appreciate this. In spite of his

spectacularly braided, frogged and tasselled Hussar
uniform (his military career, like his adacemic, had
proved, in the words of the Prince of Wales, 'simply
a waste of time'), Eddy looked vapid, apathetic, indolent. Of the energy of his father and the vivacity of his
mother, he showed no trace; his charm of manner
was all that he had inherited and even then he was
obliged to bestir himself in order to exercise it.

How this amorphous young man was ever going
to be moulded into a future sovereign posed a seemingly insoluble problem. Eddy was interested in nothing other than the pursuit of pleasure. His various
dissipations (amongst which, it was rumoured, could
be counted a visit to a male brothel) were further
sapping his already inadequate strength. What was
to be done? While the Prince of Wales urged an
extended tour of the Empire (despite the fact that
Eddy had returned from the last such tour in a state
of near collapse) and Queen Victoria plumped for
a tour of the capitals of Europe (against which the
all-too-knowing Bertie firmly set his face), Princess
Alexandra favoured a more conventional remedy:
Eddy must marry and settle down. A good, sensible
wife was what he needed.

This line of action the irresolute young man was
only too ready to follow. Whatever his faults, Eddy
was never rebellious. If the Prince were 'properly
managed and is told he *must* do it', claimed a member of his father's household, then marry he would.
But who was he to marry? On this question the

young man's mother and grandmother—Princess Alexandra and Queen Victoria—were at odds. Where the Queen favoured a German bride, the Princess of Wales did not. Alix wanted no part in the setting up of a German princess on the British throne.

Unfortunately for her, however, Eddy's first choice was just such a German princess: his cousin, Princess Alix of Hesse. But then, even Alexandra had to allow that the girl's father, Grand Duke Louis of Hesse, was almost as anti-Prussian as she was (had he not sided with Austria in the Austro-Prussian War of 1866?) and that her mother, the late Princess Alice, had been one of Queen Victoria's daughters. Indeed, in every other way Alicky, as she was called, seemed suitable; exactly the sort of serious-minded girl that was needed.

Alicky proved, in fact, a shade too serious-minded on this occasion. She turned Eddy down. Only if she were forced to marry him, she declared, would she do so; but she felt sure that they would not be happy.

With Alicky out of the running, Queen Victoria came up with another German princess: Eddy's cousin Mossy. Mossy was Princess Margaret, the youngest child of the Empress Frederick. With Mossy's sister Sophie having just married Crown Prince Constantine, why should Mossy not marry this other grandson of old King Christian IX? But this time it was Eddy who did the turning down. With his ado-lescent-like ability to fall in and out of love—and in again—in the same week, Eddy had already forgotten

Alicky and had fallen for someone else. This time he had his mother's whole-hearted support,

For his latest love was French. She was Princess Hélène of Orléans, the twenty-one-year-old daughter of the Comte de Paris, at present living in exile in England. Alexandra's championship of this match was the height of folly. Princess Hélène might have had the looks of a future queen but in almost every other way she was unsuitable. For one thing, she was a Roman Catholic; for another, her father was a pretender to the French throne. But backed up by his adoring mother and three no less adoring sisters, Eddy persisted in his unwise courtship. When Princess Hélène, dazzled at the prospect of becoming a queen and apparently besotted by this languid and seductively-mannered Prince, agreed to change her religion in order to marry him, the Princess of Wales was delighted. After all, Dagmar had embraced Orthodoxy, so why should Hélène not embrace Protestantism? In the autumn of 1890, at Mar Lodge, the Scottish home of Eddy's sister Louise, now Duchess of Fife, the couple became engaged.

This was all very well, but how was the disapproving Queen Victoria to be told? Princess Alexandra had the answer. Astutely feminine as ever, she advised the couple to go at once to the Queen and take her into their confidence. They must ask for her help. The ruse worked perfectly. The sentimental old Queen, touched by the sight of the happy pair, gave them her blessing, She promised to see what could be done about the situation.

Princess Hélène's father proved not nearly so sympathetic. The Comte de Paris would not hear of the proposed change of religion. Nor, when Princess Hélène made a personal appeal to the Pope, would he. The only way for them to marry would be for Prince Eddy to renounce his rights to the throne. This, not even the romantically-minded Princess of Wales was prepared to sanction. The engagement was broken off and the couple parted.

This was not to be Hélène's only opportunity of winning a crown for herself. Having failed to marry one of Alexandra's sons, she was to be given the chance of marrying one of Dagmar's. The Tsar and Tsaritsa were to favour her as a wife for their eldest son, the Tsarevich Nicholas. But in this case Nicholas was to fight shy of the idea. Instead, Hélène married the Duke of Aosta, cousin to King Victor Emmanuel III of Italy and, having let the crowns of both England and Russia slip through her fingers, spent the rest of her days plotting tirelessly to get her hands on the Italian crown for her husband.

While Princess Alexandra was imagining that her poor son was suffering from a broken heart, the feather-brained Eddy had embarked on yet another affair. To a beauty by the name of Lady Sybil St Clair Erskine, he was writing a series of muddle-headed love letters. He would not at one time have thought it possible, ran one of his naïve observations to the lady, to be in love with two people—Hélène and herself—at the same time; but now he found himself in this exceptional position. Did she, he wondered, love him a little in return?

Even if she had—or even if she had not—Lady Sybil would not have been allowed to marry Prince Eddy. For by now the Princess of Wales had decided on a bride for her son: he was to marry Princess May of Teck.

2

Princess May was the only daughter of the Duke and Duchess of Teck. In choosing her as the future bride for her son, Princess Alexandra had been obliged to compromise on the matter of nationality. For Princess May's father, the dark and irascible Duke of Teck, was German while her mother, the fat and ebullient Duchess, was a member of the British royal family. Thus, while the Duke of Teck was the son, by a morganatic marriage, of Duke Alexander of Württenburg, the Duchess, like Queen Victoria herself, was a granddaughter of King George III.

Of the shortcomings of her parents, the twenty-four-year-old Princess May seems to have inherited none. Where her father was cantankerous and moody, she was calm and even-tempered; where her mother was capricious and extravagant, she was steady and prudent. Princess May might be reserved, but she had considerable depth of character and surprising self-confidence.

She was also very good-looking. In short, May was exactly what was needed for Prince Eddy.

And it took no time at all for Prince Eddy to be convinced of this. As pliable and romantic as ever, the young man not only agreed to the marriage but obliged everyone by falling in love with May. He even went so far as to propose to her a month before the date set for him to do so. On 3 December 1891, at Luton Hoo—the home, significantly, of the Danish Minister at the Court of St James's—Eddy and May became engaged.

Princess Alexandra was delighted. That May (who, besides being fond of Eddy, had a strong sense of royal obligation) was the '*right bride*', Alexandra had no doubt; 'and the fact of her being English,' she could not resist reminding Queen Victoria, 'will make all the difference.'

Her delight did not last long. Just over a month later, when Princess May and her parents were at Sandringham to celebrate Prince Eddy's twenty-eighth birthday, he fell ill. It was influenza. This quickly developed into pneumonia and for six days, in his tiny bedroom, the Prince lay dangerously ill. During all this harrowing time, his distraught mother hardly ever left his side. Although fully alive to her son's faults, Alexandra was devoted to him; the thought that he might be taken from her was almost more than she could bear.

Yet he was taken. By the dawn of 14 January 1892, it was realized that he was dying. Soon after half past nine that morning, surrounded by the shocked and exhausted members of his family, he died.

Although, it must be admitted, the death of Prince Eddy was one of the best things that could have happened as far as the future of the British throne (and of Princess May) was concerned, it came as a terrible blow to his family. Princess Alexandra, in particular, was heartbroken. It had all been so unexpected, so sudden. A mere week before, on his birthday, he had been able to come downstairs to look at his presents. The picture of him returning upstairs was to remain imprinted on his mother's mind for years to come. 'I still see him all the time before my eyes,' she afterwards wrote to her parents, King Christian and Queen Louise, 'as he went up the stairs for the last time in his life and turned his head to give me his friendly nod, which I must do without forever now.'

It was while in this state of deep depression that Princess Alexandra was obliged to go to Copenhagen for her parents' golden wedding, in May 1892. And although neither she nor her husband attended any of the brilliant public ceremonies, the Princess, as always, drew comfort from being in the midst of her warm-hearted relations.

3

For the family of King Christian IX, the stage was now being set for one of history's repeat performances. A generation before, in March 1865, Dagmar's fiancé—the Tsarevich Nicholas, heir to the Russian throne—had died. Dagmar had promptly become engaged to the new heir. Considered suitable for one brother, there seemed no reason why she should not be equally suitable for another. And so it had proved. Indeed, Dagmar's marriage to Alexander was known to be highly successful. Why then, should not the sons of Dagmar's sister Alexandra follow this precedent? Why should May not marry the new heir to the British throne: Eddy's brother George?

He was certainly a better proposition. Where Prince Eddy, like his father, had tended to take after the Hanoverian side of the British royal house, Prince George resembled his mother's family: he was frank, modest, artless and uncomplicated. He had inherited, in full, the Danish family's bantering form of humour. 'Even the Captain,' wrote the Princess of Wales from aboard the *Osborne* on one occasion, 'says "Oh how I miss Prince George's chaff" ! ! !' And, unlike his brother, Prince George was stable, diligent and conscientious. He would undoubtedly make a better king.

That Prince George, twenty-six at the time of his brother's death, should get married, was becoming increasingly important. Were he to die (as he had almost done, from typhoid, a few weeks before Eddy's death) the succession would pass to his sister Louise, who had recently married the Duke of Fife. And, with the best will in the world, no one could imagine

Louise as a queen regnant. If Eddy would have made a poor king, Louise would make an infinitely poorer queen. As immature and ill-educated as her sisters, Victoria and Maud, Louise was more diffident than either. She was married, moreover, to a commoner, and had only one child, a daughter. No, the answer would be for Prince George to marry and start a family as soon as possible.

In the meantime, he was being hastily groomed for his future role. Shortly after Prince Eddy's death, Queen Victoria created him Duke of York ('Fancy my Georgie boy...now being a grand old Duke of York', wrote Alexandra) and was packed off to Heidelberg to master what his mother scathingly called 'that old *sauerkraut*, the German language'.

She was hardly less scathing about the girl whom her son at one stage considered marrying: his cousin, Missy. Missy was Princess Marie, the eldest daughter of Queen Victoria's son Alfred, Duke of Edinburgh. However attracted George might be to the golden-haired Missy, Princess Alexandra was having none of it. The reason for her disapproval was the usual one: Missy was too German. Because her father was the heir to the duchy of Coburg, Princess Marie and her sisters were being educated in Germany; Princess Alexandra, remembering that her son had once mentioned a preference for an English, as opposed to a German, consort, never let slip an opportunity of reminding her son of the regrettable fact of Missy's German education.

'*Entre nous*, talking about *her*!' ran one of Alexandra's effusions on the subject of Missy, 'it is a pity those children should be entirely brought up as Germans. Last time I saw them they spoke with a very strong foreign accent…they won't *even know* that they have ever been English—particularly as they have been confirmed in the German church.'

But for once, Prince George refused to be guided by his mother. He was quite prepared to marry Princess Marie, German accent or not. In 1892, some months after Prince Eddy's death, Missy was asked if she would consider marrying Prince George. To Princess Alexandra's delight, she would not. Instead, Missy became engaged to Prince Ferdinand, heir to the Romanian throne and became, in time, that most flamboyant, conceited and effusive of twentieth-century sovereigns, Queen Marie of Romania. If Eddy's death had saved England from an extremely ineffectual king, Missy's refusal of Prince George's proposal saved the country from an extremely bizarre queen.

With Missy ruled out, everything seemed to point to a match between George and May. Queen Victoria certainly favoured it. Princess Alexandra, although appreciating its advantages, could not yet resign herself to the idea; it appeared so unromantic, so unseemly, so calculated. Prince George and Princess May felt the same way. Although they were not indifferent to each other, they were acutely distressed and embarrassed by the situation. Both modest and somewhat inarticulate young people, they could not bring themselves to discuss the matter.

At this point, the Princess of Wales did the most sensible thing in the circumstances. In the spring of 1893 she took the bemused Prince George on a cruise. Together with his sisters Victoria and Maud, George accompanied his mother, aboard the *Osborne*, to Athens. There was nothing like a dose of her Danish relations, reckoned Alexandra, for cheering anyone up. And she was right. Despite the weather, which Crown Princess Sophie of Greece reported as being 'too vile for words', the British royals enjoyed their stay in Athens immensely. The Princess of Wales was always happy in the company of her brother, King George, and the rough and tumble of Prince George's Greek cousins did his depressed spirits the world of good.

More valuable, however, were his talks with his beloved aunt, Queen Olga of the Hellenes. Amidst the turbulence of the Greek royal household, Queen Olga was like an island of calm—motherly, affectionate, sensible, tactful. Together, the practical Greek Queen and the uncertain British Prince discussed his future. Queen Olga, who had long ago taken a liking to the reserved and self-contained Princess May, strongly advised George to propose to her. He must do so as soon as he returned to England.

And this he did. On 3 May 1893, at the home of his sister, the Duchess of Fife, Prince George and Princess May became engaged. Princess Alexandra, still slightly disconcerted by the situation, had delayed her return home until after the engagement. That she approved of her son's choice, there was no doubt; what the sentimental, and self-centred, Alexandra could not face was that the memory of her adored Eddy was somehow being slighted and that she was about to lose her no less adored Georgie.

The wedding in the Chapel Royal on 6 July 1893 found her no less melancholy. Despite the presence of so many members of her family, headed by King Christian IX and Queen Louise, the Princess of Wales seemed mournful. In her gleaming white satin and shimmering diamonds, she looked pale, wan, ethereal. Her smiles were brief and bitter-sweet. 'Poor Aunt Alix looked rather sad in church,' reported the Tsarevich Nicholas to his mother, Alexandra's sister Dagmar, 'one can quite understand why.'

CHAPTER NINE

1

'I was immediately struck—as everybody was—' wrote a British member of parliament on seeing the Tsarevich Nicholas in London at the time of Prince George's wedding, 'with his extraordinary resemblance to the Duke of York. It is curious how persistent some family strains are. The little royalty of Denmark has created more replicas of the original type than any other living Royal House. And thus when you see the children of one Danish princess, you see the very picture of the children of the other princesses...'

Nicholas and George, the sons of Dagmar and Alexandra, were certainly astonishingly alike. They were both short and slender, with neatly trimmed beards, brushed-up moustaches, centre partings and clear blue eyes. They could easily have been taken for twins, certainly brothers. Indeed, on the occasion of Prince George's wedding, the Tsarevich had frequently been mistaken for the bridegroom.

And not only did the cousins look alike but their personalities were not dissimilar. The sons of overwhelming fathers and adoring mothers, they were both rather diffident young men: well-mannered, kindly and shy. By no means intellectual, they were not unintelligent. Each possessed a stubborn streak; both were diligent, conscientious and honest.

Of the two, Nicholas was probably the weaker character. As such, he stood in awe of his forbidding father, Tsar Alexander III, and was devoted to his lively mother. It was from her that he had inherited all his more winning traits—his gentleness, his friendliness, his considerable charm. He even shared her love of dancing and her taste for society. Like Alexandra, Dagmar continued to treat her son as a child long after he had grown up. 'My dear little soul, my boy,' she would write to the adult Tsarevich; while he would call her 'my sweet darling Mama'. To be parted from each other, even temporarily, would be like a 'horrible nightmare'. 'I cannot think of it without tears,' wrote Dagmar on one occasion, 'and your dear face, so sad and bathed in tears, is constantly before my eyes...'

The Empress was the greatest influence in Nicky's young life. In her tactful, ultra-feminine way, Dagmar managed her timid son no less thoroughly than she did her stolid husband. It was she who advised him, who encouraged him, who tried to make him conscious of his responsibilities. 'Never forget that everyone's eyes are turned on you now, waiting to see what your first independent steps in life will be,' she wrote when he took up command of a squadron of Horse Guards at the great military camp at Krasnoe

Selo. 'Always be polite and courteous with everybody so that you get along with all your comrades without discrimination, although without too much familiarity or intimacy, and *never* listen to flatterers.'

To this the always dutiful Nicky answered, 'I will always try to follow your advice, my dearest darling Mama.'

And later, when in the company of one of his ebullient Greek cousins, Prince George, Nicholas went off on a world tour and complained to his mother of the heat and boredom of official receptions in British India, Dagmar lost no time in reminding him of his duties. 'I'd like to think,' she wrote, 'you are very courteous to all the English who are taking such pains to give you the best possible reception, shoots, etc. I quite see that the balls and other official doings are not very amusing, especially in that heat, but you must understand that your position brings this with it. You have to *set your personal comfort* aside, be doubly polite and amiable, and above all, never show you are bored. You will do this, won't you, my dear Nicky? At balls you must consider it your duty to *dance more* and *smoke less* in the garden with...the officers just *because it is more amusing.* One simply cannot do this, my dear, but I know you understand all this *so well* and you know my only wish is that *nothing* can be said against you and for you to leave a good impression with everybody everywhere.'

That Nicky was accompanied by his cousin George—Greek Georgie—on this tour was not looked upon as an unmixed blessing by Dagmar. She knew the behaviour of her Greek nephews only too well. And when she heard that George was to remain by her son's side as he journeyed back home through Siberia, she became increasingly alarmed. 'It would be nice for you to have his company in your *free* moments, but don't let him play his little jokes in front *of others* or do things which might shock people, because *you* must remember what you represent, and I don't want the *smallest* thing to be held up against you. So you must impress on him quite *seriously* not to play the clown there. I am sure you understand, my beloved Nicky, all this really means a lot to me. On board ship it was quite different...but in Siberia it is *official*, and you must not forget that for a moment.'

It was as well that the Empress was taking some trouble with her son for the Emperor certainly was not. Having very little faith in the Tsarevich's abilities, Alexander III was making no effort to initiate the young man into affairs of state. Dutifully, and with one eye on the clock, Nicholas would attend ministerial meetings but he was never entrusted with any position of real authority. Nor did his father ever think of taking him into his confidence. In any case, with the Tsar still in his forties, there was no hurry: presumably Alexander III had another twenty-five years or so of active life ahead of him.

To Nicholas, his father remained a remote, almost God-like figure. Once, after a day's exercise with his squadron, the exhausted Tsarevich took off his boots and flopped into bed. Just as he was about to fall asleep, his father came into the room. 'You can imagine my terror,' Nicky afterwards told his comrades, 'when I saw the Tsar before me and I had no boots on.'

The only things, it seems, that Nicholas inherited from his father were his prejudices. With the Tsar as an example and the bigoted Pobedonostsev as a mentor, the easily influenced Nicky was soon as reactionary as either of them. He was violently nationalistic: all other nations were inferior to the Russians. The Germans (and in this one senses his mother's influence as well) were especially to be looked down on: Nicholas was forever making little jokes about their pomposity, bombast and lack of polish. From both parents, too, came the Tsarevich's anti-Semitism. On spending a few days with his Uncle Bertie and Aunt Alix at Sandringham, Nicholas was astonished that the Prince of Wales should have even Jews amongst his rather racy collection of house-guests. His more enlightened English cousins tried to chaff him out of his stand-offishness; 'but I tried to keep away as much as possible,' he assured his approving parents, 'and not to talk'.

To the worldly and relatively democratic Prince of Wales, the flaws in his nephew's character were only too apparent. Nicholas was too narrow-minded, too autocratic, too hesitant. The Prince used to describe the Tsarevich as amiable, but 'weak as water'.

2

With her son being denied, and not really wanting, any serious employment, the Empress decided
that it was time he was married. At present he was
simply leading the life of any other aristocratic young
Russian officer: he drank, he danced, he went to the
theatre, he kept a mistress. If nothing else, reckoned
Dagmar, Nicky could marry and secure the succession. But in this, and for the first in her life, the
Tsaritsa came up against her son's streak of intrac-
tability. Easily guided in all else, Nicky refused to be
guided in this matter of a wife.

Dagmar had at least two candidates. One was that
tall, dark, distinguished Princess Hélène, daughter
of the Comte de Paris, whose romance with Prince
Eddy of Wales had floundered so badly. The other
was Princess Margaret of Prussia, daughter of the
Empress Frederick and sister of Princess Sophie:
that Sophie who had married Nicky's cousin, Crown
Prince Constantine of Greece. Of the two, Dagmar
favoured Hélène; and she favoured her for the very
reason that her sister Alexandra had once favoured
her: Hélène was French, not German.

'Mama made a few allusions to Hélène, daughter
of the Comte de Paris,' wrote Nicholas in his diary on
one occasion. 'I myself want to go in one direction
and it is evident that Mama wants me to choose the
other one.'

The direction in which Nicky was so anxious to go was not only different from that wanted by his mother, it was the very one to which she was most strongly opposed. For the Tsarevich had fallen in love with the girl whom his late cousin Eddy had once wanted to marry, Princess Alix of Hesse.

Nicholas had first met this daughter of the Grand Duke of Hesse when she had come to St Petersburg for the wedding of her sister, Ella, to one of the Tsar's brothers, Grand Duke Serge. They had met again, some years later, when she had spent six weeks with her sister in St Petersburg. He had been twenty-one at the time, she seventeen. The two of them had fallen deeply in love. With his 'gentle charm and that kind caressing look in his eyes', the handsome Nicky had been all but irresistible to Alix, while she, with her reserved manner and considerable beauty—her pale skin, her sea-green eyes and her red-gold hair—was no less attractive to him. 'My dream,' he confided in his diary, 'is some day to marry Alix H.'

It was a dream which his mother had no intention of letting come true. That Princess Alix was a German was not the strongest of Dagmar's objections to the girl. There were other, more serious ones. For one thing, Alix of Hesse was not nearly important enough for a future Tsaritsa; for another, she had—as far as Dagmar was concerned—a most unfortunate personality.

Alix of Hesse was everything that the Danish royalty disliked. She was dull, humourless, unsmiling. Her beauty was of the cold, statuesque variety; she moved like an automaton, she dressed like a schoolgirl. Of the poise and charm and sparkle of the Danish princesses, she had nothing. When set against them, she appeared gauche, tongue-tied and haughty. Where they were all surface, she was all depth: introspective, sensitive, self-critical, intelligent. She took life extremely seriously, and her religion, which was Lutheran, she took most seriously of all.

Yet Alicky possessed one trait which the warm-hearted Danish royal family lacked—an inner fire. Behind that quiet façade beat a passionate heart; about people, and ideas, Alix of Hesse could feel very strongly indeed.

It was, perhaps, this combination of reserve and ardour which drew the diffident Tsarevich to her. Before long, he was determined to marry this obscure and unsophisticated German princess. In spite of his parents' arguments (amongst which was the valid one that Alicky would never forsake her Lutheranism for Orthodoxy) Nicky remained adamant. If he could not marry Alix, he announced to his mother, he would not marry at all.

3

'Natural vivacity and an optimistic temperament,' wrote Baron von Samson-Himmelstierna of Dagmar, 'have enabled Marie Feodorovna, in spite of a nervous excitability, to cheer her husband in the midst of his incessant conflicts with himself and the world.'

By creating what the Tsar enjoyed most—an unpretentious domestic atmosphere, not unlike that of her Danish girlhood—Dagmar was able to relieve some of the strain of his position. Visitors to Russia, overwhelmed by the magnificence of the public ceremonial, would be astonished at the simplicity of the private life of the imperial family. Lady Randolph Churchill described the hall of the palace at Gatchina as 'worthy of an old English country house, full of comfortable writing-tables, games and toys; I even spied a swing. In this hall their Majesties often dine, even when they have guests, and after dinner the table is removed and they pass the remainder of the evening there. The Emperor and Empress elect to live with the greatest simplicity in the smallest of rooms...' It was startling, she continued, 'to see the Tsar standing, while supper is going on, talking perhaps to a young officer who remains seated all the time.'

Into this natural atmosphere, Dagmar's relations fitted very well. Indeed, Alexander III was far happier in the company of his wife's family than he was amongst his own indolent, ambitious and luxury-loving grand-ducal relations. The 'Greek crowd' were especially welcome; to the Russian imperial children, the family of King George I was looked upon as the 'most exciting'. Queen Olga, says one of Dagmar's daughters, 'looked a saint and her serenity did us all much good'. The Greek Queen never moved without a mass of exquisite Greek embroideries which she sold to her Russian relations to raise money for her many charitable organizations in Greece.

Distinctly less saintly were her sons. During one Russian holiday, the assembled royal children all thrilled to the whispered news that Greek Georgie, then aged fourteen, was having an affair with one of the Greek nursery maids. The fact that not all the children understood precisely what 'having an affair' entailed, rendered the news no less exciting.

But the holidays offered more naïve pleasures than this. There was the wonderful miniature railway laid out in the grounds of Gatchina, the picnics in the long northern summer twilights, the drives in quaint old Russian carriages with the seats set back-to-back, the sight of the fountains in the formal park at Peterhof, and the thrill of seeing the Imperial Ballet from St Petersburg dancing on a floating stage on the lake, 'while the whole court gathered there to watch them, the women in exquisite dresses, the men in their picturesque uniforms'.

The children all adored the Empress. 'To us boys,' writes one of her Greek nephews, 'she was kindness itself and always treated us like her own children.' An inveterate matchmaker, Dagmar was always trying to forge links between her own and her husband's families. In 1889 she had engineered a match between her brother-in-law, the Tsar's youngest brother Grand Duke Paul and her niece Alexandra, daughter of

King George of the Hellenes. 'No one,' wrote one of the bride's brothers, 'can imagine the brilliance of the functions at the Russian Imperial Court. This marriage was a glittering pageant from end to end.'

But within three years these scenes of brilliance had changed to those of mourning. While the Russian, Greek and Danish royal families were on their annual Danish holiday, word came that the Grand Duchess Alexandra was dying in childbirth. Her parents—King George and Queen Olga—hurried to Moscow, arriving there just in time to see her die. The rest of the family followed later, in a special funeral train. For three days and nights the train rocked its way across Europe from Copenhagen to Moscow where, in a special hall at the Moscow station, the body of the Grand Duchess Alexandra lay covered by a cloth of gold lined with ermine. The coffin was put aboard the train and carried on to St Petersburg for burial. King George was particularly upset by this sudden death of his daughter. She was said to have been his favourite child.

Dagmar, too, had her sorrows. A source of continuous distress throughout these years was the condition of her second son, the tubercular George. He by now lived permanently at Abbas Touman, in the distant Caucasus. Each year, in early spring or late autumn, she visited him. Of her three sons—Nicholas, George and Michael—this middle one was the most intelligent, with a sharp wit, a generous nature and a winning personality. Despite his illness,

he had something of his mother's vivacity. This buoyancy made the sight of him all the more difficult for
Dagmar to bear. 'Poor Georgie!' she once wrote to
Nicholas. 'Life is really too sad for him; it is wonderful with what fortitude he bears it, without a murmur
of complaint. I am so deeply grieved by this that the
tears come to my eyes when I think of it...'

Occasionally, when he seemed to be showing
signs of improvement, Dagmar would take him to
Copenhagen on holiday. Like her sister Alexandra,
she had great faith in the therapeutic powers of
these Danish family gatherings. Surely the delights
of her native Denmark—the warmth of her father's
court, Uncle Freddie's pavilion on the beach at
Charlottenlund, the company of the Danish and
Greek and English cousins—would have a beneficial
effect on the boy? But before long he would be spit-
ting up blood. He would have to be hurried back to
the dry air of the Caucasus. 'It really is *too* sad and I
am utterly miserable about it and grieved to the heart
to part with him again..." she would write.

But she kept her grief private. In public Dagmar
always showed a smiling face. No one seeing her
fulfilling her ceremonial duties ever imagined that
she had a care in the world. 'Court life,' as one of
Dagmar's daughters said, 'had to run in splendour,
and there my mother played her part without a single
false step.' Dagmar adored the flash and glitter of
the St Petersburg season; dancing and dressing up
were her passions. As soon as Christmas was over, she

would begin to agitate for a return from Gatchina to St Petersburg, while the Tsar would be dreaming up every sort of excuse to delay their departure.

The season always opened on New Year's Day with a great ball at the Winter Palace. Nothing was allowed to rob the Empress of the delights of this occasion. Once, after the invitations for what was to be a particularly brilliant ball had already gone out, news reached St Petersburg of the death of an Austrian archduke. This would mean court mourning and the cancellation of the ball. Dagmar was in despair. But not for long. Remembering an earlier occasion when the Austrian court had not bothered to mourn the death of a Russian grand duke, Dagmar hit upon a way whereby she could both retaliate and have her ball. She re-issued her invitations. The ball was to be *un bal noir*, with all the ladies wearing black.

Her diamonds glittering against the black velvet of her dress, Dagmar was able to dance to her heart's content.

But, in the ordinary way, white and silver were the colours the Empress preferred for her ball dresses. Under the eye of the formidable Princess Hélène Kotchoubey, Mistress of the Robes, and with five maids bustling in and out, Dagmar would dress in what she always referred to as her 'imperial panoply'. Her white gown would be encrusted with brilliants; diamonds would flash at wrist and throat and ears; sometimes she wore as many as ten ropes of pearls;

her high-piled dark hair would be crowned by a massive diamond tiara.

'During palace balls,' says one observer, 'it was the Empress who was the centre of attention on the dance floor while the Emperor stood silently to one side, frowning and obviously unhappy.' She was a tireless dancer; the dashing Polish mazurka was her favourite. 'I danced and danced. I let myself be carried away,' she once admitted joyously.

When the Tsar, bored beyond endurance, felt that the ball had gone on long enough, he would begin ordering the musicians, one by one, out of the ballroom. Eventually, only one drummer would be left on the dais, 'too frightened to leave, too frightened to stop playing'. If the guests insisted on dancing to this solitary drummer, the Tsar would begin to turn off the lights. At this the Empress, with unruffled charm, would turn to the guests and say, 'Well, I suppose the Emperor wants us all to go home.'

CHAPTER TEN

1

By the last decade of the nineteenth century, the annual gatherings of King Christian IX's family had come to be regarded as events of extreme significance. Few could believe these meetings were not politically momentous. In an age when sovereigns still wielded—or appeared to wield—considerable power, this dynastic coming-together was surely more than a manifestation of family affection. Could there by any doubt that the monarchs of Greece and Russia, strolling beneath the copper-coloured beeches at Fredensborg, were discussing the affairs of the Balkans? Or that the King of Denmark and the Prince of Wales were hatching some anti-German plot as they puffed together at their great cigars? Who could believe, as the tiaras flashed in the candlelight, that the Empress of Russia, the Princess of Wales and the Duchess of Cumberland were not planning further dynastic aggrandizement? Surely it could not all be as innocent as it seemed.

Even the foreign diplomats stationed in Copenhagen, who should have known better, could not help suspecting that something was afoot. 'The comings and goings of European monarchs round the venerable King,' wrote the less gullible son of one French minister, 'created an artificial stir which was the delight of the chancelleries. If the Tsaritsa accelerated her yearly visit by forty-eight hours so as to find her brother, King George of the Hellenes, still at home, cypher telegrams flew to all corners of the globe raising the familiar spectre of the Eastern Question. If the future King Edward VII made a detour so as to visit his father-in-law, then a new Anglo-Russian policy was in the making.'

Most suspicious of all was the German Chancellor, Prince Bismarck. To him, who always tended to over-estimate the influence of royalty, Fredensborg was 'Europe's Whispering Gallery', with Queen Louise as the arch-intriguer. He credited the Danish Queen with far more influence than she in fact possessed; he simply could not believe that she was not continually working against him.

For such fears, there was very little ground. The family jamborees were every bit as guileless as they appeared. In fact, King Christian IX actively dis-couraged any political talk among the members of his wide-ranging family. At the first mention of any of those perennial *fin-de-siècle* political topics—the Balkans, Fashoda, Dreyfus—the old monarch would change the subject. The prevailing atmosphere might have been anti-German (or, at least, anti-Prus-sian) but it remained an atmosphere only: there was almost nothing in the way of active intrigue against the Second Reich. They may have said a great deal but they did, and could do, nothing.

No, rather than exchanging political opinions, the members of the family were far more likely to be regaling each other with stories of their latest, apparently side-splitting adventures. Each day seemed to bring yet another encounter worth repeating.

There was the story about the new young sentry, a country boy, who refused the mild-mannered King himself admittance to the palace. 'But I live here. I am the King,' protested the old monarch in vain.

Then there was the one about Crown Prince Frederick—Uncle Freddie—who, riding a bicycle for the first time, was obliged to raise his hat in greeting two curtsying old ladies, and promptly landed on top of them.

The Tsar of Russia, the King of Greece and the Prince of Wales—Uncle Sacha, Uncle Willie and Uncle Bertie—out for a walk in the park of Fredensborg Castle, once came across a man who had lost himself in the woods. Not realizing who they were, the stranger asked them to show him the way out of the park. The illustrious trio accompanied him to the gates, talking all the while of inconsequential matters.

'I've very much enjoyed my walk with you gentlemen and I hope we shall meet again,' said the stranger as he parted from them, 'may I ask your names?'

'Certainly,' answered King George. 'I'm the King of Greece, this is the Prince of Wales, and this is the Emperor of Russia.'

'And I,' said the stranger with a sceptical smile, 'am Jesus Christ.'

2

But every now and then some dynastic manœuvre would seem to bear out the suspicion that everything was not quite as innocent as it looked. The marriage of King Christian's youngest son, Prince Waldemar, was a case in point.

Thus far, only one of King Christian's children had married a German. This was his daughter Thyra, whose husband, the ugly Duke of Cumberland, was even more violently anti-Prussian than the rest of them. Then, in 1885, Prince Waldemar made—from Bismarck's point of view—a still more pro-vocative match: he married a French princess. She was Princess Marie of Orléans, daughter of the Duc de Chartres and niece of the Comte de Paris, pre-tender to the French throne. That her family was not a reigning one was neither here nor there; she was French, and that was enough for Bismarck. With Franco-Prussian hostility the most constant factor in late nineteenth-century politics, Waldemar's choice of bride looked like nothing so much as a slap in the face for Germany.

There was, in fact, some slight justification for Bismarck's apprehensions. Once established in her husband's boyhood home, the Yellow Palace,

Princess Marie revealed herself to be an ardent French patriot, violently anti-German. A woman of great verve and charm, Princess Marie did whatever she could to further the cause of France, republic though it might be. She was in close and constant touch with the members of the French Legation in Copenhagen. A vast tricolor hung from the ceiling to the floor of her drawing-room at Bernsdorff.

This was the Princess's one political enthusiasm; for herself, she was not ambitious. Like her husband, the modest and attractively-mannered Waldemar, Marie was quite content to remain in the background. Neither hankered after a throne. When, in 1886, the recently vacated Bulgarian throne was offered to Prince Waldemar, husband and wife were appalled. The country was far too unstable and, with Bulgaria always at loggerheads with Greece (where Waldemar's brother, George, was King), the position would be an impossible one. 'Nothing would induce me to go down there—ever!' was Marie's robust comment on the offer.

To have so dedicated a patriot at the influential Danish court was a source of great satisfaction to the French government. No more than the Germans could they appreciate just how a-political were these Danish family gatherings, or just how little pressure Princess Marie was able to exert. These were the years in which the old European system of alliances was beginning to break up: the years in which the stage was being set, as it were, for the First World

War. For most of the 1880s the astute Bismarck had kept Germany, Russia and Austria loosely tied together by the 'Three Emperors' Alliance', thus leaving France out in the cold. Towards the end of that decade, however, France, in its search for an ally against Germany, began an ardent wooing of Russia. But the Tsar Alexander III, who had very little love for Germany, had even less for France; thus, when in 1887 Bismarck proposed a renewal of the alliance, Alexander agreed. But France was not to be put off. Nor was Alexander entirely indifferent. 'Russia,' as one writer so graphically put it, 'did not withdraw her cheek; but France did all the kissing.'

During the Tsar's visit to Denmark that year, the French government decided to make yet another overture. The death of the Russian writer, Michael Katkov, gave them their excuse. Katkov had been a fanatical hater of Germany and a passionate advocate of an alliance with France. He had always been a great favourite with Tsar Alexander III. To his funeral the French Ligue des Patriotes sent their President, Paul Déroulède; on the coffin of *l'ami de la France*, the Frenchman laid a gigantic wreath. Coming back from the funeral in Russia, Déroulède stopped off at Copenhagen to see the Tsar. He was armed with what have been called the 'most alluring offers' from the French Minister of War. But Alexander was having none of him. The gates of Fredensborg remained firmly closed.

Thwarted, Déroulède approached Princess Marie. Surely she could plead the French cause with the Tsar? But she neither could nor would. Princess Marie might be heart and soul with Déroulède but she knew better than to badger the Tsar, especially when he was on holiday.

Her discretion was not always of so high an order. On a later occasion, the French Princess proved much less tactful. By the early 1890s the international situation had radically altered. The ebullient Kaiser Wilhelm II, having rid himself of Bismarck, decided not to renew the always uneasy alliance between Germany and Russia. This, of course, encouraged the Tsar to look towards France; amongst other things, Russia urgently needed French loans. By 1893 a secret military convention had been negotiated between the two nations. All that remained was for Alexander III to sign the treaty. In this, the Tsar was proving more than usually bovine. No amount of prompting by the French Prime Minister, Casimir Périer, or his ambassador in St Petersburg, could overcome the Tsar's tardiness. By the time Alexander and Dagmar set out for their annual Danish holiday, the treaty had still to be ratified.

This delay proved too much for Princess Marie. No sooner had the Tsar's yacht tied up in Copenhagen harbour, than Marie marched up the gangplank and blurted out. 'Why don't you hurry up and ratify the alliance with France?'

Alexander was appalled. Having pacified Marie with a few evasive remarks, he begged King Christian IX to see that he was not harassed by political questions while on holiday. The King promptly despatched an equerry to Paris. In future, asked the old King, would the French government please approach his son-in-law, the Tsar, direct and not through his daughter-in-law, Princess Marie? 'We were mute with surprise,' protests one member of the French government; as well they might be, for on this occasion they had certainly not enlisted the help of the patriotic Princess.

In due course, however, the treaty was signed. Germany became increasingly isolated and although there was as yet no suggestion of the future *entente* between England and France, the members of King Christian IX's family had the satisfaction of knowing that most of them were still on the same side.

3

The holiday of 1893 was the last that Tsar Alexander III spent in Denmark. Early in the new year he began showing signs of failing health. Although he had turned only forty-nine that year, Alexander looked and felt years older. The strains of his position was proving too much for him. Not only did this simple-minded man not have the mental ability to cope with his monumental task, but the ever-present threat of assassination was breaking his nerve. Only during the Danish holidays could he be free of the atmosphere of danger; in Russia every other day seemed to bring news of fresh subversion, of mass arrests, of bloody insurrections, of dastardly plots. Every public appearance became a nightmare, every journey a hazard.

Once, on the long journey back from the Caucasus, a great crash shattered the imperial train. The family had been at luncheon in the dining car; their carriage was ripped open and the heavy iron roof caved in. With truly Herculean strength, the Tsar supported the sagging roof so as to enable the others to crawl out to safety. Above the screams of the wounded and the clash and clang of iron, the little Grand Duchess Olga could be heard shouting, 'Now they'll come and kill us all!'

Dagmar, dusty and bleeding but only slightly hurt, proved no less heroic than her husband. Once she knew that he and the children were safe, she rushed to the aid of the wounded. Twenty-one people had been killed in the crash and scores wounded, some of them hideously. For five hours, until a relief train arrived, the Empress carried water, washed and bandaged wounds and gave comfort. The cause of the crash was never uncovered. It might have been the work of revolutionaries; it might have been an accident.

On the Tsar and the Tsaritsa, the effect of this catastrophe was profound. 'For weeks,' wrote one observer, '[the Empress's] highly-strung nerves were unable to recover from the impression of those terrible pictures of destruction.'

This constant threat of assassination, coupled with the Tsar's worsening health (early in 1894 he suffered a severe attack of influenza) made it essential that the succession be secured. With Nicholas, the Tsarevich, remaining adamant about marrying Alix of Hesse, his parents finally gave their consent. In April 1894 the young man went to Coburg to represent his father at the wedding of Alix's brother, Grand Duke Ernest of Hesse. Here he set about wearing down Alicky's reluctance to forsake her Lutheranism.

Into this problem of a match between Nicky and Alicky, half the royalty of Europe, from Queen Victoria down, duly plunged themselves. The German relations were particularly anxious for the marriage. In a letter to his mother, Nicky rattles off the nicknames of those pressing—Ernie, Ducky, Aunt Michen, Aunt Ella *et al.* Finally, in the face of this onslaught, Alicky's resistance was broken down. 'I can't tell you how happy I am,' reported Nicholas to Dagmar, 'and how sad at the same time that I am not with you and can't take you and dearest Papa to my heart at this moment.' Alicky, he assured his no doubt sceptical mother, was quite changed. 'She is gay and amusing, talkative and *tender.*'

King Christian IX of Denmak, the courtly and
unaffected Father-in-law of Europe

Queen Louise cf Denmark

A family on the threshold of greatness, at the time of Princess Alexandra's engagement to the Prince of Wales in 1862. *Left to right, back row:* Princes Frederick, Christian (later King) and William. *Front row:* Princess Dagmar, Prince Waldemar, Princess Louise (later Queen), Princess Thyra and Princess Alexandra

The lovely Princess Alexandra, photographed
before her marriage to Bertie

Princess Dagmar on the day of her marriage
to the Tsarevich Alexander

Princess Thyra, afterwards Duchess of
Cumberland and *de jure* Queen of Hanover

The young King George I making his triumphant
entry into Athens in October 1863

The wedding of Dagmar to Alexander in
the Winter Palace, St Petersburg

The pleasure-loving Prince of Wales at the age of thirty-four

King George I and Queen Olga of the Hellenes with their
British nephews, Princes Eddy and George, in Athens, 1882

The Greek and British royal families photographed in a studio railway carriage at Wiesbaden. *Left to right*: Princess Maud of Wales, King George I of Greece, Princess Alexandra holding Princess Marie of Greece, Queen Louise, Queen Olga, Prince Nicholas of Greece, Princess Victoria of Wales, Princess Alexandra of Greece, Crown Prince Constantine of Greece, Princess Louise of Wales, Prince George of Wales, Prince George of Greece, Prince Eddy of Wales

Some of the family photographed at Fredensborg during the
gathering of 1883. Holding hands in the centre of the group are
(*left to right*) Princess Thyra, the Empress Marie (Dagmar) and
Princess Alexandra. Standing behind them are (*left to right*) King
Christian IX, Queen Louise, Tsar Alexander III, Queen Olga
(obscured), King George I, Prince Waldemar, Crown Prince
Frederick and Crown Princess Louise

Tsar Alexander III

Dagmar, Tsaritsa of Russia, in middle age

Prince Waldemar, amiable and unpretentious
youngest son of King Christian IX

King George of the Hellenes

The fifty-two-year-old Princess of Wales with her daughter
Princess Maud and Prince Charles of Denmark, afterwards King
Haakon VII of Norway

Crown Prince Frederick of Denmark with
his bride, Princess Louise of Sweden

King Christian IX in old age

The funeral procession of King Christian
IX in the streets of Copenhagen

Royal mourners at Roskilde Cathedral. *Left to right:* King George
of the Hellenes, the Duchess of Cumberland, Queen Alexandra,
the Dowager Empress of Russia (obscured), King Frederick VIII,
the Duke of Cumberland

The new King, Frederick VIII, appearing on the
balcony (*right*) of the Amalienborg Palace

A sketch of Queen Alexandra, King Edward VII, King Frederick
VIII and Queen Louise at a gala performance at Covent Garden,
1906

The enduringly youthful Queen Alexandra at the age of seventy

A photograph taken at Cowes, 1909, showing the strong physical resemblance between the first cousins, Nicky (Tsar Nicholas II) of Russia and George, Prince of Wales (afterwards King George V)

King Constantine I of the Hellenes, son of George I
and grandson of King Christian IX of Denmark

Princess Victoria (*left*) with her mother, Queen Alexandra, and her aunt, the Dowager Empress of Russia, at the Air Force Pageant, Hendon, June 1921

Dagmar, touched by her son's obvious happiness, did her best to match his enthusiasm. Alicky, she instructed, was not to call her merely 'Aunty-Mama'; she was to call her—as Princess Alexandra was called by her children—'Motherdear.'

The girl was despatched to England, where, under the benevolent eye of her grandmother, Queen Victoria, some attempt was made to mould her into a future Tsaritsa. It was arranged that she and Nicky would marry in the spring of the following year, 1895.

In the meantime, Alexander and Dagmar had sanctioned the marriage of another of their children: in July 1894 their eldest daughter Xenia married her handsome cousin Sandro, Grand Duke Alexander.

Not all the glitter of the occasion, however, could hide the fact that the Emperor was seriously ill. He had lost weight, he moved more slowly, his feet started to swell. The doctors—in whom, anyway, the Tsar had very little faith—could suggest nothing other than a change of air. The annual journey to Denmark was cancelled and the family went to the Tsar's hunting lodge at Spala, in Poland. Here, at the insistence of the Empress, Alexander was examined by the celebrated Professor Leyden. The specialist diagnosed nephritis. He could hold out very little hope of recovery. All he could do was to advise yet another change of air: the Tsar must set out at once for a warmer climate. Queen Olga of Greece offered her sister-in-law the use of 'Mon Repos' on Corfu but the Empress decided to make first for Livadia, their own palace in the Crimea. However, not all its delights—the balmy, grape-scented air, the riotously flowering shrubs, the still and shimmering sea—could lessen the Tsar's suffering. By the middle of October it was clear that Alexander was dying.

The Tsarevich Nicholas, appalled at the prospect of succeeding to the imperial throne so soon, sent for Alicky. Travelling as an ordinary passenger, she crossed Europe by train, arriving at Livadia on 22 October. Here this gauche girl from Darmstadt found herself all but ignored. It was the assured and beautiful Empress who commanded all the attention. Indeed, it was during these ten days at Livadia—the last ten days of the Tsar's life—that the foundations of the future unfortunate relationship between Dagmar and Alicky were laid. As the Tsar's life ebbed away, the Tsaritsa seemed to come into her own: everyone consulted her, everyone deferred to her, everyone sympathized with her. Dagmar might be sick with grief and worry but she remained mistress of the situation. Of the shy young Tsarevich and his equally shy fiancée, practically no notice was taken.

But if Nicholas was prepared to put up with this state of affairs, Alicky was not. She might be reserved but she could be resolute. Within a few days of her arrival, she was giving evidence of her resentment of the way in which her fiancé—the future Tsar—was being passed over in favour of his mother and uncles. 'Be firm and make the doctors come to you every day and tell you how they find him...' she instructed her fiancé, 'so that you are always the first to know. Don't let others be put first and you left out. You are Father's dear son and must be told all and asked about everything. Show your own mind and don't let others forget who you are...'

On 29 October, Dagmar wired her sister Alexandra and, the following day, the Prince and Princess of Wales set out for the Crimea. They arrived too late to see the Tsar alive. On 1 November, with Livadia shrouded in a damp and sinister mist, Alexander III died.

'I feel the end approaching,' he had whispered to his wife. 'Be calm. I am quite calm.' Soon after, with his great head resting on Dagmar's shoulder and his family gathered around him, he died.

'Everything seemed hushed,' remembered his daughter Olga. 'Nobody sobbed. My mother still held him in her arms. We all rose as quietly as we could, crossed the room, and kissed my father's forehead and hand. Then we kissed my mother. It seemed as though the fog outside had entered the room. All of us turned to Nicky and kissed his hand for the first time.'

Dagmar's son, old King Christian's grandson, was now Tsar Nicholas II.

The realization, both of his father's death and his own position, threw the young Nicky into a state of torment. 'My God, my God, what a day,' he confided to his diary that evening. 'The Almighty has called to Him our adored, dear and deeply loved Papa. My head is going round. I cannot believe it. The truth seems so improbable and terrible...He died like a saint. Oh, God help us in these sad days! Poor, dear Mama!'

In fact, poor, dear Mama was bearing up better than most. During all the elaborate ceremonial of the funeral, Dagmar behaved magnificently. The presence of her sister Alexandra (whose youthful appearance, as she stepped from the funeral train, caused one minister to mistake her for the new Tsar's fiancée) was invaluable. 'Alix is everything in the world to [Dagmar] just now,' reported the Prince of Wales to Queen Victoria.

but there were other relations on hand to comfort her as well: her brothers, King George of the Hellenes and Prince Waldemar of Denmark and, of course, her father, King Christian IX. Indeed, the old King's fatherly pats on the Dowager Empress's back during the funeral gravely discomforted the punctilious Russian master of ceremonies.

Only after the funeral did Dagmar break down. But even now, she was not allowed to indulge her grief for long. A week later, Nicky and Alicky were married. For the occasion, court mourning was set aside; in her white, lavishly embroidered dress and glittering jewels, the Dowager Empress far outshone the younger, more beautiful but stiffly-mannered bride. But the long and complicated ceremony was a strain. Dagmar was reminded, only too poignantly, of her own wedding day. Again it was King Christian who comforted his daughter when she almost broke down. 'Her eyes were red with weeping,' says Princess Radziwill, 'her whole appearance was one of complete dejection, she was quite broken down. Her father in vain did his best to comfort her. It was a touching sight seeing the old man trying to sustain her.'

Nicky, too, was deeply distressed at his mother's grief. In the days following the wedding—for there was no honeymoon—he did all he could to console her. 'He is too good, dear, loving and kind,' wrote Alicky, 'and his affection for his mother is touching, and how he looks after her, so quietly and tenderly.'

CHAPTER ELEVEN

1

To find partners, and particularly royal partners, for King Christian IX's vast brood of grandchildren was no easy matter. With so many Danish or half-Danish princes and princesses on the market, it was inevitable that some of them should marry each other.

The old King's eldest son, Crown Prince Frederick, had no less than eight children to marry off. Luckily, the young princes and princesses had inherited very little of their mother's plainness or narrow-mindedness; try as she might, poor, upright Crown Princess Louise simply could not compete with the rumbustious atmosphere of the other royal households. Her own homes—the Crown Prince's Palace at Amalienborg, and Charlottenlund by the sea—might be run as strictly and as stiffly as any upper-class Victorian household, but once the court was invaded by her children's English or Greek or Russian cousins, her influence tended to go by the board.

None the less, there was one ideal which Crown Princess Louise shared with her husband's frothier relations and that was that the children be brought up as simply as possible. There was no coddling or spoiling. No less than in the other royal households, the Crown Prince's children ate plain food, slept on hard beds and spoke when they were spoken to.

The second son, Prince Charles, endured an even hardier upbringing than the rest of them for, at the age of fourteen, he joined the navy. Having talked his reluctant mother into allowing him to have an anchor tattooed on his arm (she insisted that it be done at home, by a naval captain, and not in one of those questionable-looking boats berthed in the old fish market), Prince Charles set off on a trial voyage as a volunteer cadet. From the start, he loved the navy. The long cruise over, the Prince wrote, and passed, his entrance examination for the Naval Officers' School. For the following three years Charles lived the rough-and-tumble life of any other cadet—studying in the winter and cruising in the summer. In the year 1893, at the age of twenty, he passed out as a second lieutenant. Not until three years later did Charles become a first lieutenant. This was due to the fact that his father, in true Danish democratic fashion, insisted that his son should not be favoured in any way. When asked why he had remained a second lieutenant so long, the young Prince would say, in his wry way, 'Lack of strings and influence'.

Prince Charles was an attractive young man; in many ways a typical Dane, tall, slender, fair-haired and blue-eyed. He was also a level-headed youngster, conscientious beyond his years. And, like all Christian IX's family, he was frank and unaffected, unostentatious in his way of life and unsophisticated in his tastes. Amongst his knock about relations, he was eminently at home.

It was not surprising, then, that this open and artless young man should choose a bride from amongst his many girl cousins. Nor that he should settle on one of the daughters of the Prince and Princess of Wales. For, of all the cousins, the English and the Danish had the most similar backgrounds. Princess Alexandra certainly remained the most closely associated with her own country; it was she, in fact, in her determination to keep her daughters from marrying German princelings, who encouraged the match between her second daughter, Maud, and her nephew, Charles. If her daughter must get married (and Alexandra was in no hurry for this) then let it be to one of the family.

In 1895, during the course of the annual reunion at Fredensborg, Charles proposed and Maud accepted.

The news infuriated some of Charles's equally eligible Greek cousins. Not only had Maud always been a great favourite in the family but, as a daughter of the future King of England, she was considered to be an extremely desirable *parti*. 'Why Charles, and not me?' demanded Prince Nicholas of Greece in mock indignation. 'All I got as an answer,' he says, 'were some well-chosen epithets I dare not repeat.' Could it be, he wondered, that cousin Maud still bore a grudge against him? Once, during a squabble at Bernsdorff, she had banged him on the head with a bag of peas and he had retaliated by hitting her hard with a walking stick. 'How dare you forget that you are a gentleman and strike a lady!' his Uncle Bertie had thundered. 'She hit me first,' protested Nicholas. 'That has nothing to do with it,' countered his uncle.

At twenty-five (three years older than her fiancé) Princess Maud of Wales was still quite capable of thumping a cousin over the head with a bag of peas. She might no longer be what another of her cousins called 'as delightfully wild' as she had been in girl-hood but she retained a tomboyish streak. Maud was happiest out of doors. For dogs, horses, bicycles and yachts, she had a passion. Her talk was peppered with schoolboy slang. Neither sophisticated nor cultured, Maud was a kindly, cheerful, no-nonsense creature, as full of chaff and high spirits as the rest of them. Her chief failing was that, amongst strangers, she was painfully shy. Away from her intimate circle, she was stiff, gauche, tongue-tied. She had neither taste nor talent for public life. Only at familiar, countrified Sandringham was she ever really happy.

Given her reserve and her devotion to the English countryside, marriage to a foreign prince seemed hardly the most advisable step. Could Maud, who would be almost twenty-seven by the time she married, ever give up, not only the company of her possessive mother, but the delights of her life as an English princess. Some thought not. 'My feeling is,' wrote the Duchess of Teck, 'Maud does not care for him enough to leave England for his sake and live in Denmark, and I dread her finding this out when too late.'

Charles and Maud were married in the chapel at Buckingham Palace on 22 July 1896. The wedding was a relatively small one, more in the nature of a family gathering. Yet even this meant that royalty from as far afield as Athens and St Petersburg attended. From Copenhagen came the bridegroom's parents, the Crown Prince and Princess with their other children (old King Christian IX did not attend) and it was their eldest son, the future King Christian X of Denmark, who led Queen Victoria into the chapel. When the ceremony was over, the newly married couple made their obeisances to the seated figure of Grand-mama Queen.

The honeymoon was spent at Appleton House, on the Sandringham estate, which the Prince of Wales had given to his daughter as a wedding present. The couple were to remain there for three weeks and then join the usual family party in Denmark.

But once the couple was established at Appleton House, the Duchess of Teck was to be proved right: nothing would induce Maud to leave it. She kept postponing their departure. And Charles, who had been granted six months' leave of absence from the Danish navy, was obliged to fall in with her wishes.

By mid-August the Danish royal family had assembled at Bernsdorff to welcome the couple. By the end of the month the Princess of Wales and her still unmarried daughter Victoria joined them. By early September, King George of the Hellenes was there; by mid-September the new Tsar and Tsaritsa had arrived. But still Maud refused to budge. In the ordinary way, this family gathering would have delighted her; now the prospect of not returning to England at the end of the holiday appalled her. With her good-natured husband in tow, Maud continued her usual round; she would, presumably, have continued it indefinitely had Prince Charles's leave not expired. Not until just before Christmas did she steel herself to leave for Copenhagen.

Here the couple were given an enthusiastic welcome. Through the gaily beflagged streets and lustily cheering crowds of the Danish capital they drove to their new home beside the Amalienborg Palace. That evening they attended a banquet presided over by their grandfather, King Christian IX. In proposing the bride's health, the King expressed the hope that 'as my dear daughter Alexandra has won all British hearts, so may my grand-daughter win the hearts of the whole Danish nation'.

But during the months that followed, Maud showed precious little interest in doing so. The call of her British blood proved stronger than that of her

Danish. She hankered after England. The fact that Prince Charles was obliged to go to sea soon after his return to Denmark gave her further cause for dissatisfaction. Her complaints brought a sharp rejoinder from her mother: Princess Maud must 'on *no* account forget that she married a *Danish* Prince and a *naval* man and *he owes* his first duty both to *his country* and his profession', wrote Princess Alexandra.

It was as well that Maud did not suspect that her husband would one day have to do his duty for the dynasty too; that Prince Charles, like so many of the descendants of Europe's Father-in-law, would be called upon to wear a crown.

2

By the year 1897, the fifty-one-year-old King George of the Hellenes was grappling with a difficult situation. His Greek subjects, in their determination to free those of their countrymen still living under Turkish rule, were clamouring for action. And the island of Crete, lying south of the Greek mainland, seemed the very place where such action could best be employed. Turkish-ruled Crete had a large and unresigned Greek population; these fellow Greeks, ranted the café politicians in Athens, must be freed.

Accordingly, in February 1897, the Cretans rose up against their Turkish masters. Carried along on a positive torrent of national enthusiasm, King

George despatched a Greek force, commanded by his second son Prince George—Greek Georgie—to help the insurgents. The Great Powers, alarmed at the prospect of a war between Greece and Turkey, took instant action. They hurried naval patrols into Cretan waters and landed an international force on the island. An affronted Prince George of Greece was ordered to withdraw.

But by now Greece was in no mood to hear of withdrawals. She was spoiling for a full-scale war. Not only was she determined to keep her troops on Crete but she was intent on extending the struggle. Looking northwards, she encouraged her countrymen in Turkish-ruled Macedonia—on the Greco-Turkish border—to revolt. This they obligingly did and on 17 April 1897, Turkey declared war on Greece.

The Greeks were cock-a-hoop. Hysterical crowds surged through the streets of Athens, waving flags, roaring patriotic songs and cheering themselves hoarse for their slightly discomforted King. 'Poor Uncle Willie,' as Dagmar put it to her son Nicholas, 'cannot give in because of his people who will bring about a revolution if he changes his mind.' For if the King appreciated just how unprepared was Greece for war, his people did not. That their army was ill-organized and ill-equipped while the Turks were trained and officered by Germans, disturbed the enthusiastic mob not one jot. Greece must be restored to its former glory, and restore it to its former glory they would.

'What mattered the numerical superiority of the Turks,' asked one commentator dryly, 'when every Greek was equal to four or five of the enemy in bravery and efficiency? What had not Leonidas and Themistocles been able to achieve with their scanty followings in the glorious days of antiquity? Were not the Hellenes the present-day genuine descendants of the classical nation of heroes? Of what account was the lack of guns, cavalry, commissariat, and more, if God in His justice supported the Cross against the Crescent?'

On this occasion, however, God did nothing of the sort. Within a week the Greek army, commanded by Crown Prince Constantine, had been soundly beaten. Faced by the German-bolstered Turks, their resistance melted like butter. Within three weeks, the road to Athens lay open to the Turkish army.

Not for the first time had a member of King Christian IX's family suffered, albeit indirectly, at the hands of Germany. Kaiser Wilhelm II, who through-out the *fracas* had been denouncing the Greeks in the most violent terms, was highly gratified at the way things were going.

In mounting panic, King George turned to his relations. Here was a chance to put to some use the fact that he was connected with half the sovereigns of Europe. Those judiciously arranged marriages must surely count for something. While his daughter-in-law, Crown Princess Sophie, badgered her brother Kaiser Wilhelm II on the one hand and her grandmother

Queen Victoria on the other, King George sent frantic telegrams to his sisters Dagmar and Alexandra. Dagmar, who was in Copenhagen at the time, at once wrote off to her son, Tsar Nicholas II, ordering him 'to *insist* that Turkish troops be immediately withdrawn from Greek territory'. Princess Alexandra, no less distraught, appealed to the Prince of Wales who, in turn, appealed to the British Prime Minister, Lord Salisbury. 'If only England would lead the way and put her foot down,' argued Bertie, 'Greece may yet be extricated from the terrible position in which she is now placed.'

Alexandra turned to the Queen as well. 'The Princess of Wales came down last night in an awful stew about Greece,' reported the Queen's lady-in-waiting, Marie Mallet, 'imploring the Queen to do something to stop the war and stay the hand of the triumphant Turks.'

But, with the best will in the world, there was nothing that the Queen could do. Once again Victoria found herself trapped as she had been during Bismarck's wars of unification thirty years before: between her German and Danish relations. With her grandson, Kaiser Wilhelm II, supporting Turkey, and Princess Alexandra's family wholeheartedly for Greece, the Queen could only do what she could to bring about the peace. When the armistice was finally arranged, by an exultant Kaiser Wilhelm II, Greece was obliged to suffer considerable humiliation. Her troops had to withdraw from Crete, her northern frontier was altered to the advantage of Turkey and she had to pay a huge indemnity. Only the intervention of King George's nephew, Tsar Nicholas II, and of his brother-in-law, the Prince of Wales, prevented the terms from being even harsher. This, alas, was the extent to which King George's brilliant family connections were able to help him.

It would have needed more than this slight softening of the terms, however, to save King George's reputation. Suddenly the very crowds who had recently been applauding him to the skies turned against him. It was he, they now blithely maintained, who was responsible for the disastrous war. So violent was the feeling against the entire royal family (and not least of all against the German-born Crown Princess Sophie) that Crown Prince Constantine was obliged to relinquish his command of the army. Hurt and bewildered, the family retired to Tatoi.

They managed, none the less, to ride out this particular storm. The second time, they would not be so fortunate.

Instead of these trials bringing the Greek royal family closer together, they tended to divide them. They widened the gulf between the King and his sons. King George, for all his *bonhomie*, had always been a rather withdrawn father; his relationship with his sons had been easy but never intimate. That family sense of fun was all that he shared with them. Like so many members of the Danish royal family, King George could never appreciate that his children had grown up. So enduringly youthful in both looks and tastes themselves, these sons and daughters of King Christian IX insisted on treating their own offspring as children long after they had matured. By 1898, King George's eldest son, Crown Prince Constantine, was thirty, with three children of his own; three of his brothers were in the second half of their twenties. Yet the King never confided in them nor consulted them. About the running of the country, he kept them in total ignorance. Now, when Constantine tried to discuss the present Greek plight, and the much-needed reorganization of the army, with his father, George refused to listen to him.

This state of affairs upset Queen Olga considerably. During the annual Danish holiday following the Greco-Turkish War, the Greek Queen poured out her troubles to her sister-in-law, Princess Alexandra. 'Aunt Olga,' according to the Princess of Wales, 'is miserable about it, and cried bitterly at Copenhagen!' The Queen was afraid that her sons had become '*very* bitter' and 'very antagonistic' towards their father. It was '*very* hard for the sons,' added the possessive Alexandra blithely, 'that they are treated as children.'

3

Queen Louise of Denmark was eighty in the year 1898. For almost sixty years, ever since her marriage to the impecunious young officer who had become one of Europe's most revered monarchs, Louise had devoted herself to the interests of her family. Neither an aggressive nor a politically ambitious woman, Queen Louise had been passionately concerned with the enhancing of her family's status. Discreetly, tactfully, but persistently, with a well-worded letter here and a timely suggestion there, she had placed her children, and grandchildren, in influential positions. To Queen Victoria, she might be 'false and intriguing' but to those who knew her better, she was merely determined to do what was in the best interests of her descendants. 'Her feeling for family and old associations,' wrote the Grand Duchess of Mecklenburg-Strelitz, 'was very great and true.'

Even at eighty, Queen Louise retained something of her former prettiness; something of that doll-like elegance so characteristic of the women of her family. Her blue eyes still sparkled, her skin still glowed. But she was almost stone-deaf and was confined, for most of the time, to a wheelchair. Devoted to her rose garden at Bernsdorff, she would have one of her sons wheel her out there on good days during the summer. Her daughters, no less attentive, would carry out trays of little delicacies.

But even in these melancholy circumstances, the family sense of fun was always breaking through. One day, as Princess Alexandra, followed by her pet Pekingese, was carrying out a tray of milk and biscuits to her mother, King George passed by on his bicycle. By accident, he bumped against his sister's dog. With

the dog yelping in surprise, Alexandra flung the tray
to the ground and snatched up her pet. 'He has killed
my dog, he has killed my dog!' she shrieked. He had,
of course, done nothing of the sort. As soon as King
George's son, Prince Nicholas, realized that the dog
had not been hurt, he began to imitate the scene.
Affecting his aunt's famous limp, he re-enacted her
screams of distress. Alexandra, with her childlike
sense of humour, was delighted. Again and again, she
made her nephew repeat the performance.

Not all the hilarity in the world, however, could
disguise the fact that Queen Louise did not have
much longer to live. 'My grandmother,' wrote one
of the princes, 'was just like a candle burning itself
away'. Princess Alexandra was very anxious that her
mother should see her great-grandson, little Prince
Edward of York, before she died. She begged George
and May to bring him over to Denmark that autumn.
'In some ways it is rather tiresome that we have to
go so far for so short a time,' complained Princess
May, 'but as poor Amama is so very ill we cannot do
otherwise.'

A few weeks after this visit, on 29 September 1898,
Queen Louise died. Mentally alert to the very last, she
had had the day's newspapers read to her the evening
before. She was buried in the little town of Roskilde,
in the old cathedral in which lay the remains of all
the Danish sovereigns.

Her death saddened not only her devoted husband, but her huge family. 'The return to Bernsdorff,

the scene of so many happy family gatherings, where for many years several generations had lovingly clustered round the historic figure of a beloved mother, grandmother and great-grandmother, was sad indeed,' wrote one of her grandsons.

CHAPTER TWEVLE

1

With the death of Queen Victoria on 22 January 1901, Alexandra finally took her place as consort of the man who had inherited what the late Queen used blandly to claim was the most important position in the world.

Few women could have been less like the old Queen than the new. Queen Alexandra was almost everything that Queen Victoria had not been. Plump, plain, dowdy, serious-minded and awe-inspiring, Queen Victoria had spent almost forty years withdrawn from the public gaze. Queen Alexandra, slender, stylish, warm-hearted and feather-brained, was the most glittering figure in the Edwardian cavalcade.

At fifty-six, Alexandra was still astonishingly lovely. To look at, she was rather like a wax flower—beautiful, ageless, unruffled, impeccable. Always fashionably dressed, she had none the less perfected the style which best suited her: her high-dressed hair would be crowned by an elaborately trimmed toque; her slender neck would be encircled by a boned collar or rows of pearls; her waist would be laced to its narrowest. It was she who first popularized those hydrangea shades which, for three generations, were to be almost obligatory summer fashion for British queens and princesses. In the winter she wore violet or cherry-red velvet lavishly trimmed with fur; at night she appeared in shimmering creations of white or silver or gold. For her coronation, on 9 August 1902, she insisted on wearing exactly what she wanted, regardless of tradition or even fashion. 'I know better than all the milliners and antiquaries,' she announced bluntly. And she was right. She looked superb. Her dress was of golden Indian gauze, her train of richly embroidered, ermine-lined violet velvet; about her neck and cascading to her waist were row upon row of diamonds and pearls, amongst them a replica of the Dagmar Cross—Denmark's most famous jewel.

To her position, Alexandra brought all the grace and charm and vivacity that had so long been missing from court life. She brought also a reputation for boundless sympathy with those who were suffering. Always popular and with a talent for public appearances, Alexandra could now play her royal role for all it was worth.

So decorative and socially accomplished a queen suited the Edwardian court to perfection. For King Edward VII, having finally come into his own, was determined to make the most of things. It was true that for the political, as opposed to the public, duties of the monarchy, he had very little taste or, for that matter, talent. Queen Victoria had excluded him for too long from affairs of state for him to apply himself to them now. In any case, he was temperamentally unsuited to this aspect of his task: he lacked concentration, he hated desk-work, he was bored by formal meetings. Domestic and colonial politics interested him very little; only for foreign affairs and the armed forces did he show any enthusiasm. But into his public duties he flung himself with gusto, carrying out his obligations with extraordinary energy and *panache*. He was determined that his reign was to be the most brilliant in Europe.

All traces of his mother's dreary court were swept away. The ceremonial aspect of the monarchy was restored and expanded. Edward VII's reign was to be marked by showy state visits, spectacular openings of parliament, glittering courts, balls and banquets. Buckingham Palace became once more the principal home of the sovereign. Its reception rooms were lavishly redecorated and refurnished; its galleries and staircases were recarpeted; plans were put in hand for the redesigning of its façade and setting. Osborne House, so closely associated with the old régime, was given to the navy; Windsor and Balmoral were modernized and refurbished.

'I have no words to describe *how magnificent* it all is…' reported the enraptured Dagmar to her son Nicholas II. 'Everything is so tastefully and artistically arranged—it makes one's mouth water to see all this magnificence!' From a Dowager Empress of Russia, this was praise indeed.

Edward VII's court was forever on the move—at country houses, at race meetings, on tours of inspection, on foreign visits, at reviews or at sea. The royal couple were always on display. Society could hardly have wished for two more fitting leaders than the restless, luxury-loving, genial but impressive-looking King and a Queen who was both glamorous and dignified, gay and virtuous, amusing and kind-hearted.

But if becoming Queen had revealed Alexandra at her best, it had also revealed her at her worst. Once in a position to do exactly as she pleased, she lost no time in doing so. She became more obstinate, more unpunctual, more selfish, more capricious, more erratic. 'Mama, as I have always said,' wrote Prince George on one occasion, 'is one of the most selfish people I know.'

Her first show of stubbornness was her refusal to move from Marlborough House to Buckingham Palace. That, she assured her son Prince George, would finish her. 'All my happiness and sorrow were here, very nearly all you children were born here, all the reminiscences of my whole life are here, and I feel as if by taking me away a cord will be torn in my heart which can never be mended again.' Only with difficulty could she be persuaded to move.

Her unpunctuality continued to drive her impatient and punctilious husband to near-distraction. 'Keep him waiting; it will do him good!' she would blithely exclaim as the King sat drumming his fat fingers in the next room. She would treat her unmarried daughter, Princess Victoria, with a shameful lack of consideration. It was not that Alexandra did not love her, but that her love made her all the more possessive, demanding and selfish. Princess Victoria, wrote one of her cousins, 'was just a glorified maid to her mother. Many a time a talk or a game would be broken off by a message from my Aunt Alix, and Toria would run like lightning, often to discover that her mother could not remember why she had sent for her, and it puzzled me because Aunt Alix was so good.'

Good she undoubtedly was, but, lacking imagination, Alexandra was moved to acts of goodness only by what she saw or was told about. A wounded soldier would reduce her to floods of tears, an unhappy servant would earn her lavish sympathy, but more deserving causes often went unnoticed. She might donate vast sums to charity yet insist (for the economies of her Danish childhood had not been entirely forgotten) that her maids darn her stockings. Stories of her irrational behaviour were legion.

And, of course, Alexandra remained as immature and as empty-headed as she had ever been. With her deafness cutting her off from the brittle chit-chat which passed for conversation in her husband's circle, she preferred, as always, the company of her old companions and her simpler-minded relations. In droves, the members of the Danish royal family now invaded the English court. Not only at the tone of King Edward VII's friends but at the skittishness of

Queen Alexandra's relations would Queen Victoria
have been turning in her grave. Alexandra had never
lost that family sense of the ridiculous. Her nephews had countless stories to tell of the larks at the
Edwardian court. Even after the solemnities of her
coronation, the gorgeously dressed Queen allowed
her clamouring Greek nephews to try on her glittering crown. On another occasion, Prince Christopher
of Greece, wheeling his lumbago-crippled aunt, the
Dowager Empress of Russia, through the grounds at
Sandringham, suddenly succumbed to temptation
and sent her bathchair careering down a steep slope.
'The Empress's despairing shrieks rent the air as she
sped down to the very bottom and then, driven on
by her own impetus, was rushed half-way up the cor-
responding incline, only to start the descent again,
this time backwards,' reports the delighted Prince.
'When I rescued her she was terrified out of her wits,
but she had quite lost her lumbago.'

But there was worse still. When Dagmar, staying
at Buckingham Palace, was once again afflicted by
lumbago, Queen Alexandra decided that she must
be cheered up. Calling in one of her nephews, the
Queen bundled him into the tartan taffeta dress
which Queen Victoria had worn during her state
visit to Paris in 1855. Onto his head she tied the late
Queen's fussily feathered bonnet and into his hands
she thrust a lace parasol. She then led the boy, in
his swishing taffeta skirts, along endless corridors
and past scandalized servants until they reached the

door of the Dowager Empress's room. Having had him announced as 'Her Majesty Queen Victoria', Alix pushed him into the room. Dagmar, lumbago notwithstanding, was all but convulsed with laughter.

When Alexandra was not entertaining her relations, she would be visiting them. Twice a year she spent several weeks in Denmark. The death of her mother, Queen Louise, had by no means put an end to these family assemblies; more than ever did Alexandra feel it necessary to spend as much time as possible with her father. A secretary at the British Legation in Copenhagen describes her first visit to Denmark as Queen as something which he would never forget. 'Queen Alexandra descended from the train all in black, with long floating veils, and threaded her way through the crowd of Royalties and officials, looking younger than anyone present, with still the same fairy-tale-like grace of carriage and movement that I remembered as a child, and with the same youthful smile of welcome, and with all her delicacy of form and feature heightened by her mourning and her long black veils...'

Alexandra's enthusiasm for these Danish holidays was not, however, shared by her immediate family: not only did King Edward VII find the Danish court deadly dull but Prince George, Princess May and even the unmarried Princess Victoria had come to dislike it. This near-sacrilege Queen Alexandra put down to their being '*so* spoilt that they think everything *dull* where there is no *shooting* ! ! or where they can't do exactly as they can at home *voilà tout* ! ! !'

The truth was that Prince George, under the influence of his wife, the serious-minded Princess May, had outgrown his taste for family pranks. The times when his possessive mother, leading a pack of high-spirited relations, had burst uninvited into York Cottage, Sandringham or York House, St James's Palace, had long since been put a stop to. For anyone as conscientious as Prince George, life at the Danish court was by now a 'dawdle and waste of time'.

For Princess May, it was even worse. So organized, so industrious, so reserved herself, Princess May was exasperated by the idleness and the gregariousness of the Danish family. 'The life here is very tiring as one is all day waiting about and one has no time to one-self,' she wrote. The six-thirty dinner was a 'despair' and the 'endless evening with *cercle*' , a bore. She even went so far as to refer to 'that vile D...k' on an occa-sion when the not unintelligent Princess Victoria, always in the wake of her inconsiderate mother, was dragged off on yet another visit. 'Yes, alas,' agreed Prince George, 'poor Toria has of course to go to Denmark with Mama, it will certainly do her no good I fear and she hates it so.'

These grumblings Queen Alexandra airily brushed aside. With all the audacity of the pot calling the kettle black, she listed her children's shortcom-ings with regard to the Danish holidays. 'Naturally', she chided her son on his refusal to attend one of the family gatherings, 'it would have pleased poor Apapa *just* to have *seen* you and dear May whom he likes so much for a little here! and I as well—the whole family flattered themselves that it would have pleased you to have seen them once again...'

2

Just as the death of Queen Victoria had brought Alexandra into the limelight so, in a way, had the death of Tsar Alexander III brought Alix's sister Dagmar, the Dowager Empress, into her own.

This was due to several factors. For one thing, according to a somewhat odd Russian tradition, a dowager empress took predecence over an empress; it was thus Dagmar, and not Alicky—now the Empress Alexandra—who took the place beside the new young Tsar. For another thing, the older woman was much better equipped for the role of first lady. Not only had Dagmar been Empress for thirteen years (after having served an even longer apprenticeship) but she thoroughly enjoyed the part. Whereas Alicky, who had been pitched into the position overnight, was awkward, immature and painfully shy, Dagmar was soignée, effervescent and assured. And she was still relatively young. Forty-seven at the time of her husband's death in 1894, Dagmar—like all the members of King Christian's family—looked at least ten years younger than her age. Between the slight and sparkling Dowager Empress and her stolid daughter-in-law, there seemed to be hardly any age difference.

Quite naturally, then, it was Dagmar who continued to set the tone of the imperial court; who kept all social arrangements firmly in her own hands. While the new Empress, numb with nerves, either blushed and stammered or stood stiff and unsmiling, the accomplished Dowager Empress remained the central female figure.

The personality of the new Tsar, too, tended to increase the Dowager Empress's importance. So young, so inexperienced, so diffident, Nicky looked to his mother for guidance. This she was only too ready to give. It was not that she was bossy; it was simply that, to her, Nicholas II seemed hardly more than a schoolboy. By no stretch of the imagination a clever woman, Dagmar was none the less a quick-witted and practical one. And she knew how to handle others. With Nicky trusting so few people, he trusted his mother implicitly. After all, she had been his father's confidante; she had known and shared all Alexander III's views. As Nicholas II was determined to tread his father's narrow path, who better to guide him along it but his mother? Time and again this latest Autocrat of All the Russias would say to his ministers, 'I must ask my Matoushka about this.' And they, only too conscious of his immaturity and equivocation, would in turn suggest that it might please His Majesty to consult his Matoushka on this or that point.

It was no wonder that Count Sergius Witte, one of Nicholas II's most able ministers, could claim that 'the Emperor was entirely under the influence of his mother'. Or that society would be titillated by a cartoon of a little crowned and bearded figure in a baby chair being spoon-fed by its mother.

As a result Dagmar became, almost overnight and in spite of herself, something of a power in the land. Working through her—for, in a way, she was hardly more resolved than her son—the ministers could influence the Tsar. While his huge and intimidating uncles would try and get their way by bellowing at him, his mother could get hers by subtler methods. Yet at no stage did this suddenly increased importance go to Dagmar's head. She did not aspire to power. Her main concern was for the dynasty. About the complexities of Russian political and economic life she remained as cheerfully uninformed and uninterested as she had ever been. Her influential position made her no less ignorant and no more ambitious. Typically, her one political concern (other than her undying hatred of Germany) was with the choice of the Russian minister to the Danish court. In this, she always had to have her say. The result was that the Copenhagen post was much sought after: it was looked upon as the gateway to diplomatic advancement.

Domestically, too, the Dowager Empress remained the *prima donna*. Because Nicky and Alicky had married in such haste, no palace had been prepared for them. They thus started off their married life in the Anitchkov Palace, home of the Dowager Empress. With only half a dozen rooms at their disposal, the young couple were obliged to lunch and dine at Mama's table. When Nicholas granted interviews in their sitting room, Alexandra had to make do with their bedroom. That Dagmar remained the mistress of the home, there was no question. Her proximity meant that Nicholas spent a great deal of time with her; at first because he was sorry for her in her widowhood, and later because he had come to rely on her for encouragement and advice.

Inevitably, friction developed between the old Empress and the new. Although both Dagmar, who was naturally warm-hearted, and Alicky, who was naturally withdrawn, treated each other with consideration and respect, certain circumstances soon revealed the latent hostility between them. Once in a position of authority Dagmar, like her sister Queen Alexandra, developed a certain selfishness, a determination to get her own way. The possession of the imperial crown jewels was a case in point. The Dowager Empress, who so loved jewellery and wore it to such marvellous effect, refused to hand over the heirlooms to the younger woman. Alicky was fobbed off with some unimportant pieces, including a couple of cumbersome tiaras which merely gave her a headache when worn for any length of time. Hurt and humiliated, the Empress had to save face by claiming that she anyway preferred pearls and that her mother-in-law's dazzling collection of diamonds, rubies, emeralds and sapphires meant little to her.

With supreme confidence in her own judgement, Dagmar chose all the members of Alicky's household, including an awesome mistress of the robes. In the matter of clothes, too, the older woman always felt that she knew best. She did indeed—for whatever suited her small and graceful figure—but Alicky, in her resolute fashion, simply refused to wear the unsuitably fussy garments chosen by her mother-in-law. In time, the Empress Alexandra would come to wear her state garments with great authority but, in private, she preferred loose, fluid, somewhat unfashionable clothes, far removed from the Dowager Empress's chic and figure-hugging dresses.

The young couple's move to a home of their own—the Alexander Palace at Tsarskoe Selo, some fifteen miles from St Petersburg—considerably emphasized the lack of accord between the two women. While the Dowager Empress remained in the capital, in her world of parties, gossip and beautiful clothes, the Empress withdrew into her own, very different, world. More and more she cut herself off from other people, particularly from the brittle society so beloved of her mother-in-law. Being something of a prude, the Empress Alexandra wanted no truck with the worthless, decadent, extravagant members of the Russian aristocracy; she preferred a simple, domestic, almost bourgeois life. To the Dowager Empress's circle, she appeared woefully provincial.

Her imperial duties, too, Alexandra saw in a quite different light. Where Dagmar felt that an empress must always be on show Alicky would carry out only those public appearances which she considered absolutely essential.

In all this, Alicky was backed up by Nicky. He adored her. No less than she, he was happiest away from the glitter of his position. And whatever Alexandra's failings as an empress, she was making a brilliant success of her marriage. 'She was absolutely wonderful to Nicky...', claims Dagmar's youngest daughter, Olga, one of the few members of the family to say a good word for Alicky. 'No wonder Nicky always called her Sunny, her childhood name. She undoubtedly remained the only sunshine in the ever-growing darkness of his life.'

3

In one way only did Alicky appear to be failing Nicky: she seemed unable to produce a son. This was not for any want of trying. Between the years 1895 and 1901, Alexandra bore her husband four daughters: Olga, Tatiana, Marie and Anastasia. The birth of each of these four daughters meant sharp disappointment for the parents; to present her husband with a son, and the Empire with an heir, was Alicky's dearest wish. The wish was shared, of course, by the Dowager Empress. No less than her daughter-in-law did she want to see the dynasty securely established. Each time Alexandra was pregnant, Dagmar's hopes soared. She was lavish with advice. Nicky was to 'watch over her and look after her in every possible way'; Alicky must be certain to keep her feet warm; she was to eat, of all things, raw ham in bed before breakfast as a remedy against morning sickness.

Not all the cosseting in the world, however, was able to bring forth a Tsarevich. And by the turn of the century, the matter was becoming increasingly urgent. In the summer of 1899, Nicholas's heir—his tubercular brother George—died in the distant Caucasus. A peasant woman had discovered him at the side of the road, beside his overturned bicycle; he had died in her arms. The woman, a member of an obscure religious sect, was brought to St Petersburg to describe the young man's last moments to his distraught mother. 'I remember the tall, black-robed woman from the Caucasus, with her flowing black and white veils, silently gliding by the fountains of Peterhof' remembered Olga, 'she was a figure from a Greek tragedy. Mother was closeted with her for hours.'

Inevitably—for in imperial, mystical Russia nothing was ever allowed to be what it seemed—the young man's sudden end loosed a spate of sinister rumours about the true nature of his death. The real facts, it was whispered, were being withheld.

A year later Nicholas himself fell ill with typhoid. For a while it was thought that he was dying. The

Dowager Empress, concerned for the future of the dynasty, urged her son to declare his younger brother Michael official Tsarevich; at present he was merely Heir Presumptive, not Heir Apparent. This was duly done; although the idea of the handsome, brainless, feckless Michael—'darling Misha'—ever becoming Tsar, was laughable. None the less, the declaration further widened the gulf between Dagmar and Alicky. The Empress regarded her mother-in-law's insistence on the declaration as a deliberate slap in the face: a a move designed to underline the fact that she was incapable of producing an heir.

By now, in fact, Alicky was becoming desperate. Having submerged herself, with all the fervour of her nature, in the Orthodox religion and, more particularly, into its mystical fringe, Alexandra looked to it for an answer to her dilemma. She prayed with increased ardour, she made pilgrimages to little-known shrines, she gave audiences to bizarre miracle-workers, she consulted dubious 'soul doctors'. By 1903 a French mystic and faith-healer by the name of Philippe Vachot was in attendance on the Empress; he assured her that she was pregnant and that the child would be a boy. The French authorities, who had distinctly less faith in the self-styled doctor, advised the French Ambassador to St Petersburg that they had already prosecuted him three times for practising medicine without a licence. Alarmed, the Ambassador hurried to consult the Dowager Empress. What, he asked her, was he to do? Dagmar advised him to take the report to the Tsar himself. If she were to reveal that Vachot was an impostor, the Empress would accuse her of interfering.

On being granted an audience with the Tsar, the Ambassador was astonished to discover that Nicholas was more concerned about whether or not he should break the news to the Empress than by Vachot's criminal record. When Dagmar followed up the Ambassadors' call with one of her own, she found her son equally undecided. After all, he argued to his mother, the French police had not actually proved that the man did not have super-natural powers.

Only on the Empress's pregnancy proving to be a phantom one was Vachot sent packing. Before he left, however, the Frenchman gave the Tsaritsa one more assurance. 'You will someday have another friend, like me,' he said, 'who will speak to you of God.'

Not until 12 August 1904 were Alicky's prayers answered. 'A great never-to-be-forgotten day when the mercy of God has visited us so clearly,' wrote the exultant Nicky in his diary that evening. 'Alix gave birth to a son at one o'clock. The child has been called Alexis.'

Dagmar was no less delighted. At the magnifi-cent baptism from which, by another of those quaint Russian traditions, the Tsar and Tsaritsa were absent, she was again the leading figure. Beside her, at this christening of his great-grandson, stood her eighty-six-year-old father, King Christian IX. With more and more justification could the Danish King be regarded as Europe's leading royal patriarch.

CHAPTER THIRTEEN

1

In the year 1905 yet another crown fell, as it were, at the feet of King Christian IX's dynasty. Reluctantly, gingerly and with great circumspection, the Danish royal house picked it up. It agreed to the acceptance, by one of its members, of Europe's most recently established throne.

The throne in question was that of Norway.

For almost a century, Norway and Sweden had been tied together by an Act of Union. It was an alliance in which Sweden was unquestionably the dominant partner. Norway might have its own parliament—the Storting—but the Swedish King ruled over both countries and Sweden kept a firm grip on Norwegian affairs. Dissatisfaction with this arrangement was rife in Norway; throughout the nineteenth century relations between the two countries had become increasingly bitter. Early in the year 1905, things came to a head.

The particular bone of contention was whether or not Norway should have its own consular representation. Norway was determined that it should and

Sweden was just as determined that it should not. In March 1905, the Norwegians finally lost patience. A defiant Storting passed a bill by which the country would have its own consuls in future. The contentious bill was then sent to King Oscar II of Sweden for his sanction. This he refused to give. Thereupon the Norwegian government resigned. King Oscar II, having scrabbled about in a vain effort to form a new government, refused to accept their resignation. This was exactly what the Norwegians wanted. As their country had no government, they argued, and as the King was incapable of forming one, the King of Sweden had ceased to function as King of Norway. The Act of Union, in other words, had been dissolved. The triumphant Storting instructed the Norwegian Council of State to take over the government of the country. In June 1905, the President of the Storting formally announced the dissolution of the Union and the independence of Norway.

A more gentlemanly revolution could hardly have been imagined. More gentlemanly still was Norway's next step: it offered its now vacant throne to a member of the Swedish King's family. King Oscar, however, was not prepared to be anything like as courteous. As far as he was concerned, the Union had not yet been dissolved and the throne was not yet vacant. Norway, he announced, was in no position to offer the throne to anyone until it had fulfilled one condition. The condition was this: Sweden would recognize Norwegian independence only after the parliaments of the two countries had formally negotiated the dissolution of the Act of Union. Only then could she hawk her throne about.

But Norway could not agree. She was determined to fill the throne before negotiations began. A king, setting the seal on Norwegian independence, would gain the country international recognition and thus strengthen its hand in the negotiations with Sweden.

With this tricky question of priorities still unsolved, Norway started looking for a monarch. That she was looking for one at all came as a great relief to Europe's family of kings. Norway was known to have a strongly republican element; why, reasoned the republicans, should Norway saddle itself with another monarch? On the other hand, even among republicans, it was appreciated that the monarchies of Europe would look more kindly on the newly independent country if it were headed by a monarch. A king would give the country an air of respectability.

But who was this king to be? The Great Powers, of course, lost no time in suggesting candidates of their own. These Norway wisely refused to consider. The candidate would have to come, it was decided, from either the Swedish or the Danish royal houses. With the irate King of Sweden unlikely to accept the offer for a member of the Bernadotte family, the field was narrowed to the Glücksburgs—the dynasty of King Christian IX of Denmark.

Here there were four likely candidates: Prince Waldemar, the youngest son of old King Christian;

Waldemar's eldest son, Prince Aage; Prince Nicholas, the third son of King George of the Hellenes; and Prince Charles, second son of Crown Prince Frederick of Denmark and husband of Princess Maud of Wales.

The first three were not really suitable. Prince Waldemar, a somewhat retiring and unambitious man, was already forty-seven years old, while his wife, the more spirited and ardently Francophile Princess Marie, was a Roman Catholic. Already they had refused the Bulgarian throne. Then their eldest son, the eighteen-year-old Prince Aage, was far too young. Prince Nicholas of Greece, at thirty-three, was a good age, but being Greek Orthodox and having a Russian wife and a Russian mother, he was thought to be too much under the influence of St Petersburg. Prince Charles of Denmark, on the contrary, seemed eminently suitable. He was in his early thirties, with a son not yet three years old and a wife who was the daughter of King Edward VII of England. An added advantage was that his mother, the plain and pious Crown Princess Louise, was a Bernadotte: King Oscar II of Sweden was her uncle.

The candidate decided upon, the Norwegian government sent an emissary, Baron Wedel, to sound out the Danish royal family. As King Christian IX was away, visiting his daughter Thyra, Duchess of Cumberland, at Gmunden in Austria, it was to Crown Prince Frederick—the father of Prince Charles— that Baron Wedel presented himself. He found the Crown Prince obsessed by the idea of not upsetting the Swedish King: only if King Oscar II agreed to his son's candidacy would the Crown Prince consider it.

The candidate himself proved even less enthusiastic. The tall, gangling, easy-going and unassuming Prince Charles protested that he had no wish to become a king, that he was quite happy with his position as an officer in the Danish navy and that he hated the idea of leaving Denmark. His wife, the shy and unsophisticated Princess Maud, was even more unwilling. She had no taste for ceremonial and no talent for public life. None the less, it would not have occurred to Prince Charles to reject any formal offer of a crown. As a member of a reigning house, he had certain obligations; royal blood entailed royal duties. The members of King Christian IX's family were all imbued with an unshakeable sense of royal dedication. If the acceptance of the crown would be to the benefit of Norway, then accept the crown he would.

Thus, against his own inclinations, Prince Charles assured Baron Wedel that he would accept the offer. He would do so only if he could be of real service to the country and if his candidature had the wholehearted approval of the Norwegian people. He was not prepared to behave like an ambitious adventurer. Furthermore, his acceptance must have the approval of Denmark, Great Britian and above all, Sweden. Until the crown had definitely been refused by the Swedish royal house, the circumspect Prince Charles was prepared to make no move whatsoever.

There and then Crown Prince Frederick sat down to write a letter to his wife's uncle, King Oscar. What, asked the Danish Crown Prince, was the Swedish King's attitude to the affair? In his reply, King Oscar made his attitude crystal clear. It was what it had always been. Norway, he maintained, had no right to offer the throne to anyone until the parliaments of the two countries had formally negotiated the dissolution of the Act of Union. However, as it was extremely unlikely that any member of his own house would accept the proffered throne, King Oscar had no objection to Prince Charles accepting it—when the time was ripe.

Encouraged by this reply, Crown Prince Frederick sent the Danish Foreign Minister off to see the old King at Gmunden. With as much hesitation as any of the other members of his family, King Christian IX agreed to the future candidature of his grandson.

2

Not everyone shared the Danish royal family's somewhat lukewarm attitude towards the vacant Norwegian throne. As that summer of 1905 merged into autumn, and the King of Sweden still refused to recognize Norway's independence, the various sovereigns of Europe became increasingly agitated. Empty thrones gave them a distinctly uneasy feeling. What if war were to break out between the two countries?

Or, worse still, what if the Norwegians were to plump for a republic? Most agitated of all the sovereigns was King Edward VII of England. As Prince Charles was his wife's nephew and Princess Maud their daughter, King Edward was particularly interested in the affair. He was all for Prince Charles setting off there and then to claim the throne; the Prince was not to wait for a decision by the King of Sweden; a *fait accompli* was what was needed. In telegram after frantic telegram, King Edward urged his son-in-law to go to Norway before it was too late. If he did not, warned the English King, someone else would do so.

'The moment has now come for you to act or lose the Crown of Norway...' ran one of King Edward's telegraphic exhortations. 'I urge you to go at once to Norway, with or without the consent of the Danish government, and help in the negotiations between the two countries...The Queen is quite of the same opinion.'

The Queen was not, in fact, of the same opinion. Or if she was so then, she was not so at a later stage. During her annual autumn visit to Denmark, Alexandra came to a much better understanding of the delicacy of the situation. This prompted her to write to her impatient husband, explaining that it would be impossible for their son-in-law to fly in the face of Swedish opinion; it would lead to war between the three countries at once. Prince Charles gave his father-in-law a further reason for his hesitancy. 'I cannot go to Norway without the King of Denmark's consent as I should hurt his feelings which I must consider.'

Indeed, of all the members of the family, King Christian was proving the least amenable. The King no more hankered after this throne than he had after any of the other thrones now filled by his descendants. As with the offer of the Greek throne to his son Willie, over forty years before, King Christian was thrown into an agony of indecision. If the Norwegian throne were presented to his grandson, well and good, but the old King had no desire to spoil relations with Sweden nor, worse still, to be responsible for sparking off a war between Sweden and Norway. Prince Charles could accept the throne when King Oscar had renounced it, not before.

His caution won the day. Norway was obliged to negotiate. Talks between the two countries opened in September 1905. With these successfully concluded, Sweden recognized Norwegian independence and refused the offer of the throne for a Bernadotte. The crown could at last be offered to Prince Charles of Denmark.

The Norwegian government was delighted. Indeed, one of its representatives so forgot himself that he treated Crown Princess Louise to an ecstatic appreciation of her son's qualities of simplicity and directness, as opposed to the pomposity and ostentation of the Bernadottes. This particular Bernadotte took it in good part. Laughing heartily, the homely Louise assured him that she was in full agreement.

The matter, however, was not quite settled. Prince Charles was still proving hesitant. Worried by the apparent strength of republican sentiment in Norway (he was being inundated with republican tracts) he insisted on a plebiscite. He would accept the Norwegian crown only if the great majority of the people wanted him. He had no wish to become a party king. In his stand, Prince Charles was being backed up by his grandfather King Christian, his father the Crown Prince and his uncle King George of the Hellenes. Only his father-in-law, King Edward, proved unsympathetic. In fact, he was exasperated by this further delay: 'King Edward furious at idea of referendum,' wired Baron Wedel from London.

But furious or not, King Edward could not prevent the plebiscite. It was held on 12 and 13 November 1905. Some 260,000 voted in favour of a monarchy and some 70,000 against: a majority of more than five to one. Five days later the Storting met to elect Prince Charles of Denmark as King of Norway. The election was unanimous.

It was the ubiquitous Baron Wedel who went to break the news to King Christian XI. The Baron was led through a suite of sumptuous rooms in which only one candle flickered in each massive candelabra, allowing just enough light to show the way from one door to the next. He found the eighty-seven-year-old King in his little study, standing beside a table cluttered with photographs of his illustrious family. As the King read Wedel's telegram announcing the election results, his old eyes filled with tears.

At this poignant moment Prince Charles hurried into the room. The Norwegian Prime Minister was on the telephone, wanting to speak to Baron Wedel. The Baron was to read Prince Charles's formal acceptance of the throne to the Prime Minister. With Prince Charles standing beside Wedel, the odd little ceremony was enacted. 'With the consent of His Majesty the King, my august grandfather,' intoned Wedel into the mouthpiece, 'I intend to accept election as King of Norway, thereby assuming the name Haakon VII and giving my son the name of Olav. My wife and I pray for God's bounteous blessing on the Norwegian people, to whose honour and happiness we consecrate the rest of our lives.' Solemnly, Wedel replaced the receiver.

To the Norwegians, the phrase 'my wife and I' struck a reassuringly democratic note. They were to be still more impressed by Danish royal simplicity the following afternoon when the deputation from the Storting arrived in Copenhagen to make the formal offer of the throne. King Christian suddenly arrived at their hotel. This unexpected appearance of the sovereign completely flustered the hotel manager. 'I shall tell the President of the Storting that Your Majesty is here and wishes to speak with him,' he spluttered.

'No, you will not do that,' the King answered airily. 'I shall go up and greet him myself.' And this is what he did.

The atmosphere the following day, 20 November 1905, was distinctly more formal. In the Throne Room of the Amalienborg Palace, with its painted murals, its glittering candelabra, its gold and silver carpet, its three famous silver lions from Rosenborg and its elaborately swagged and tasselled canopy over the throne, Prince Charles of Denmark was formally offered the Norwegian crown. It was accepted, on his behalf, by King Christian. The Danish King—albeit reluctantly—had achieved a double *coup*: a grandson and a grand-daughter were now King and Queen of Norway.

CHAPTER FOURTEEN

1

For the Dowager Empress of Russia, the birth of the Tsarevich Alexis meant more than the arrival of a long-awaited grandson. It marked the end of her period of ascendancy.

Nicholas II, after ten years of reigning, was somewhat more confident of his abilities, while Alexandra having, as she believed, been given proof that God was on the side of the dynasty, was gaining more confidence in hers. Politically, husband and wife were in accord. One of Nicholas II's first public pronouncements, to the effect that he would 'maintain the principle of autocracy just as firmly and unflinchingly' as had his father, would have had Alicky's full approval. Her duty, as she saw it, was to uphold this God-given autocracy, to ensure that her newly-born son would one day inherit these autocratic powers intact. At first tentatively, and then with more and more assurance, Alexandra replaced Dagmar as the Tsar's political confidante and adviser.

As it happened, the political views of the Dowager Empress and the Empress were not in any way in conflict; like Dagmar, Alexandra had a distinctly naïve view of the situation in Russia. The real Russia, imagined Dagmar, was the Russia of the *moujiks*— those loyal, simple, humble, cap-doffing peasants who fell to their knees in the fields at the sight of the imperial train thundering across the steppes. All dissatisfaction in the country was caused by those un-Russian elements: the Jews, the journalists, the pen-pushing clerks and what the Tsar, with a curl of his lip, would refer to as 'the intellectuals'.

With this shallow assessment of the situation, Alexandra was in complete agreement; it was merely that the younger woman was more passionately interested in affairs of state and that she pressed her opinions more forcefully. Already, in domestic and social matters, Alicky had all the say. 'That is for Her Majesty to decide,' was Nicholas's customary answer to a question by a member of the household. The Dowager Empress found this trend increasingly disturbing. 'If Nicky is not careful,' she once confided, 'he will one day be saying "That is for Her Majesty to decide" to one of his ministers.'

It was a prophetic remark.

So convinced of the rightness of their outlook and happy only in the company of their immediate family, Nicholas and Alexandra cut themselves off, more and more, from the company of others. This included the Dowager Empress. In the smug, priggish, self-contained and unsophisticated atmosphere of Tsarskoe Selo, Dagmar found herself ill at ease.

With Alexandra taking everything, including herself, so desperately seriously, all gaiety seemed to have fled from the imperial circle. As a result, the Dowager Empress found herself becoming lonelier by the year.

By now, all Dagmar's children had left home. Her eldest daughter Xenia was married to Grand Duke Alexander and had a family of her own. In 1901 Dagmar had married off her youngest daughter Olga to a highly unsuitable husband: Prince Peter of Oldenburg, who was not only fourteen years the girl's senior but who, by all accounts, had no interest in women whatsoever. 'I shared his roof for nearly fifteen years,' claimed Olga afterwards, 'and never once were we husband and wife.' Some said that Dagmar, with her streak of selfishness, had organized the match to ensure that by marrying a prince who lived in Russia, Olga would remain at her mother's beck and call. Indeed, just as Dagmar's sister Alix always had her unmarried daughter Victoria by her side, so would Dagmar always have Olga close at hand.

A few years later Dagmar's youngest son, the feather-brained Michael who, unlike his brother-in-law the Prince of Oldenburg, was only too interested in women, made an even less suitable alliance. He fell in love with a twice-divorced daughter of a Moscow lawyer. When the shocked Nicholas II refused to give him permission to marry ('I will never give my consent', he assured his no less shocked mother) the happy-go-lucky Misha simply set up home with her.

Nor were Dagmar's troubles confined to the domestic scene. In February 1904 Russia was drawn into a disastrous war against Japan. Nicholas II had been egged on to this folly by the vainglorious Kaiser Wilhelm II; against the Kaiser's exhortations, Dagmar's somewhat muddled protestations went unheeded. Although she was as anxious as any for the glory which a successful war would reflect on the dynasty, the Dowager Empress wanted no truck with Wilhelm's schemes. She disliked him intensely. When the Tsar was obliged to make the Kaiser an admiral in the Russian navy, he had to summon up all his tact to break the news to his Prussian-hating mother. 'I think, no matter how disagreeable it may be,' he wrote, 'we are obliged to let him wear our naval uniform... *C'est à vomir* !'

Moreover, with Britain interesting herself in Japan and with Dagmar still dreaming of some future Anglo-Russian alliance, she was anxious to avoid a possible *fracas* with her sister Alexandra's country. As it was, Alix's sympathies on this occasion were with Japan. 'For a wonder in this war Motherdear is for the Japs!' reported Princess May. 'She is not nearly so Russian as she was...'

The war was an unmitigated disaster for Russia. Both on land and at sea, she was humiliatingly defeated. And there was worse to follow. By the beginning of the year 1905, the entire Empire was in a state of dangerous unrest. Appalled by the war's death toll and by the shocking conditions in factories and on the land, the people were crying out for some say in the government. They wanted a fully representative assembly—a Duma. On the morning of 22 January a good-natured crowd, led by a sympathetic priest, marched on the Winter Palace to present a petition, listing their grievances, to the Tsar. They were fired on by the panic-stricken troops guarding the Palace. From thenceforth the day was to be known as 'Bloody Sunday' and Tsar Nicholas II, who was not directly to blame, as a blood-stained tyrant.

The disaster plunged Russia into deeper turmoil. For a year the country was in a state of violent unrest. Dagmar's brother-in-law, the reactionary Grand Duke Serge, was blown to bits in Moscow. The Black Sea Fleet mutinied. There were murders, strikes, riots and uprisings throughout the Empire.

By all this Dagmar was appalled and bewildered. 'I have suffered so much and so intensely that I feel at least ten years older in this short time...' she wrote to her son from Copenhagen. 'It is still hard for me to believe that all this is happening in Russia.'

To avert a full-scale revolution, something had to be done. Either, advised the Tsar's ministers, the rebellion must be crushed, or Russia given a constitution. The Dowager Empress, encouraged by her more liberal Danish relations, added her voice to those who advised the Tsar to grant a constitution. Reluctantly, he agreed to do so.

By the Imperial Manifesto of 30 October 1905, Russia ceased to be an absolute autocracy and became a type of constitutional monarchy.

The first Duma was opened in the Throne Room of the Winter Palace in the spring of 1906. The scene was one of vivid contrasts: between the gorgeously dressed members of the imperial family, attended by the clergy, the uniformed councillors of state, senators, diplomats and courtiers, and the newly-elected members of the Duma, some of them in workers' blouses and breeches. The atmosphere was uneasy. Whether or not the granting of a constitution had been a step in the right direction, few members of the imperial family seemed able to decide. Neither the Tsar nor the Tsaritsa had much faith in it and the Dowager Empress was as uncertain as either of them. Her husband, after all, had always believed in iron-handed autocracy; away from the assurances of her more enlightened Danish relations, Dagmar was not so certain that he had not been right. 'No *patriotism* on one side, no *authority* on the other—it is simply frightful,' she exclaimed. '*God Almighty* alone can lead us out of this chaos and save our country—perhaps with *His* help the Duma will bring better times...'

But she did not really believe it. Indeed, the opening of the Duma seems to have been the one occasion when Dagmar's customary aplomb and gaiety deserted her. She was, runs one somewhat effusive account, 'extremely moved and agitated. Her eyes were red, and she kept putting up her handkerchief as if to wipe away tears. She keenly observed the assembly, as if trying to read their countenances, to guess what lay behind them. The Socialist group attracted her attention quite particularly, and she watched it the whole time, with something akin to anxiety in her lovely dark eyes, which then wandered towards her son, resting on him with passionate yearning and sadness. Her countenance was perfectly dignified, and yet a whole tragedy lurked in her figure as it bent under the blessing of the Metropolitan.'

Dagmar's reservations were shared by her sister Alix. 'I fear the Constitution which at last poor Nicky had been forced to grant has come too late,' she wrote, 'and then God only knows what will happen.'

2

By the year 1906 the eighty-seven-year-old King Christian IX of Denmark was generally regarded as the grand old man amongst Europe's royal houses, the Nestor of Sovereigns. He might not have been the most important monarch and he was definitely not the brightest, but he was the most respected. Certainly no Continental king had so many brilliantly placed descendants as he; there was hardly a court in Europe into which his children or grandchildren were not proliferating. For someone as modest, as unambitious and as relatively humbly born as King Christian, it was a remarkable achievement.

Unwittingly, too, Christian IX had earned for himself another distinction: by the end of his reign he was being looked upon as the model of a democratic king. This, for a natural autocrat and a conservative, was a hardly less remarkable achievement. Here, also, things had happened in spite of, rather than because of, any measures on the part of the King. Christian IX had always been a constitutional monarch but throughout most of his reign, Denmark was governed by a strongly conservative cabinet, backed by the upper house of the Rigsdag—the parliament—and appointed by the autocratically-minded King. Christian's gentle nature belied an ingrained respect for authority. But, with the lower house of the Rigsdag becoming more liberal with each election, there was increasing friction between right and left. Only in 1901, after prolonged, complicated and bitter conflict, was a true parliamentary democracy introduced. By this so-called Change of System, it was established that the King must choose his cabinet from the majority party in the lower house. Thus, in the summer of 1901, King Christian IX with, it must be admitted, considerable reservation, appointed his first liberal cabinet.

The triumphant liberal Prime Minister, summoned to the palace by the King, found himself agreeably surprised by his sovereign's modest demeanour and friendly manner. But there were limits, he was to discover, to the monarch's approachability. Christian IX's affable way masked a profound awareness of the dignity of his position. When the politician so far forgot himself as to slap the old King cheerfully on the back, he was rewarded with a look of the utmost astonishment.

As the King grew older so, of course, did life at the Danish court become duller. Only his daughters, it seems, refused to believe that it was not still the greatest possible fun. 'Queen Alexandra was so much pleased with this visit,' wrote one long-suffering member of her suite, 'that it seemed churlish to complain.'

King Edward VII's assistant private secretary, young Frederick Ponsonby, visiting Copenhagen for the first time in 1904, was appalled at the boredom and the formality and the leadenness of it all. The evening, he says, was the worst part. Dinner was served at the impossibly early hour of six-thirty and both before and after the meal, the old monarch would move slowly round the circle of guests, saying an appropriate—or, more often, inappropriate—word to each, Ponsonby, frantic for something to talk about to the old man, hit upon the idea of reading up an out-of-date biography of the monarch and of then asking him questions about his early days. The King was delighted. Like all old people, his memory of the distant past was much clearer than of more recent events and he plunged happily into his reminisscences. Each night, having greeted the others with unusual perfunctoriness, the King would hurry back to Ponsonby to continue their talk. 'You will remember General Stewart,' he would start, and Ponsonby, not wanting to spoil things by admitting that General Stewart had died some thirty years before he was born, would let him ramble merrily on.

The after-dinner *cercle* over, the men would escape to their rooms for a quick smoke, but would be obliged to return to the drawing-room for cards. As the King could not play bridge, the company would be forced to play loo or whist, and not for stakes. The old monarch preferred to play with his three daughters. There they would sit on their little gilt chairs, the King looking so sage and seigneurial in his evening dress, his daughters so sophisticated in their gleaming jet and flashing diamonds, all playing games that would not have taxed the mind of a schoolchild.

At ten the company would be 'mercifully released'. This would be the moment for King Edward VII to make for his own rooms where, with three companions, he would play bridge for high stakes until the early hours.

'The Danish suite,' says Ponsonby, 'were all charming and entirely agreed that these evenings were a nightmare, but they said that the old King had gone through this programme for so many years that it was quite impossible to change anything now.'

The story would be told of how, in order to give the public the impression that the royal family was still as vivacious as they had ever been, the King and his children would carry on a simulated conversation as they sat in their box at the theatre. 'One, two, three,' the King would say, 'Four, five,' would reply one of the princesses. 'Six, seven, eight, nine, ten,' would add another, notoriously talkative, one.

However sluggish King Christian might have been intellectually, physically he was still amazingly vigorous. Maurice Baring, Third Secretary at the British Legation in Copenhagen, would often see the octogenarian King out riding; 'he looked on horseback, so extraordinarily young was his figure, like a man of thirty', says Baring. Ponsonby describes him, at eighty-six, as 'still sprightly'. And Jusserand, the new French Minister, professed himself astonished at the liveliness of the monarch to whom he had to present his credentials.

'He once showed us, in detail,' continues Jusserand, 'his living rooms on the ground floor of his palace, full of curious old furniture collected by him, portraits of ancestors, engraved crystals, huge silver mugs, proportionate to the thirsts of former days; but he had especially a large collection of notes, scrapbooks, newspaper cuttings concerning Danish politics; each document marked and annotated by himself. An implacable memory, still further fortified by these aids, prevented him forgetting anything, either services rendered or wrongs inflicted, whereas a man in politics should sometimes be able to forget.'

The chief thing which the King, and his family, were unable to forget, was the perfidy of Prussia. Forty years after the Schleswig-Holstein War, the wound remained as raw as ever. Of this, Kaiser Wilhelm II was only too conscious. No less than Bismarck could Wilhelm II believe that the Danish family assembled for any reason other than to intrigue against Germany. Suspicious, thin-skinned and forever over-estimating royal powers, the Kaiser watched the comings and goings of King Christian's family with continuing alarm. An ambassador had only to carry a private letter from Alexandra to Dagmar for Wilhelm to cry out to heaven that he was being conspired against. Edward VII had only to visit his father-in-law for the Kaiser to warn Tsar Nicholas II that 'the arch mischief-maker of Europe is at work again…'

Yet such was Wilhelm II's nature, so anxious was he to be loved and feared at the same time, that he never missed an opportunity of ingratiating himself with the Danish family. At the height of the crisis over the choice of Prince Charles of Denmark for the Norwegian throne, when Wilhelm was actively working against Charles's candidature, he descended on Copenhagen and pretended to be all in favour of Prince Charles accepting the throne. Nothing, he assured Princess Maud, would delight him more. He even lifted their little son onto his knee and addressed him as '*Der Kronprinz Norwegens*'.

On another occasion he came to Denmark for King Christian's birthday and on leaving, made a point of sending a flowery telegram to the old King's grandson, Tsar Nicholas II. 'Just leaving,' ran the fulsome phrases, 'having spent a few delightful days with the whole family at Copenhagen. Your dear grandfather was kindness itself. Your beloved mother and Aunt Alix quite spoilt me, both looking so young, everybody of the royal family tried their utmost to make me feel at home, so that I have no words for thanking them.'

What Kaiser Wilhelm II did not know was that Princess Alexandra had declared herself 'furious' that he would be there 'to spoil the family party', and that Princess Thyra, on hearing that he was due to arrive, had left Copenhagen the day before.

The Tsar was not taken in by the Kaiser's telegram. 'Deeply moved, isn't he,' he wrote with heavy sarcasm to his mother. 'That is because his dearest wish to get into the Danish family circles has at last been fulfilled, so there is no end to his delight.'

Dagmar did not need to be reminded of Wilhelm's duplicity. 'It makes me too angry—it even gives me palpitations as I write about it...' she once exclaimed.

But even the apprehensive Kaiser Wilhelm II must have realized that the days of 'Europe's Whispering Gallery' were drawing to a close; that these gatherings about the aged King could not continue indefinitely. Christian IX, no matter how vigorous, could not live forever.

Yet, to the very end, the Danish King was astounding his companions with his verve. On the morning of 29 January 1906, King Christian received various people in audience, including the ninety-year-old actress, Louisa Phister, with whom he chatted for over an hour. After that he had lunch. When his daughter Dagmar, who was visiting him at the time, asked if he were tired, he answered, 'No, not at all, not more than an old man is allowed to be.' With that, he put his arm around his daughter's waist and exclaiming, 'Come, you shall see!' danced her around the room. The dancing over, he announced that he was going into the next room to fetch a cigar; when Dagmar offered to fetch it for him, he answered, 'No, thank you, certainly not.'

But when he came back with his cigar, he looked pale and was perspiring heavily. Alarmed, Dagmar made him lie down and sent for his doctor. The doctor having administered a few drops, the King felt better; he was even able to joke with his son Waldemar, who had also been summoned. When Dagmar suggested cancelling dinner, her father would not hear of it.

Still worried, Dagmar left the room to scribble a note to her brother, the Crown Prince. During her brief absence, the King gave a deep sigh, and died. It was three o'clock in the afternoon.

As soon as the news was released, the bells of Copenhagen began to toll. Gradually, from steeple to steeple, the sad clanging was taken up. By evening, every belfry in the land was ringing out for the passing of the Father-in-law of Europe.

PART THREE
AUTUMN

CHAPTER FIFTEEN

1

The death of King Christian IX marked the end of the Danish family gatherings. There was very little about the new King, Frederick VIII—and considerably less about his wife, Queen Louise—to attract the relations to the Danish court. With the pious and by now somewhat eccentric Louise as hostess at Amalienborg, Bernsdorff and Fredensborg, all traces of gaiety were swept away. By comparison with the new régime, even the last, stiff, dreary days of the old seemed positively scintillating. 'We had to undergo a series of very old-fashioned state functions which were homely but boring,' complains a member of King Edward VII's suite. Nothing, he says, 'of any great interest was discussed'.

Yet King Frederick VIII, like his brothers and sisters, was a man of enduringly youthful looks and considerable charm. He was also a man of good sense. Sixty-two at the time of his accession, Frederick certainly came to the throne well prepared: the most valuable lesson imbibed during his long apprenticeship was of the need for a constitutional monarch to keep within the limits of his position. A natural conservative, who often found these limits irksome, Frederick VIII none the less had the intelligence to abide by them. His accession speech, to the effect that he prayed for 'the good fortune to arrive at an understanding with the people and their chosen representatives on all that tends to the good of the people' was not all rhetoric; he fully realized that he must not oppose a gradual liberalization of the régime. Fighting down his own inclinations, Frederick tried to identify the throne with whatever progressive movements were going.

He was very conscious too, of a need for the popularization of the monarchy. Where old King Christian IX had never actually sought public approval, Frederick VIII went out of his way to gain popularity. He made countless tours, he delivered eloquent speeches, he espoused charitable causes, he never forgot a face. He battled for the rights of those Danes living in German-ruled Schleswig; he threw himself into the granting of greater independence for Iceland; he presided over such popular measures as the extension of the franchise and the additional taxation of the rich. Indeed, to some, the new King seemed rather too willing to swim with the liberal tide. 'He seemed anxious for popularity,' runs one jaundiced comment, 'and to gain this he was quite willing to don the cap of liberty and promise anything to his people.'

Be that as it may, by his involvement and his adaptability, Frederick VIII ensured that the dynasty

remained on the throne long after other, more autocratic, monarchs had tumbled.

With so many close relations in the various courts
of Europe, Frederick VIII enjoyed a reign that was
marked by a constant coming and going. He paid
a state visit to England where he was taken on the
customary royal round: a banquet at Buckingham
Palace, a luncheon at Guildhall (only by listening
carefully to his speeches could one realize that he was
speaking English, not Danish), a review at Aldershot
and a gala performance at the opera—to hear Melba
and Caruso. He went to Stockholm where he was able
to smooth the feelings of his wife's family, still ruffled
after the affair of the Norwegian crown. Displaying
more political realism than the rest of his relations,
he visited Kaiser Wilhelm II in Berlin. It was through
the resulting friendlier relations with Germany that
he was able to ease the lot of the Danes in Schleswig.
With forty members of the Rigsdag he visited Iceland,
where he is said to have 'enjoyed a larger measure of
popularity than any Danish King'.

And if Frederick's myriad relations no longer
massed together for their annual holidays in Denmark,
they continued to pay shorter, more formal visits.
Royal yachts still lay at anchor off Copenhagen and
the railway station still presented a picture of mingled
pomp and confusion as the royal mob milled about
on the platform, kissing, shaking hands and trying
to find the right carriages. Under the new reign, the
Amalienborg Palace was considerably altered and

improved, although there remained a tendency for the royal luggage to go astray. King Edward VII, always obsessed with the correct clothes for every occasion, found this fault particularly maddening. He could hardly bring himself to go down to dinner in the unbecomingly short jacket and tight breeches of the Danish uniform in which he had arrived a few hours before.

To the way of life of his sisters, Alexandra and Dagmar, Frederick's accession made one significant difference. Still anxious to continue their annual Danish holidays, but ill-at-ease in the company of their sister-in-law Louise, the sisters decided to buy a home of their own in Denmark. They found one at Hvidore, by the seashore, some miles out of Copenhagen. The elaborate house, which one visitor described lyrically as a 'milk white Italian villa' and another as the most 'ghastly property' he had ever seen, delighted the two women. In no time the rooms of the Villa Hvidore were a cheerful clutter of fussy furniture, potted plants, family photographs and yapping lapdogs. Above the chimney-piece was engraved 'East, West, Home's Best'. 'The two sisters,' wrote the visiting Infanta Eulalia, 'who adore each other, are absolutely happy in each other's society, and in the simplicity of the life they lead. They welcomed me with enthusiasm, kissed me, and were quite excited to have somebody to whom they could show their little home.' The visitor had to see it all—their writing tables, their favourite chairs, their kitchen garden, the kettle with which they made their own tea.

From the walled garden, a passageway, cut under the public road, gave access to a private stretch of beach. On fine autumn days the Queen of England and the Dowager Empress of Russia could be seen, in their forward-tilted straw boaters, hunting for pieces of amber among the pebbles.

'It is most unfair,' the Queen would exclaim, eyeing her sister's larger pile of amber.

'I always pick up more than you do,' would be the Empress's triumphant rejoinder.

'They are Danes,' was the Infanta Eulalia's comment on this show of schoolgirlish rivalry, 'and they have never lost the love of simplicity which is the most notable characteristic of the people of Scandinavia.'

2

For Queen Alexandra, the end of the family jamborees made precious little difference to the frequency with which she was able to see her relations. Luckily, she was married to a man who adored both entertaining and travelling, be it informally or in state. Thus not only were the members of her family constantly braving the Channel crossing in order to visit her, but she was forever setting out on yet another cruise that would unite her with some crowned relation.

In the spring of 1906, King Edward and Queen Alexandra visited the Queen's favourite brother,

King George of the Hellenes. Alexandra had paid an unofficial visit to Athens the year before but this was to be a state occasion, a return visit for the one that the Greek King had paid to London in November 1905. The first five days of the stay were spent privately at 'Mon Repos', King George's home on the island of Corfu. While on Corfu, the King and Queen were reunited with their son and daughter-in-law, George and May (now Prince and Princess of Wales), who were on their way home from an official tour of India. 'You may imagine how pleased we were to see each other again,' wrote Princess May. 'The King looks well but Motherdear looks very sad and tired after her great sorrow…'

The great sorrow, of course, was the recent death of King Christian IX; indeed, the Greek court was still in mourning for the father of both Queen Alexandra and King George. 'We ladies all wore high black gowns and long crape veils and looked very lugubrious!' noted Princess May.

None the less, the air, the sunshine and the company of her adored brother George and his family quickly restored Alexandra's spirits. The Greek royal family, claims Frederick Ponsonby, 'were all delightful'. Like a pack of excited schoolchildren, the royal family went sightseeing: to the Acropolis, to the British School of Archaeology, the Athens Museum, the Theatre of Dionysus, the Theseus Temple and the Olympic Games stadium. There were informal lunches beneath the trees at Tatoi, dinners *en famille* and a state banquet for a hundred and eighty.

With all the visitors, King George was a great favourite. His buoyancy and his naturalness charmed them all. During his state visit to England the year before, he had impressed Frederick Ponsonby by his complete lack of pomposity. Ponsonby, climbing into a carriage beside the King, had suddenly realized that contrary to Continental tradition, he would be sitting on the right, instead of the left, of the visiting monarch. 'Sit down,' said George to the hesitating Ponsonby. 'I know you don't have any nonsense of that sort in England.'

There were limits, though, to King George's leniency. On the occasion of this visit to Athens, the debonair Lord Charles Beresford, commanding the battleship squadron of the British Mediterranean Fleet, neglected to change into full dress uniform to receive the Greek King. At this implied insult, even King George felt obliged to complain to his brother-in-law; the outraged King Edward (who anyway disliked Beresford) lost no time in reporting him to the Admiralty Board.

Of his brother-in-law's political acumen, King Edward had a very high opinion. He considered King George 'intelligent and well up in European politics'. As international affairs were the only brand of politics that really interested King Edward, he was able to appreciate the Greek King's diplomatic skills.

George certainly needed all his wits about him for Greece, then, as always, was embroiled in squabbles with its Balkan neighbours. For the most part, King George could ignore these rumblings ('he attached no importance to anything anyone had said or done in the neighbouring countries', reports a member of King Edward's suite) but Turkey always presented a more formidable problem.

At this moment, the most burning issue was the once Turkish-owned island of Crete. King George's second son, Greek Georgie, had been appointed High Commissioner in Crete after the disastrous Greco-Turkish War of 1897. His high-handed rule ('Prince George of Greece out-Sultans the Sultan' proclaimed one British press headline) antagonized the four Protecting Powers—England, France, Italy and Russia. While the despotic Prince George was behaving as though union between Greece and Crete was simply a matter of time, the Powers were coming to the conclusion that he must be replaced. But it was a delicate situation. 'I was given to understand...' wrote a newly appointed British consul general in Crete, 'that the Prince was the favourite nephew of King Edward and Queen Alexandra and that it must be my particular job to let him down lightly.'

Now, during this Greek visit, both King Edward and his minister in attendance took the opportunity of raising the Cretan question. It was eventually decided that the Greek King would be asked to nominate a new commissioner in the place of his son.

Before the year was out, however, the situation had resolved itself. An uprising on the island, led by a local politician by the name of Eleftherios Venizelos, forced Prince George to resign his office. For the first time, but by no means for the last, had the fiery Venizelos decided the fate of a member of the Greek royal house.

The five-day state visit over, the *Victoria and Albert* sailed away from Greece. 'Frankly speaking,' says one of King Edward's entourage, 'we none of us enjoyed it except perhaps the Queen, who loved being with her brother.'

3

Queen Alexandra enjoyed her state visit to Scandinavia, in the spring of 1908, just as much. On this occasion the usual Danish holiday was extended to include Sweden and Norway. In the Norwegian capital of Christiania—later Oslo—Queen Alexandra was able to stay with the new King and Queen of Norway: her nephew Haakon and her daughter Maud. Of the three Scandinavian courts, the Norwegian was the least brilliant. For one thing it was very new; for another, the tone of the country was highly democratic, almost republican; and, perhaps most important of all, neither the King nor the Queen had the slightest taste for ceremonial.

The Kongens Slot—Royal Palace—in which the royal visitors were housed, was a vast, inconvenient, barrack-like structure, originally designed for ceremonial purposes only. The rooms might be magnificently proportioned but they were quite uninhabitable. At the time that Haakon and Maud had first taken up residence there, the huge building had boasted only one bath and no lavatories. All the water had to be carried up from the kitchen in the basement and all the slops carried down. Most of the furniture, which had been the personal property of the King of Sweden, had been carted back to Stockholm. The royal couple had been obliged to make do with such furniture as they brought with them from Copenhagen, and with what the Norwegian government had been able to pick up in sales.

At the time of the visit of the British sovereigns, the palace was still far from habitable. There were not nearly enough bathrooms and the staff was quite unable to cope with such things as an obligatory banquet. Although Queen Alexandra could put up with this happy-go-lucky atmosphere, the more punctilious King Edward was soon showing signs of his notoriously short temper. Once, as the royal party was strolling back from some expedition, a pack of local photographers became so persistent that King Edward exploded and ordered them to be cleared away. Undaunted, the photographers sent their pictures to the palace the following day; to the surprise of the King's suite, the King and Queen bought them all.

It was the attitude of King Haakon, however, that most astonished King Edward's entourage. Always slightly discomforted by the Danish royal family's easy-going ways, they were positively shocked by King Haakon's lack of majesty. The only way to win popularity and combat republicanism, explained Haakon, was to conduct himself with the utmost simplicity. He was even contemplating travelling about the streets of his capital by tram. Against any such notion, the British argued vehemently. A monarch, they advised, must conduct himself like the captain of a ship; he must be a 'Delphic Oracle'; he must 'get up on a pedestal and remain there'. And, whatever he did, he must never travel by tram.

King Haakon, as was his way, listened but said very little in reply.

Queen Maud was equally unpretentious. But whereas her husband had inherited the family's easy public manner, she had not. Her shyness and her stiffness came from her British, not her Danish, ancestry. In anyone, these failings were unfortunate; in a queen, they were disastrous.

Yet away from the intimidating eyes of strangers, Maud could be delightful—high-spirited, warmhearted, easily amused. She might not have inherited the Danish family's social grace but she had her full share of its sense of fun. Indeed, in an intimate circle, Maud was regarded as nothing short of hilarious. She had the family talent, too, of creating a cheerful domestic atmosphere. Her private apartments—like her mother's—were a cosy clutter of family photo-graphs, family gifts and conventionally pretty paint-ings. The Norwegian royal ménage, of Haakon, Maud and little Olav, was one of the happiest and most harmonious in Europe.

For Queen Alexandra, the visit was a delight. Once more she was amongst uncomplicated, unintel-lectual people whose speech she could follow. With the visit assuming, as one of King Edward's suite put it, 'a family rather than an official character', every-thing went off splendidly.

The next reunion, a few months later, was in an altogether different style. In the summer of 1908, King Edward and Queen Alexandra visited the Queen's nephew, Tsar Nicholas II.

Whereas the Norwegian visit had had no politi-cal significance, the Russian was decidedly politi-cal in character. An Anglo-Russian convention, by which Britain became loosely allied to Russia, had been signed the year before. This meeting between the King of England and the Tsar of Russia would therefore set the seal on the agreement between the two countries. With Russia and France already allied, and with Britain having established an *entente cordiale* with France (towards the realization of which, the Francophile King Edward had made a considerable contribution) the three states were now in alliance.

It was an alliance which the Germans viewed with the gravest distrust. Already, to Kaiser Wilhelm II, King Edward VII was 'the Encircler'; a satanic schemer intent on ringing Germany with enemies. The main purpose of the British King's showy state visits, imagined his nephew, was to isolate the Second Reich in a hostile Europe. This proposed meeting with the Russian Tsar was merely another move in his machiavellian game.

For the two sisters, Alexandra and Dagmar, an understanding between their respective adopted countries was the realization of a life-long dream. It was thus only fitting that they should be present at this proposed ceremonial meeting between the husband of one and the son of the other. The meeting was to take place at sea; the yachts would anchor off Reval—now Tallin—in the Gulf of Finland.

The North Sea crossing of the *Victoria and Albert* was extremely rough. Almost the only passenger not to be affected by the weather was Queen Alexandra. Looking as soignée as ever, she braved the crazily-tilting decks. Even when, on one occasion, a particularly violent lurch flung her to the floor and sent everything on the tea table—urn, teapot, dishes, plates, cakes, biscuits and a shower of sugar—tumbling into her lap, she treated it all as a great joke.

By the time they reached Reval, the weather had cleared. Here were anchored the sumptuously appointed imperial yachts, the *Standart* carrying the Emperor and Empress and their children, and the *Polar Star* carrying the Dowager Empress. The meeting lasted for two days. While the ministers talked, the royals exchanged visits. Arm in arm the monarchs strolled along the spotless decks (Nicholas seemed particularly relaxed in the company of his genial uncle) while the women sat talking in the shade of the awnings. In stiffly starched, short-skirted white dresses and huge hats trimmed with *broderie anglaise*, the four beautiful young archduchesses sat decorously beside their mother, the Empress Alexandra; their four-year-old brother, the sailor-suited Tsarevich Alexis, posed stiffly for Queen Alexandra's box camera. There were banquets, concerts and dancing on deck under the strange, red, northern sky which remained light until half past eleven at night.

If Alexandra and Dagmar were, as always, delighted to be in each other's company, the Tsaritsa appeared altogether less happy. Beside these two older, yet more light-hearted and simple-minded women, Alicky seemed sad, introspective, tortured. She was unable to free herself of the pressures of both her public and her private life.

For by now the Empress of Russia knew that her son—the handsome, adored, long-awaited Alexis—was a haemophiliac: a sufferer from that dreaded bleeding disease which could bring death at any moment. She was already embarked on what one of her intimates would call her 'long Calvary'. It was a journey that was to affect, disastrously, the lives of all the Russian imperial family; not least of all that of the Dowager Empress.

4

Very little involved in these family junketings was Princess Thyra, the Duchess of Cumberland. For year after year the good-natured Thyra and the irascible Ernest lived out their quiet life at Gmunden in Austria. In the year 1908, he turned sixty-three, she fifty-five. With Ernest hating travel and happy only in his *lederhosen*, the pliant Thyra had had to adjust her life to his. This was something at which the daughters of King Christian had always been adept.

There had been a time, of course, when the couple had known more activity. With six young children, this had been inevitable. The rampaging Greek royal youngsters, on their way home to Athens from their Danish holidays, used to spend a week or two at Gmunden. Dagmar had sometimes brought her young family, and Frederick and Waldemar theirs. When Alexandra and her three daughters came to Gmunden, the unsophisticated local Austrian officers, roped in for dances at the château, 'were always asking the mother to dance, imagining that she was one of the daughters'.

But those days had long since gone. The Cumberlands had now settled down to a relatively uneventful life. Their home, perched on a pine-covered hill, boasted the most magnificent view: over the village of Gmunden on the shores of the Trauensee to the high, wooded mountain, the Trauenfels, towering beyond. 'Gmunden,' wrote one of Thyra's nephews, 'is beautiful and picturesque in fine weather, but when the rainy season begins, even as children we were impressed by its gloominess.' Something of this gloom pervaded the house as well; certainly life within its walls tended to be somewhat old-fashioned. There would be staid musical evenings or gargantuan dinners at which, says one guest, 'an unbelievable number of courses followed one another, with an iced sherbet half-way through to give the illusion of renewed appetite.'

Yet no matter how stodgy the entertainments or how anti-social the host, Princess Thyra always managed to save the occasion by her grace. Years with a difficult husband had not soured the extraordinary sweetness of her temperament and, like her sisters Alexandra and Dagmar, Thyra was slender, erect and elegant. On special occasions, she would sport her famous diamond necklace with its huge cross; it was, says that experienced diplomat, Daniele Varè, 'the most beautiful diamond necklace I have ever seen... the stones were all the same size and glowed like a rainbow round her neck'. At times like these, Thyra looked no less a sovereign than did her sisters.

And, of course, this is what they all considered her to be. The Duke of Cumberland, for all his eccentricity of dress and demeanour, regarded himself as *un roi en exil.* He was, he would stoutly maintain, the King of Hanover and his wife was the Queen; their household at Gmunden was the Hanoverian court-in-exile. That Prussia had abolished the throne of Hanover and sequestrated the last Hanoverian King's private fortune was something that the Duke of Cumberland could not forget. Nor was the Duchess of Cumberland likely to forget that Prussia had despoiled her native Denmark in 1864; there were limits, it seems, to the sweetness of even her nature.

The antipathy which both Ernest and Thyra had felt for King Wilhelm of Prussia they had by now transferred to his grandson, Kaiser Wilhelm II. The Duchess of Cumberland had only to hear that the Kaiser was due to visit Copenhagen for her to pack up and leave. While the alacrity with which Ernest managed to disappear whenever Wilhelm II was in the neighbourhood had earned him the nickname of 'the Vanishing Duke'. Nothing, it seemed during the early years of the century, would ever reconcile the Duke and Duchess of Cumberland to the German Emperor.

5

In Copenhagen, a Prince who could have been a King—Thyra's brother Waldemar, who had once refused the Bulgarian throne—was living an equally unspectacular life. In the year 1908, Waldemar turned fifty. Except for the pince-nez perched firmly on his nose, he looked like a younger, slimmer, more book-ish version of his brother-in-law, King Edward VII. With that, however, the resemblance ended. Prince Waldemar was a relaxed, discreet, modestly-mannered man, quite content with his career as an admiral in the Danish Navy and with his home in the Yellow Palace: the very palace in which his father had lived before becoming King. His political attitudes were liberal; his air, like that of all the men of the Danish family, was amiable and unaggressive.

Very different was his wife, Princess Marie, that Francophile daughter of the Duc de Chartres. Her interests by no means ended with her ardent and active championship of the cause of her native France. 'In everything that went on,' wrote a French Minister to the Danish court, 'she took a hand, were it a charity ball, a line in steamships, any work, any business, she was in direct correspondence with the Emperor of Russia, who signed his answers Nicky, with the powerful Russian Minister Witte, President Loubet, Mr Delcassé and many others...'

She took a more than conventional interest in the education of her five children; the four sons were brought up as Protestants, the daughter a Catholic. She painted, she modelled, she sculpted; her private drawing-rooms, which she used as studios, were always teeming with birds, dogs, flowers, fruit and vegetables. An accomplished horsewoman, she delighted in riding with two horses harnessed tandem ahead of hers; no number of falls ever dampened her enthusiasm. She joined the Copenhagen fire brigade and proudly wore their uniform. On one occasion her guests were understandably startled when, at the clanging of an alarm bell, the Princess rushed from the room to re-appear with a fireman's helmet on her blond curls. Shouting her apologies, she hurried off to fight a fire which had broken out aboard a ship in the harbour.

'Her début at a court where, with great simplicity of manners, there prevailed a rather stiff, old-fashioned etiquette, had been difficult,' claims the French Minister, 'but she overcame all obstacles and was beloved by all...'

Yet Princess Marie was clearly wearing herself out. Her body had never been a match for her enthusiasm. Often she would be at her desk until four in the morning, scrawling those letters by which she hoped to bring about more speedily a Continental alliance against Germany. When she was warned to take things more quietly, she would answer that she had no wish to spend her old age in a wheelchair.

That wish, at least, was granted. Princess Marie died suddenly, at the age of forty-four, in 1909. The death of this energetic Princess almost broke her gentle husband's heart. He had been devoted to her. For a long time Waldemar could not bring himself to have her buried at Roskilde among the other Danish royalty. Her coffin was kept in the Sailors' Church in Copenhagen, so that he could visit it more easily. He was to outlive her by thirty years.

CHAPTER SIXTEEN

1

Stubborn in so many things, Queen Alexandra was most stubborn in her attitude towards Germany: 'So my Georgie boy has become a real, live, filthy, blue-coated, *Pickelhaube* German soldier!!!' she exclaimed on the occasion that her son, Prince George, was made an honorary colonel of a Prussian regiment. It had been, she was none the less quick to add, his misfortune—not his fault.

Nor did the personality of Kaiser Wilhelm II do anything towards softening Alexandra's intransigency. Loud, brash, humourless, conceited, arrogant, Wilhelm II was everything that she disliked. Set against the well-bred menfolk of her own family, he appeared unspeakably vulgar. She was in full agreement with those who imagined that he was simply waiting for an opportunity to plunge Europe into war; his bite, she had no doubt, was every bit as bad as his bark. Thus, into any measures aimed at counteracting Germany's growing might, Queen Alexandra flung herself wholeheartedly.

These were the years in which Germany was building up her fleet. Jealous of British naval might and anxious to become a world power, the Second Reich was determined to establish itself as a great maritime power. This Britain, as Mistress of the Seas, hotly resented. As a result, a frantic and expensive naval race had developed between the two countries. It was a race in which Alexandra's emotions were deeply involved.

In her longing to see Britain keeping ahead of Germany, the Queen had a redoubtable ally in the ebullient and mandarin-faced Sir John Fisher, First Sea Lord. Fisher, like Alexandra, loathed Germany. No less than she, he had never forgotten what he referred to as Britain's betrayal of Denmark, when she had allowed Prussia to wrest Schleswig-Holstein from Denmark; nor that the vital Kiel Canal cut through territory that had once been Danish. Indeed, Fisher had a plan whereby, in the event of war with Germany, Britain would land troops in Schleswig-Holstein and seize the Kiel Canal.

That such a man should have the support of the impetuous and single-minded Queen was only to be expected. Throughout the years that he was battling to build up Britain's navy she was his unquestioning champion. It was Fisher who originated the Dreadnought; his plan was to build four new ones each year. Therefore when, in 1906, the Liberal Government balked at the idea of building even three Dreadnoughts, the Queen was hardly less determined than the First Sea Lord that the original plan be adhered to. She never let slip an opportunity of referring to it, even in jest. To Fisher's request that he be given a seat on the royal train on one occasion that summer, the Queen telegraphed back, 'Yes with pleasure I will give you a seat in my train if you will give us a fourth Dreadnought.'

Fisher's reply was no less to the point. 'Humbly beg to inform Your Majesty that four Dreadnoughts will be built and building on Your Majesty's next birthday…'

And when that birthday came round, the First Sea Lord's telegram was equally gallant. 'Your Majesty is sixty-two today may you live until you look it is the fervent wish of your humble admirer.'

The rivalry between Britain and Germany was not yet of so serious a nature that their respective monarchs needed to avoid one another. Although King Edward VII and his nephew Kaiser Wilhelm II said a great many uncomplimentary things about each other in private (and, for that matter, in public) there was no open breach between them. The British King and the German Kaiser met, officially and unofficially, several times during Edward's reign ('there was always a feeling of thunder in the air' whenever they met, admitted Frederick Ponsonby) and, provided no contentious topics were discussed, the meetings could be got through safely.

But, as yet, King Edward had paid no state visit to Berlin. For a man so addicted to the pageantry of state occasions (and Kaiser Wilhelm II was hardly less addicted) King Edward's slowness in visiting the German capital did not pass unremarked. After all, he had already paid state visits to France, Russia, Austria, Spain, Italy, Greece, Portugal, Denmark, Norway and Sweden; his official visit to Kiel could hardly count as a great state occasion. How could this so-called 'Peacemaker of Europe' hope to retain his reputation if he failed to visit the capital of the one sovereign who was generally regarded as the main threat to the peace of Europe?

One did not need to look far for the cause of the King's tardiness in visiting Berlin. There were few things Queen Alexandra would rather not do than go to the German capital in state. She could never have prevented her husband from going but she would never have encouraged him. But for even so wayward and obstinate a woman as she, Alexandra appreciated that her position entailed certain sacrifices. Thus, when it was finally arranged that King Edward VII was to visit Berlin in February 1909, Queen Alexandra agreed to accompany him.

She saw to it, however, that everyone should know that she was being 'dragged' there.

2

Yet for Queen Alexandra personally, the state visit to Berlin was a tremendous success. Having agreed to go, she obviously decided that she would make the best of it. In the train carrying the royal party through Germany, she was in excellent form. Throughout dinner she kept the company diverted with her chatter. When a sudden lurch of the train scattered a trayful of quails over her, leaving one perched on her wig, she assured her amused companions that she would arrive in Berlin *coiffée de cailles*.

Two incidents, guaranteed to appeal to both the Queen's childish sense of humour and her streak of malice towards the German imperial family, marked the ceremonial arrival in Berlin. Kaiser Wilhelm II had been determined that the visit should be one of unparalleled magnificence: nothing must be allowed to detract from the pomp and dignity of the occasion. As the royal train slid into the Lehrter Bahnhof, there were solemnly waiting, on the beflagged and red-carpeted platform, a host of dignitaries, headed by the royals in full panoply. By some mischance, however (and one must assume that it was mischance) King Edward had moved into the Queen's carriage; he thus alighted a good hundred yards down the platform from where the imperial family was so decorously assembled. Queen Alexandra must have been more than a little amused to see the discomforted German royals, all fluttering plumes, clanking swords and hitched-up skirts, come dashing down the platform to receive them.

The next incident, from Alexandra's point of view, was even more gratifying. As the procession of carriages moved through the streets, the horses drawing the second carriage, carrying the Queen and the German Empress, suddenly jibbed, reared and stopped dead. Nothing could get them to move forward. This meant that, in full view of the public, the royal ladies had to alight from their carriage and clamber into another hastily vacated one, thus holding up the entire procession. The Kaiser was furious. That this should happen at all was bad enough, but that it should happen in front of the horse-conscious British was doubly infuriating. 'The Queen...' says one of the British suite, 'was secretly pleased at the contretemps.'

Throughout the three-day state visit, Alexandra never put a foot wrong. Amongst all the glitter of the occasion (and the imperial court, despite its showiness, was not without a certain brilliance) none shone more brightly than she. She looked superb. Although old enough to be the German Empress's mother, she was said to be looking more like her daughter. The Empress Auguste Viktoria—Dona to the family—was a staid, matronly, over-dressed creature, very different in type from the women of the Danish royal family. 'Thank God the German visit is over...' the Tsar Nicholas II had once written to his mother. '[Dona] tried to be charming and looked very ugly in rich clothes chosen without taste. The hats she wore in the evening were particularly impossible.' These impossible hats, in fact, were all chosen by the Kaiser: at the beginning of each season, Wilhelm would put on display all the hats he had decided on for his submissive and adoring wife. Beside this opulently dressed and doll-like Empress, the slender Queen Alexandra in her velvet coats, fur toques, spotted veils and huge muffs looked radiantly young and smart.

That the Queen played a larger public role than was customary during this Berlin visit was due to a distressing fact: King Edward was far from well. He tired easily; he felt puffed and fretful. He could only just manage to force himself on from one function to the next. There was no doubt that the succession of brilliant but exacting entertainments—the luncheons, the gala dinners, the receptions, the balls, the reviews—was proving too much for him. One day, after luncheon at the British Embassy, he suddenly collapsed. It was feared that he might have suffered a stroke. But once his doctor, Dr James Reid, had loosened the tight collar of his Prussian uniform, the King recovered. King Edward, announced the doctor, had suffered a bronchial attack.

To save her husband further strain, Queen Alexandra took over some of his less important duties. She carried them out with all customary grace. Frederick Ponsonby, watching her move amongst the audience during the *entr'acte* at the ballet (it was *Sardanapalus*, written by the Kaiser) was filled with admiration for the way in which she addressed a few words to each person. Although she could not, of course, hear anything that was being said in reply, she charmed everyone. 'I have never seen anything better done,' he claims.

Queen Alexandra returned home no better disposed towards Germany than she had ever been; not that it would have mattered if she were. Politically, she was of very little consequence. She had certainly played her part in turning her husband against Germany and its ruling family, but that was as far as her influence went. And, in any case, King Edward's opinions, or preferences, carried hardly more weight than hers. His tireless and much publicized journeyings from court to court and from capital to capital were having very little effect on the European situation. He was not nearly as powerful a diplomatic force as many imagined him to be. A more harmonious relationship between the British and German royal families would have made very little difference to the course of events. Their mutual antipathy did not cause the rivalry between Britain and Germany; it merely happened to coincide with, or mirror, it. By now, both royal families were anachronisms.

Much more important than their personal feelings was the fact that they happened to preside over rival power blocs. Against such a situation, the quality of the relationship between the British and German reigning houses mattered very little. That Queen Alexandra had nursed a life-long hatred for the country with which Britain was gradually being drawn into conflict was incidental. It was gratifying, but it was incidental.

3

Dagmar, the Dowager Empress Marie of Russia, joined her sister Queen Alexandra for King Edward's usual Mediterranean cruise in the spring of 1909. As always, the two women, both in their sixties, behaved with all the skittishness of schoolgirls on a day's outing. 'You cannot imagine how I am enjoying myself here,' wrote Dagmar from Italy to her son Nicholas, 'everything is so beautiful and interesting that words cannot express it.'

Landing at Naples, the royal party took a special train to the lower slopes of Mount Vesuvius. Here were waiting some donkeys which the Queen, quite unbeknown to the King, had ordered to carry them to the rim of the crater. Nothing, announced the sixteen-stone King Edward, would induce him to mount one of those little donkeys; nor had he the slightest intention of walking up the mountain. But as Alexandra was determined to see the crater, she and Dagmar, with the long-suffering Frederick Ponsonby in tow, went jogging up the rough pathway.

In no time the two women had cantered off into the distance, leaving their companion to urge his much slower donkey to catch them up. Before he could do so, however, a shrill blast of the train whistle announced that the King wanted them to return. Forcing his donkey on, Ponsonby came to within shouting distance of the Queen. The King wanted them to turn back at once, he cried. But Alexandra was having none of it. There was no point in going only half way up, she answered, and continued blithely on her way. Discomforted, Ponsonby fell back. A series of even shriller blasts from the train impelled him into action again. The King was obviously working up to one of his monumental rages. This time, in the face of Ponsonby's earnest entreaties, the Queen agreed to turn back. But by now the Empress was a mere speck in the distance. Only after a stumbling, spine-jolting ride could the secretary reach her to tell her to return. Extremely disappointed, Dagmar had no option but to consent. She, too, knew something of her brother-in-law's impatience. By the time the three riders arrived back at the train, the King was 'boiling with rage'. Unable to vent it on either the Queen or the Empress, he did so on the head of poor, innocent Ponsonby.

King Edward returned to England, while Alexandra and Dagmar sailed on to see their brother George in Greece. The sisters were reunited again, that autumn, in their new home at Hvidore. When the Queen returned to England after this Danish holiday, she found herself facing a disturbing situation. The King looked old and ill; he was also deeply concerned about a conflict which was developing between the House of Commons and the House of Lords. It was a conflict which directly involved the sovereign. There was a strong possibility that he would have to use his royal prerogative to create new peers to ensure the passing of legislation to curtail the powers of the House of Lords. Extremely loath to do any such thing, the King tried to find a compromise solution. He even talked, in moments of despair, of abdicating. In fact, the dilemma was not to be resolved until after his death.

But such was King Edward VII's nature that, despite failing health and political worries, he insisted on keeping to his usual time-table. In the spring of 1910 he went for his annual holiday at Biarritz; with him went his long-standing mistress, Alice Keppel. No sooner had he arrived there than he collapsed. He was obliged to remain, if not in bed, in his rooms. Queen Alexandra, who was about to visit her brother George yet again, begged him to leave that 'horrid Biarritz' and accompany her. He refused. With the constitutional crisis still unresolved, he had to be ready to return home at any moment. Alexandra, determined not to miss the chance of even a few days in the company of one of her relations, sailed on to Corfu without him. The political situation held steady and not until 27 April did King Edward arrive back at Buckingham Palace.

Alexandra, by then, was on Corfu. She had not been there long before she had word to say that the King was very ill. Immediately she left for home, arriving in London on the evening of 5 May. Only on seeing her husband did she appreciate that he was dying.

On the following day, King Edward rejected the informal clothes which his valet had laid out for him and insisted on wearing a frock coat. But he spent most of the day in an armchair, fighting for breath. In the afternoon, he suffered a series of heart attacks. Clearly, he had not many more hours to live. With characteristic generosity, Alexandra included Mrs Keppel among those whom she allowed into the room to take leave of the King.

Just before midnight on 6 May 1910, King Edward died. He was in his sixty-ninth year.

Amongst the host of royalty who came flocking to London to take part in King Edward VII's spectacular funeral procession were a great number of Queen Alexandra's close relations. Indeed, four of the nine kings who rode behind the coffin were members of her immediate family—descendants of the late King Christian IX of Denmark. The new King of England, George V, was his grandson: King Frederick VIII of Denmark and King George I of the Hellenes were his sons; King Haakon VII of Norway was another grandson. And a Russian grand duke represented yet another of his grandsons, Tsar Nicholas II.

Just as Alexandra had rushed to her sister Dagmar's side on the death of Tsar Alexander III, so did the Dowager Empress now hurry to London to be with the newly widowed Queen. For three months Dagmar remained with her sister. Although her presence afforded Alexandra great comfort, it was not altogether beneficial. Loath to give up any of the privileges of her former position, Queen Alexandra was encouraged, indeed incited, by her sister to hang on to them. Alone, Alexandra was wilful and capricious enough; egged on by the equally self-willed but more practical Dagmar, she became worse. In Russia a dowager empress took precedence over an empress, and Dagmar saw no reason why a dowager queen should give way to a queen. Queen Mary thus found herself facing the very predicament which the young Tsaritsa Alexandra had faced some fifteen years before.

In the matter of jewels, too, there was cause for friction between the old consort and the new. Just as Dagmar had tried to lay claim to all the imperial jewellery, fobbing off the new Tsaritsa with a few inferior pieces, so did she encourage her sister to keep as much as she could. No one seemed to know which pieces belonged to the Queen of England and which to Queen Alexandra personally. As, by the terms of King Edward's will, his widow was left to decide which of the pieces she wanted, considerable diplomacy was needed to ensure that Queen Mary received a fitting share.

And again, as the Dowager Empress had lived on in the Anitchkov Palace after her husband's death, with the new Tsar and his wife occupying a mere half a dozen rooms, so did Alexandra remain in Buckingham Palace, while the new King and Queen had to make do with Marlborough House. Nothing seemed able to budge her. She would make the move, she assured her son and daughter-in-law, in her own good time. When Kaiser Wilhelm II, displaying unwonted tact but customary verbosity, tried to talk her into making a move, Alexandra let him flow on unchecked. 'Willy dear,' she said sweetly, when his stream of talk had finally dried up, 'you know that you always speak rather indistinctly; I am afraid I have not heard a single word you were saying.'

Queen Mary, who throughout this trying period behaved with the utmost forbearance, did allow herself the luxury of complaining, in private letters, to her Aunt Augusta, the redoubtable Grand Duchess of Mecklenburg-Strelitz, about 'Aunt Minny's' interference. Aunt Augusta proved much less forbearing. 'Oh! were *I* there instead of Minny!!' she wrote, 'more I dare not say.'

But more she did say. 'May the pernicious influence soon depart,' she wrote on another occasion, '*then* I hope all will come right.'

CHAPTER SEVENTEEN

1

King Frederick VIII, no less than his sister Queen Alexandra, was alive to the menace of the Second Reich. He was meeting it, however, in a quite different fashion. Where Alexandra's husband, and now her son, reigned over the most powerful nation in Europe, Frederick reigned over one of the weakest. Not even as a joke could he send telegrams demanding yet another Dreadnought. King Frederick was obliged to come to terms with Germany, not to compete with it. Although his feelings, and those of his countrymen, were anti-German, he could not afford to move openly into the Anglo-French camp; Denmark must remain on friendly terms with its mighty neighbour. She shared a common border with Germany; the German-dominated Baltic sea washed her shores; there were Danes living in German-ruled Schleswig-Holstein.

So, fighting down his own inclinations, Frederick VIII did what he could to keep Germany well-disposed towards his country. One of his first state visits had been to Berlin. With Germany just as anxious to gain Danish support as was Denmark to keep German friendship, Frederick had been warmly received. Although he did not enter into any alliance with Germany, Frederick had little difficulty in persuading the Kaiser to adopt a more lenient attitude towards the Danes in Schleswig-Holstein. And Kaiser Wilhelm II, with an eye ever open to a possible Danish alliance, referred to Frederick as 'a friend with whom he had been united for many years by ties of mutual esteem'.

There were other ties as well. King Frederick's heir, Crown Prince Christian, and Kaiser Wilhelm's heir, Crown Prince Wilhelm ('Silly Willy' to the British royal family) were married to sisters. And a closer, more significant bond still would be forged in the spring of 1913, when the Kaiser's only daughter, Princess Victoria Louise, was to marry Ernest Augustus, Duke of Brunswick-Lüneburg, who was King Frederick's nephew: the son of his sister Thyra, Duchess of Cumberland. With this marriage, not one, but two dynastic feuds would be patched up. For not only was the bridegroom's mother, Princess Thyra, a member of the hitherto unremittingly anti-Prussian Danish royal family, but his father was the Duke of Cumberland whose rightful kingdom, Hanover, had been snatched by Prussia in 1866. The magnificent marriage celebrations, which would bring to Berlin so many of old King Christian IX's descendants, including King George V of England and Tsar Nicholas II of Russia, would seem to mark the end of the old dynastic antagonism and the beginning of a new era. Yet, in little over a year, Europe would be at war, with Kaiser Wilhelm II on the one side and the majority of King Christian IX's descendants on the other.

Not trusting to a mere easing of relations with Germany, Frederick VIII applied himself to the defence of Denmark. The country must be strong enough to discourage the Second Reich from thinking in terms of simply marching in and taking over in the event of a general European war. In this sphere, as in others, the impatient King experienced considerable frustration. Having, much against his will, to keep within his limits as a constitutional monarch, Frederick was unable to push through his schemes: against bickering, vacillating, vote-conscious politicians and the rise and fall of a series of governments, he could make no headway. The whole question of Denmark's defence system ended in an unsatisfactory compromise.

In the spring of 1912, King Frederick VIII, with Queen Louise and their youngest children, spent a few weeks in the South of France. The sixty-eight-year-old King, who suffered from a weak heart, had not been well; it was hoped that a holiday would set him up again. It did. Feeling much better, Frederick started out for home during the second week of May; at Hamburg the family broke their journey to put up at the Hamburger Hof for a few days. On the evening of 14 May, just before ten o'clock, the King decided to set off for a walk. Why he should have gone out into the streets of Hamburg alone, unattended by even an aide, is uncertain; perhaps it was simply another example of the informality of the members of the Danish royal family.

As King Frederick was crossing the Gänsemarkt, he suddenly staggered. A stranger, who turned out to be a doctor by the name of Seeligmann, hurried up to help. The King seemed to recover and, declining the doctor's offer of assistance, assured him that he felt better and that he would walk on. A few seconds later he collapsed. Dr Seeligmann, helped by a policeman, bundled the unknown man into a cab and told the driver to take him to the nearest hospital. King Frederick VIII died in the cab.

At the hospital, the body was put into the mortuary. As the King carried no sort of identification, no one had any idea who he was. At the Hamburger Hof meanwhile, his family and companions were becoming increasingly uneasy about his continued absence. Having unsuccessfully searched the streets themselves, they contacted the police. Not until four in the morning were they told about the unknown man lying in the hospital mortuary. The King's body was brought back to the hotel. On the following day it was put aboard the royal yacht, *Dannebrog*, at Travemünde, and carried to Copenhagen.

King Frederick VIII had reigned for less than six and a half years. His eldest son succeeded him as King Christian X.

2

In the years before the First World War, the Dowager Empress Marie of Russia was one of the most dashing royal figures on the European scene. With her son and daughter-in-law, the Tsar and Tsaritsa, living such self-contained and secluded lives, Dagmar felt free to indulge her love of constant movement and diversion.

In Russia, where she was very popular, she lived an active public and social life. Combining kindness of heart with shrewd common sense, the Dowager Empress took a more than conventional interest in those great charitable organizations of which she was the head. Under her practical guidance, the multi-faceted 'Department of the Institutions of the Empress Marie' and the Society of the Red Cross were reorganized and expanded. Her generosity was legendary; her Treasurer was in a state of almost permanent despair. She was for ever petitioning her long-suffering son on behalf of others.

Of great comfort to Dagmar were the children of her daughter Xenia and her son-in-law Sandro— Grand Duke Alexander. With the Tsaritsa intent on keeping her husband's relations at arm's length, Dagmar saw comparatively little of her son Nicholas's five children. To Xenia's children, therefore, she was very close.

Extremely energetic, Dagmar was always setting out on yet another journey: to the Crimea, to the

South of France, to her sister Alexandra in England or her brother George in Greece, to her beloved Hvidore in Denmark. She travelled in great state. Swathed in furs, or cool in silk, she would step from her luxurious train or her superbly appointed yacht, *Polar Star;* often she would be trailing a suite of over two hundred people. During their stays abroad, this considerable suite would stock up with foreign goods—silks, cigarettes, playing cards—which they would then, contrary to court regulations, smuggle back into Russia. On one occasion the Master of the Court decided to put a stop to the practice by fining them. Smiling her radiant smile, Dagmar announced that she would pay all these fines from her personal account. As her personal account was the responsibility of the same Master of the Court, the poor official found himself paying the very fines which he had just levied.

Chic, smiling, with a buoyant nature and an ability to win hearts, the Dowager Empress wanted for nothing; she lived in a world of unquestioned opulence. 'The daughter of Christian and Louise,' as one of her contemporaries put it, 'has become inured to luxury and splendour. But at heart she remained the sane-minded Princess Dagmar, who accepted the good things of this world with keen pleasure yet never considered them essential.'

Insouciant the Dowager Empress might have seemed to those who did not know her well, but during all this period she was a deeply troubled woman.

Several things were causing her distress. Her youngest daughter Olga, whom she had coerced into marriage with Prince Peter of Oldenburg, had fallen in
love with someone else. It had been, quite literally,
a case of love at first sight. The minute the twenty-
two-year-old Olga set eyes on a tall, fair young officer
by the name of Nicholas Koulikovsky at a review, she
decided that she was going to divorce her husband
and marry him. She promptly told her husband the
news. Prince Peter, who had not the slightest sexual
interest in his wife nor, for that matter, in any other
woman, was not in the least put out. Although he
could not agree to a divorce (his 'own dignity and
the family name' would not allow it) he had another
suggestion to make. He would appoint Koulikovsky
as personal aide-de-camp and the young man could
move into their home. To this extraordinary suggestion, the besotted Olga agreed. A *mènage à trois* was
thereupon set up in the Oldenburg home.

Distressing as this arrangement might have been
for the Dowager Empress, such was the moral code of
the day that the fact that the Grand Duchess Olga was
living under one roof with two men was considered
preferable to the scandal of a divorce.

But Dagmar was not to be spared such a scandal
with her youngest son, Michael. For years, to the
anguish of his mother, Misha had been living with
his twice-divorced mistress. To both the Dowager
Empress and the Tsar, the idea of divorce was shocking in the extreme: 'even the loss of a dear person

is better than the general disgrace of a divorce', declared Dagmar on one occasion. Then suddenly, in the autumn of 1912, Michael wrote to his mother to tell her that he had finally married his mistress. She was thunderstruck. 'It is unbelievable!' she poured out to Nicholas. 'I can hardly understand what I am writing—it is so appalling in every way that it *nearly* kills me!' She begged for the marriage to be kept '*absolutely secret*'. Otherwise she would not be able to show her face in public.

Nicky was no less appalled. 'Between him and me,' he assured his mother, 'everything is now, alas, at an end.'

But, sad to say, it was Nicholas himself who was causing the Dowager Empress the deepest pain. He had become enmeshed in the most extraordinary situation. Its source lay in the illness of his son, the Tsarevich Alexis.

On Dagmar's daughter-in-law, the Empress Alexandra, the young Tsarevich's haemophilia had had a devastating effect. Few diseases are more harrowing for a mother to witness. With the blood of a haemophiliac lacking the qualities necessary to cause it to coagulate and so stop its flow, any wound can be fatal. Even an apparently harmless bump could lead to an internal haemorrhage, with the blood flowing unchecked to form painful swellings. Worst of all was the bleeding into the joints. This meant, as well as the most ghastly pain, a crippling of the affected limbs. For this frightening affliction, there was no cure.

Thus, time and again, the Tsaritsa would be forced to sit by, watching her little boy suffer agonies and never knowing when he might die.

An additional source of anguish for Alicky was the knowledge that it was she who had passed the disease on to her son. For a peculiarity of the disease is that it occurs exclusively in males and is carried by females. It was through the English not the Danish side, of the imperial family that the affliction had been transmitted. The Empress had inherited it from her mother, Princess Alice of Hesse who, in turn, had had it passed on by her mother Queen Victoria. The disease had apparently originated in Victoria herself: a spontaneous mutation had occurred in her genes. Through the old Queen's daughters and grand-daughters, the so-called 'royal disease' had been spread throughout the courts of nineteenth-century Europe.

As there was nothing that the doctors could do to alleviate, much less cure, her son's illness, the Empress Alexandra turned, more and more, to God. Where her mother-in-law, the Dowager Empress, had taken her conversion to the Orthodox faith in her stride, Alicky had embraced it with all the ardour of her nature. Always susceptible to the mysticism of the Orthodox religion, she now flung herself, heart and soul, into this twilight world. Within it, she was certain that she would find the miracle that was necessary. God would cure her son and make him, in time, the autocratic Tsar of Holy Russia, if only she could find the way to Him.

By the year 1912, Alicky was convinced that she had indeed found the way. Her link with God was that traditional Russian figure, the *starets*—a Man of God. In this case he was an unkempt, earthy, tangle-bearded, lank-haired, evil-smelling, hypnotic-eyed peasant by the name of Rasputin.

Ever since he had first been introduced to the Empress in the autumn of 1905, Rasputin had strengthened his hold over her. It was a hold that was due mainly to the fact that he could bring a measure of relief to her son's sufferings. How he managed to do this is uncertain. A possible explanation is that, with his hypnotic eyes and his self-confident presence, Rasputin was able to create the aura of tranquillity necessary to slow the flow of blood through the boy's veins. Where the demented mother and the dithering doctors merely increased the tenseness of the atmosphere around the suffering child, Rasputin calmed him and sent him to sleep.

And the *starets*, to Alexandra's eyes, had other attractions. Besides his aura of mysticism, she liked his peasant qualities: his unaffectedness, his frankness, his simplicity. To her, this plain-speaking *moujik* represented the Russian people: the loyal, devout, unchanging Russia of her imaginings.

Before long, she had developed an implicit faith in his powers. Through him she was joined, not only to the Russian people, but to God. If she wished her son Alexis to live, she must be guided by God, speaking through Rasputin.

3

The Dowager Empress was spending her annual holiday in Denmark that October when she received the news that her eight-year-old grandson was suffering from a particularly violent attack. The Tsar and his family were at Spala, the imperial hunting lodge in Poland. With the blood flowing into the boy's groin to cause a huge swelling, Alexis was in the most excruciating pain. There was nothing that the hastily summoned doctors could do. It seemed that death must come at any moment.

'The days between the 6th and the 10th were the worst,' wrote Nicholas to his mother. 'The poor darling suffered intensely, the pains came in spasms and recurred every quarter of an hour. His high temperature made him delirious night and day; and he would sit up in bed and every movement brought the pain on again. He hardly slept at all, had not even the strength to cry, and kept repeating, "Oh Lord, have mercy on me." '

By 10 October it was agreed that the end was near. The last sacrament was administered and a bulletin, so worded that the next one would announce the Tsarevich's death, was sent out.

But miraculously, it seemed, the boy recovered. Only afterwards was the Dowager Empress able to hear the full story of this apparent miracle. On the night of 10 October, Alicky had telegraphed Rasputin for help. He had answered immediately.

'God has seen your tears and heard your prayers. Do not grieve. The Little One will not die. Do not allow the doctors to bother him too much.'

'Within an hour,' says Grand Duchess Olga, who was with her mother in Copenhagen, 'my nephew was out of danger. Later that year I met Professor Fedorov, who told me that the recovery was wholly inexplicable from a medical point of view.'

Perhaps not wholly inexplicable. There are several possible explanations. The bleeding might have stopped of its own accord. Or the necessary atmosphere of calm might have been created when the Empress, acting on Rasputin's advice, prevented the doctors from further frantic ministrations. She herself, reassured by Rasputin's message, may have transmitted her newly-found feeling of tranquillity and confidence to her son. This relaxed and optimistic atmosphere, coinciding with a natural easing of the flow of blood, may well have saved Alexis's life.

Given this proof of Rasputin's miraculous powers, Alicky's faith in him became unshakeable. In her eyes, from henceforth, 'Our Friend', as she called him, could do no wrong.

For the Dowager Empress, Alicky's blind reliance on the *starets* was deeply disturbing. So matter-of-fact herself, Dagmar had scant belief in his powers. She could only see the incalculable harm he was doing to the imperial family. For had Rasputin merely been what Alicky believed him to be—a simple Man of God with an ability to relieve the Tsarevich's sufferings—Dagmar might not have minded his intimacy with the court so much; it was his reputation outside the court that was doing the dynasty so much damage. The truth was that Rasputin—and the name means debauchee—was a drunken, uncouth, loud-mouthed lecher. Before long, St Petersburg was seething with stories of his outrageous behaviour. No woman was safe with him. Inevitably, his name was amorously coupled with that of the Empress. Scurrilous pamphlets about them were secretly printed and circulated. Obscenities were scrawled on walls. Smutty rhymes were repeated. That he and the Empress were lovers, many were ready to believe.

And even more worrying for the Dowager Empress—who had the interests of the dynasty deeply at heart—was the fact that Rasputin, through the Tsaritsa and through the weak-willed Tsar, was beginning to meddle in affairs of state. Appalled, not only at the scandalous stories that were circulating, but at the growth of this sinister influence, Dagmar received the current Prime Minister, Vladimir Kokovtsev. For an hour and a half the two of them discussed the affair. Weeping bitterly, Dagmar promised Kokovtsev that she would speak to her son about the *starets;* but she held out little hope of success. 'My poor daughter-in-law does not perceive that she is ruining both the dynasty and herself,' cried Dagmar. 'She sincerely believes in the holiness of an adventurer and we are powerless to ward off the misfortune which is sure to come.'

Dagmar's intervention could achieve nothing. Nicholas, firmly under Alexandra's thumb, would not listen to his mother. He was 'so pure of heart', she confided to the President of the Duma, who had also sought her help, 'that he does not believe in evil'.

The Prime Minister was no more successful with the Tsar than his mother had been. Indeed, his report to Nicholas on Rasputin's reputation and activities infuriated Alexandra. She would hear no word against the *starets*. Nor would she rest until she had coerced her pliant husband into dismissing the offending Kokovtsev.

Dismissed, Kokovtsev was once more sent for by the Dowager Empress. He found her more distraught than ever. 'You must understand my fears for the future,' she told him. 'My daughter-in-law does not like me; she thinks that I am jealous of her power. She does not perceive that my one aspiration is to see my son happy. Yet I see that we are nearing some catastrophe...'

Vladimir Poliakoff, in his study of the Dowager Empress, has summed up this conflict between Dagmar and Alexandra. It was not, he says, 'the ordinary tug-of-war between the mother and the wife of a man—it had a deeper meaning. Marie Feodorovna stood for the precise forms of the logical Western mind, whilst the Empress Alexandra represented the cloudy, formless mentality of the Orient. In a mysterious way the shock between the two feminine influences symbolized the combat between East and West. The East won, and the result of its victory was tragedy.'

CHAPTER EIGHTEEN

1

Friends, seeing the sixty-eight-year-old King George of the Hellenes during his Danish holiday in 1912, found him looking old and careworn. 'His face,' says one of them, 'was scored with deep lines on each side of the mouth, and his clear blue eyes, usually so lively, were veiled in the deepest gravity, almost in melancholy.'

King George had reason to look grave. Greece was once more on the brink of war. Again, of course, the enemy was to be Turkey, but this time Greece was much better prepared than she had been in 1897. This was due, very largely, to the efforts of the new Prime Minister, Eleftherios Venizelos; the same Venizelos who had been responsible for ousting Prince George of Greece from his position as High Commissioner in Crete, several years before. Since then, Venizelos had shown himself to be an astute, ambitious and patriotic politician. In 1910 he had become Prime Minister.

As much as, if not more than, most of his country-men, Venizelos was fired with the spirit of the 'Great

Idea'—the unification and regeneration of all the Greek peoples. Once he had become Prime Minister, he applied himself to two important tasks: the revision of the constitution and the reorganization of the army. For if Greece was once again to know greatness, she must have a stable government and a strong army.

In all his activities, Venizelos had the unqualified backing of King George. Although he interfered with the politicians as little as possible, the King welcomed anything that might render them less quarrelsome; and, as much as his Prime Minister, George appreciated that the humiliating defeat of the Greco-Turkish War must be avenged. Greece must prepare for war. When Venizelos reinstated Crown Prince Constantine as Commander-in-Chief of the army, the King was delighted; he might sometimes have been at loggerheads with his son in the past, but George knew how well fitted Constantine was for the post. Not only was the Crown Prince a man of considerable military ability but he was extremely popular with the troops. And then, as *Diadoch*, or heir, the Greek-born Constantine was endowed with an almost mystical prestige, such as his Danish-born father could never equal.

While Constantine devoted himself to the military preparations, Venizelos applied himself to the diplomatic. Before she could again face Turkey, Greece must come to an understanding with her Christian neighbours, Bulgaria and Serbia. By the summer of 1912, Venizelos had arranged military alliances between the three Balkan states. By the autumn, they were ready for war.

King George returned to Athens from his Danish holiday on 9 October 1912. He was given a tremendous welcome. This time, however, the mood of the people was quite different from what it had been fifteen years before, on the eve of the Greco-Turkish war. There were no hysterics. Like the efficient and well-trained army which was even then massed on the Turkish frontier, the Athenian crowd was serious, restrained, filled with a sense of national purpose. King George was quick to feel this. Stepping on to the palace balcony, he addressed the great sea of people below.

'From my inmost heart,' he cried, 'I thank you for the welcome you have given me. I feel convinced that the Hellenic nation, whose patriotism I have recognized since the very first day of my long reign, will once more do its duty. Your calm and manly attitude is worthy of the seriousness of the moment. I have the greatest confidence in the patriotic feeling of my people and my Government. May Almighty God protect and bless our beloved country.'

This time, God did indeed seem to be on the side of the Greeks. The campaign was glorious. Crown Prince Constantine, assuming personal command of the army, gained one victory after another. Everywhere the Turks were forced back. And as the Greeks surged triumphantly forward, so did their King follow in their wake. Too old, by now, for active campaigning, he was tireless in carrying out those subsidiary duties: inspecting troops, visiting hospitals, keeping up morale. 'Of all the journeys he had made in his eventful life,' writes one of his companions, 'this was certainly the one that filled the King's heart with the greatest joy and pride.'

But his most glorious moment was yet to come. In November, Salonika, the capital of Macedonia, which had been ruled by the Turks for over four hundred years, was liberated. On 12 November 1912, King George, followed by Crown Prince Constantine and the Prime Minister, Venizelos, rode in triumph through the acclaiming streets. The great victory was celebrated with a *Te Deum* in the Byzantine cathedral. 'The sun,' wrote one ecstatic observer, 'had risen on a new people and a new country. Who could now deny the right of Greece to a great future?'

Who indeed? And within three months, the greatness of that future seemed more assured still. In January 1913, Janina, the capital of Epirus, fell to the Greeks. Turkey, soundly beaten, was obliged to withdraw almost entirely from Europe. Constantinople and its outskirts remained its only European possession. By the end of the Balkan Wars, the size of Greece would have almost doubled. The 'Great Idea' was becoming a reality.

2

For King George, these were wonderful days. Since his entry into Salonika he had been living in a villa in the Macedonian capital. To a friend, who had last seen him in Copenhagen, looking old and care-worn, the King seemed like a different person, 'Now I saw before me a slight, active figure, with the elastic-ity of youth, dressed in a tight-fitting khaki uniform: the face beamed with pleasure, the eyes sparkled with life, and about the mouth, half-hidden by the fair moustache, played the smile I remembered so well, in which kind-heartedness, humour and a hint of good-natured mockery were wonderfully combined.'

The friend had brought him letters of congratu-lation from his family in Denmark: from his nephew, King Christian X; from his sister-in-law, Queen Louise; from his brother, Prince Waldemar. With a 'radiant expression', the King read their fulsome praises. Even Kaiser Wilhelm II, said the King, had been obliged to send his sister, Crown Prince Constantine's wife, Sophie, a telegram of congratulation on the fall of Salonika. The telegram had been typically effusive. 'Hurrah! Hurrah! Hurrah!' it had read.

'Now,' said the King to his companion when he had finished his letters, 'we'll have lunch, it's one o'clock. You shall have a good Danish beefsteak and onions.'

At lunch, the King, who could switch with aston-ishing ease from Greek to Danish to German to French and to English, used Danish—which only his sons and not his officers could understand—to make an important announcement. On 26 October that year, he would be celebrating the golden jubilee of his reign; it was almost fifty years since, as a boy of seventeen, he had first come to Athens. Having celebrated his jubilee, he would step down. 'Yes,' he said, 'I'm going to abdicate. It is quite time for my son to take charge. He has reached the right age, and he possesses a vigour that I can no longer boast of. His popularity is now immense, and he has gained for himself a position, abroad as well as at home. His time has arrived.'

As the lunch party was about to break up, one of the generals warned the King about the dangers of his habit of strolling through the streets of Salonika as freely as he was accustomed to doing in Athens.

'My dear General,' interrupted the King good-naturedly, 'don't let me have that sermon over again. I am a fatalist. When my hour comes it will be no use, even if I immure myself in my house and put a thousand Evzones on guard outside.'

And so, later that afternoon of 18 March 1913, King George, accompanied by an aide, set out for his usual walk. On their way towards the harbour, they passed a squalid café, the 'Pasha Liman', from which emerged a raggedly dressed man who looked closely at them as they passed. At the old White Tower, which marked the end of their walk, the King and his companion turned. When they repassed the café, the man was still there. The King had just walked by him when the man drew out a revolver and shot the King in the back. The bullet pierced his heart. Within seconds, King George was dead.

The aide-de-camp grabbed the assassin by the throat and held on to him until two policemen had come running up. The man turned out to be mentally deranged. While awaiting trial, he committed suicide.

In less than a year after King George's brother, Frederick VIII, had died in the streets of Hamburg, George had been killed in the streets of Salonika.

The King's body was carried back to Athens by sea. For three days the coffin, draped in the Greek and Danish flags, lay in state in the Metropolitan Cathedral. It was then taken to the King's beloved Tatoi. Half a mile from the summer palace rose a little hill known as Palaeolcastro, from which King George and Queen Olga had often watched the sun set over the plain of Attica. On this hill, which King George had chosen as his last resting place, a chapel was being built; Queen Olga had always feared that as soon as this mausoleum was completed, death would find an occupant for it. It was here that King George was buried.

The news of the murder of her favourite brother upset Queen Alexandra considerably. Yet not quite so much, it seems, as to make her lose her sense of proportion. When a Danish friend sent Alexandra an enormous laurel wreath, asking her to have it laid on King George's tomb, the Queen was thrown into a quandary. How could she possibly get this huge wreath to Greece? And if she did not, what could she do with it? With surprising good sense, she resolved her dilemma. One of her favourite lap dogs had recently died and was buried in the grounds of Marlborough House. So sending for a manservant, Queen Alexandra gave her orders.

'Hawkins,' she said in her charmingly distracted way, 'you see that wreath? Too much trouble to send it out to Greece; put it on dear little Beauty's grave in the garden.'

PART FOUR
WINTER

CHAPTER NINETEEN

1

The opportunity for a revenge against Germany, for which King Christian IX's family—and particularly his daughters Alexandra and Dagmar—had waited so eagerly, came almost exactly fifty years after the Schleswig-Holstein war. Prussia had thrashed Denmark in the summer of 1864; the First World War started on 4 August 1914.

Its outbreak found five of King Christian IX's grandsons on European thrones: King George V of Great Britain, Tsar Nicholas II of Russia, King Haakon VII of Norway, King Constantine I of Greece and, of course, King Christian X of Denmark. These five monarchs might not all have been fighting on the same side but at least they were not fighting against each other. Greece, Norway and Denmark declared their neutrality at the opening of hostilities; only later in the war, in circumstances that would cost King Constantine his throne, would Greece take up arms against Germany.

Of King Christian's six children, only his daughter Thyra, Duchess of Cumberland, happened to be in the opposing camp; throughout the war she and her husband, the eccentric Duke Ernest, remained quietly at Gmunden. Yet they could not hope to avoid all involvement in the struggle. After all, one of their sons was married to Kaiser Wilhelm II's daughter; and their eldest daughter, Marie Louise, was the wife of Prince Max of Baden who, in 1918, during the chaos of the final days of the Kaiser's reign, would, for a brief spell, become Chancellor of the Second Reich.

The eve of war found the Dowager Empress of Russia with Queen Alexandra at Marlborough House. A snowstorm of frantic telegrams from Russia finally convinced Dagmar of the seriousness of the international situation and, at the end of July 1914, she packed up and set off for home. But she had left it too late. As her luxurious train came gliding into Berlin, she was told that she could go no further. With Russia and Germany mobilizing, the line to St Petersburg was closed to her. The Empress, having made no secret of her dislike of Germans, was hardly popular in Germany. Now she was obliged to sit behind the drawn curtains of her saloon while the platforms surged with troops, all yelling insults at the sight of the Russian imperial insignia on the carriages.

Eventually, after several hours in this nerve-racking situation, the Empress was told that she must leave the country as speedily as possible. She could either go back to England, via Holland, or to Denmark. She chose Denmark. With all blinds drawn and all doors locked, her train travelled towards the Danish frontier. Often it was held up for military convoys; sometimes it was surrounded by hostile crowds.

Reaching Denmark, Dagmar decided to continue on to Russia immediately. As the Baltic was also closed to her, she crossed to Sweden and by travelling to the far north, close to the Polar Circle, she was able to link up with the Finnish railways. On the frontier of the Russian Empire, she was received with usual ceremony and from here was able to travel on, in customary state, to St Petersburg.

With the military and political aspects of the war, Dagmar did not involve herself unduly. Her personal popularity proved a great asset in her work for the Red Cross. Like all the women of the imperial family, including the Empress Alexandra, the Dowager Empress devoted a great deal of her time and energy to hospital work. Two of her children, other than the Tsar, were in the thick of things: her youngest son, the wayward and unsuitably married Michael, was the head of a cavalry division; her youngest daughter, the hardly less unsuitably married Olga, was nursing in a hospital at the front.

But try as she might, Dagmar could not avoid becoming entangled in the increasingly complicated political situation. At the core of the troubles was her daughter-in-law, the Tsaritsa. While things were going well at the front, Alexandra confined herself to hospital work. But when, in the spring of 1915, the

Russians started falling back before the Germans, the Tsaritsa began involving herself in the Tsar's affairs. Encouraging her, indeed inspiring her, was Rasputin. Her faith in him remained absolute. Between them, they coerced the Tsar into dismissing the Supreme Commander, Grand Duke Nicholas, and taking over personal command of the army himself. Then, with Nicholas attending to the Russian forces at the front, Alexandra applied herself to the government at home. Henceforth the affairs of the Empire were to be managed by Alexandra and Rasputin.

The results were disastrous. With her firm belief in the upholding of autocracy, the Tsaritsa saw to it that her compliant husband dismissed any minister who advocated a slight relaxation of this ideal. And even ministers of unquestionable loyalty to the Tsar fell from power because of Rasputin's antipathy towards them. One word of criticism about Our Friend's dissolute way of life or dangerous influence in affairs of state was enough to end a career. The vacant places would be filled by any nonentity fortunate enough to have won Rasputin's approval.

And, in addition to controlling affairs in St Petersburg, Alexandra and Rasputin turned their attention to the front. The harassed Tsar was deluged by a stream of instructions on the conduct of the war. As none of this advice, coming direct from God, via Rasputin and the Empress, seemed to be making the slightest difference to the chaotic conditions at the front, Alexandra was soon being accused of betraying the Russian cause. The military disasters could only be explained, it was said, in terms of betrayal. Alexandra and Rasputin, aided by the puppets they had put into power, were working against Russia. Before long the Empress, who had never been popular, was loathed by all sections of Russian society. As hunger and dissatisfaction spread, so did the cry against the 'traitress' and 'the German whore' become louder.

Appalled, various statesmen and politicians turned to the only other person capable of influencing the Tsar: his mother. They begged her to speak to her son. She went, but it was hopeless. Nicholas listened, but agreed to nothing. Against the power of Alexandra and Rasputin, the Dowager Empress was helpless. Her mission a failure, Dagmar decided to withdraw from the scene. She closed the Anitchkov Palace and retired south, to the ancient city of Kiev, in the Ukraine.

The Tsaritsa was not sorry to see her go. 'It's much better Motherdear stays on at Kiev,' she wrote in one of those hundreds of letters with which she bombarded her devoted husband, 'where the climate is milder and she can live as she wishes and *hears less gossip*.' By gossip, no doubt the Tsaritsa meant the criticism of herself and Rasputin.

In Kiev, Dagmar settled into a little, old-fashioned palace on the banks of the Dnieper River. Also in the city were two members of her family: her son-in-law Sandro—husband of her eldest daughter Xenia—and her youngest daughter Olga, whose hospital had been moved back as far as Kiev. It was while Dagmar was there that Olga's unconsummated marriage to Prince Peter of Oldenburg was finally annulled by the Tsar. It left her free to marry Colonel Nicholas Koulikovsky. The 'exceedingly modest, almost secret ceremony' was performed in a little chapel on the outskirts of the city. 'May God give her every happiness,' wrote the still somewhat unresigned Dagmar to the Tsar. 'She herself is more than happy.'

Also to Kiev, to visit his mother, came her youngest son, the debonair Grand Duke Michael and, in October 1916 the Tsar, with young Alexis, arrived for a few days' stay.

'I was shocked to see the change in Nicky, so pale, thin, and tired he looked,' wrote his sister Olga. 'My mother was worried about his extreme quiet.' But as always, when the Empress Alexandra was not present, mother and son quickly resumed their comfortable, harmonious relationship. 'Mama was very kind and charming,' reported Nicholas to Alexandra. 'In the evenings, during our games of "puzzle", we had long talks.'

On the nature of these talks, one can only speculate. It is certain that Nicholas would have listened to no further criticism of Alexandra and that his loving, tactful mother would not have pressed him too far.

Nicholas's return to headquarters left the imperial party feeling more depressed and helpless than ever. 'We presented a pathetic group'; wrote Grand Duke Alexander of Dagmar, Olga and himself, 'there we were, mother, sister and brother-in-law of the Emperor, the three of us loving him not only as relatives but as faithful subjects, willing to do everything he could ask of us, well aware of his virtues and shortcomings, cognizant of the approaching upheaval, and yet wholly incapable of opening his eyes!'

2

The Tsar had not long returned to headquarters when the party at Kiev heard the most sensational news: Rasputin had been murdered. He had been murdered, moreover, by young Prince Felix Youssoupoff, the husband of Dagmar's grandchild Irina, daughter of Xenia and Sandro. Dagmar's first reaction to the news was a characteristic 'No! No!' She was to be more astonished still to learn the details of the crime.

In December 1916, Prince Youssoupoff, having decided that the survival of the monarchy depended on the removal of the *starets*, had entertained Rasputin in the cellar of his palace. According to Youssoupoff, the entertainment consisted, in the main, of plying the guest with poisoned cakes and wine. With the robust *starets* surviving these particular delicacies, Youssoupoff tried shooting him at point-blank range. As this proved hardly more effective, Rasputin was again shot at, savagely kicked in the head and pounded with a club. His apparently lifeless body was then roped in a curtain and thrown into the frozen River Neva. When the corpse was brought up three days later, it was discovered that the *starets* had still had enough strength to free one of his roped hands. He had died, almost incredibly, of drowning.

If the Tsaritsa and, to a lesser extent, the Tsar, were appalled at Rasputin's murder, the Dowager Empress and the rest of the family were greatly relieved. Even Nicholas's mild punishment of Youssoupoff and his fellow conspirators—banishment from St Petersburg—they considered too severe. In a collective letter to the Tsar, his relations begged him to show more leniency and, more important still, to take advantage of Rasputin's disappearance to liberalize the régime by appointing a responsible ministry.

Nicholas refused both requests. 'I allow no one to give me advice,' ran his indignant reply.

No one, that was, other than the Empress. Those who imagined that the death of Rasputin would put an end to her political influence were proved quite wrong; she played a more active part than ever.

The Dowager Empress could do nothing about the regrettable situation, other than to let her son know, as tactfully as possible, that he had all her sympathy. 'My thoughts never leave you,' she wrote, 'and I can well understand that these last few months have weighed very heavily on you. That worries and distresses me terribly. You know how dear you are to me and how hard it is for me not to be able to help you. I can only pray to God for you, that He support and inspire you to do all you can for the good of our dear Russia.'

What that good should be, she had no more idea now than she had ever had. Dagmar's views on the Russian situation had always been the conventional views of the majority of the aristocracy; and of so many members of ruling castes before and since. All revolutionary fervour, as far as she was concerned, was the work of agitators. To its real causes she was as blind as the rest of them. And blind she was to remain. 'The Revolution,' she would doggedly explain afterwards, 'was not a national movement. It was entirely beyond the comprehension of the *moujiks*. Agitators, working on their ignorance, transformed them into revolutionary *canaille*, and took advantage of their ancestral humility to force them into accepting a régime against which their strange but utterly faithful souls rebelled. The Revolution of Trotski and Kerensky was not Russian but Jewish...'

Her daughter Olga was to prove more perceptive. 'We still imagined,' she afterwards said, 'that the armed forces and the peasants would come to our support. It was blindness and worse; and how many of us paid with our lives for the blunder!'

The storm broke on 8 March 1917. There was some rioting in the streets of St Petersburg. News of these disturbances filtered through to the Dowager Empress in Kiev but so quickly did the situation deteriorate that Dagmar was utterly unprepared for the news that was broken to her a mere week later.

On 15 March 1917 she heard that her son had just abdicated.

In the drawing-room car of the imperial train, which had been halted at Pskov as Nicholas was hurrying back to cope with the revolutionary situation in the capital, the Tsar had renounced the rights to the throne of himself and his invalid son.

Dagmar was horrified. 'The news of Nicky's abdication came like a thunderbolt,' wrote her daughter Olga. 'We were stunned. My mother was in a terrible state...'

Those around her were no less dismayed. 'Nicky must have lost his mind,' growled his brother-in-law Sandro. 'Since when does a sovereign abdicate because of a shortage of bread and partial disorders in his capital?...He had an army of fifteen million men at his disposal. The whole thing...seemed ludicrous.'

It was far from ludicrous. There had, by then, been nothing else that Nicholas could do. By 13 March the capital had been in the hands of the revolutionaries. The imperial government had collapsed and power had passed to the Duma. On the following day the Tsar's last bastion, the Imperial Guard, had pledged allegiance to the Duma. With both the political leaders in the capital and the generals commanding the various fronts urging Nicholas to abdicate, he had had no choice. Without the support of either the politicians or the army, Nicholas was helpless.

To the Dowager Empress, this sudden rejection of her son was incomprehensible. 'My unfortunate

Nicky may have made some mistakes,' she exclaimed, 'but to say that he is an enemy of the people. Ah, never, never...'

Her youngest son Michael, to whom the hapless Nicholas had bequeathed his rights, was no more acceptable. Whatever Misha's virtues, he was not of the stuff of which successful Tsars were made. His reign, in fact, lasted a few hours only. On the very day that he became Tsar, he abdicated.

Having overcome the initial shock of the news of Nicky's abdication, Dagmar decided to hurry to his side. She set off almost immediately. His rights having been signed away, Nicholas had returned to headquarters, at Mogilev, to take leave of his troops. It was here that his mother arrived to see him. Her train halted alongside the imperial platform and a few minutes later Nicholas was driven up in his car. Slim, smartly uniformed and with his cap stylishly tilted, Nicky entered her saloon. He looked pale, but otherwise unchanged. Mother and son were alone for two hours. 'She never told me of the subject of their conversation,' wrote Sandro afterwards. When Sandro eventually entered the carriage, he found the Dowager Empress sobbing bitterly and her son standing motionless, 'looking at his feet and, of course, smoking'.

Dagmar remained at Mogilev for three days. For her, it was a time of terrible ordeal; the worst, possibly, of her life. She, who was usually so vivacious, so insouciant, so practical and so regal, went to pieces completely. She cried almost continuously. 'I have never seen her in such a state,' wrote Grand Duchess Olga afterwards. 'She could not sit still for a moment...she understood nothing of what had happened. She blamed poor Alicky for just everything.'

On 21 March, the third day of Dagmar's stay at Mogilev, Nicholas heard that, for his own safety, he was being made a prisoner and taken back to Tsarskoe Selo. Mother and son lunched together alone that day. At three o'clock the train carrying the deputation that was to arrest him and take him back arrived at Mogilev. Less than an hour later, they came to claim him. Having assured his mother that he would be seeing her again soon, he covered her face with kisses. Then, leaving her carriage, he crossed the platform and entered his own train. The whistle shrilled, the carriages lurched and slowly his train drew out. Across the width of the platform and through the billowing smoke, mother and son looked at each other. With an expression that was 'infinitely sad', Nicholas waved goodbye. Dagmar, her face wet with tears, made the sign of the cross.

She would never see him again.

CHAPTER TWENTY

1

Queen Alexandra's gratification at the fact that none of her immediate relations, other than her sister Thyra's family, were on the opposite side during the war, was short-lived. Before the end of the struggle, those family ties had come to matter not at all. That Alexandra's son, King George V, was a first cousin to both Tsar Nicholas II of Russia and King Constantine I of the Hellenes, could not prevent either of them from losing their thrones. For all the difference it made to their personal fortunes, these grandsons of King Christian IX might just as well have been on opposing sides. Politically, their kinship counted for nothing.

With Queen Alexandra's Scandinavian relations there was, of course, no trouble. It was true that she was unable to see her daughter, Queen Maud of Norway, and that she could not visit her relations in Denmark. But she managed, by a round-about route, to exchange letters with her nephew, King Christian X. She was for ever exhorting him to maintain his anti-German stance; the Scandinavian kingdoms must be kept out of Germany's 'clutches', she declared; the 'hateful Huns' must be crushed. When the Danish King wrote suggesting that Copenhagen might be the right place for a peace conference after the war, Alexandra considered it an excellent idea. What a triumph for Denmark that would be. However, she hastened to add with characteristic vehemence, 'we must thrash them first of all'.

Causing her much more anxiety were the fortunes of her nephew, King Constantine. The assassination of King George of the Hellenes in 1913 had brought his son Tino to the throne at a time of great national triumph. And more triumphant still were the months that followed. For a second Balkan war, in the summer of 1913, was as successful as the first. With these successes, King Constantine was prepared to rest content. Greece, exhausted and depleted, needed to consolidate her spectacular gains. When the First World War broke out, Greece declared her neutrality. In his determination to remain neutral, Constantine was backed by the General Staff and the majority of the Greek people.

He was not being backed, however, by his Prime Minister and architect of Greek resurgence— Venizelos. Still pursuing the 'Great Idea', Venizelos was all for joining France and England. With Turkey allied to Germany, there seemed no reason why Greece could not, by joining the Entente Powers, finally win Constantinople from the Turks.

Greece promptly split into two irreconcilable camps. It was a situation of which the Entente Powers, anxious for Greek support, took immediate advantage. From now on they lost no opportunity of lauding Venizelos and denouncing King Constantine. The most obvious way of denigrating the King was to accuse him (and his wife, the Kaiser's sister, Queen Sophie) of being pro-German. Nothing that Constantine could say in his defence—including the fact that he sprang from a violently anti-German dynasty—carried any weight. No story about his pro-German sympathies was too bizarre to be believed.

In October 1916 Venizelos, working hand in glove with the French, staged an uprising in Salonika. Setting up a rival government to the royal government in Athens, he declared war on Germany. When Constantine still refused to abandon his neutrality, the Allied fleet bombarded Athens and imposed a blockade.

By all this, Queen Alexandra was appalled. Ready, in the ordinary way, to applaud any action which the Allies might take (and to believe any story against Germany) she could not stomach this cavalier treatment of her nephew Constantine. In letter after anguished letter to her son, King George V, she begged him to do something about 'poor, excellent, *honest* Tino'. She simply could not believe that her nephew was pro-German (and in this she was quite right) or that what the Allies were doing in Greece was defensible. Indeed, King George V had his doubts. In a letter to the British Prime Minister, the King asked whether they were 'justified in interfering to this extent in the internal government of a neutral and friendly country?' He declared himself astonished at the way the French were treating those Greek soldiers who, in refusing to join Venizelos's revolutionary movement, were remaining loyal to King Constantine and his government.

But there was worse to come. In June 1917, the French, in the name of the Allies, presented Greece with an ultimatum. King Constantine must abdicate (and could choose a successor from among any of his sons other than the Crown Prince, who was considered equally 'pro-German') or Athens would be bombarded and Greece occupied. Constantine had no choice. He was determined that no blood should be spilt on his behalf. Naming his second son, Prince Alexander, as his successor, King Constantine left the country and went into exile.

Queen Alexandra, of course, was more upset than ever. Time and again she pestered her son to intervene personally on Tino's behalf. That there was nothing that King George could do, she refused to believe. Deafer even than those who do not wish to hear, Alexandra blithely ignored all his protestations of helplessness. 'I simply cannot make Motherdear hear, much less understand, anything at all about Greece,' complained the harassed King.

Indeed, King George had to tread very warily in this matter. Already he was being obliged to live down the embarrassing fact that, not only Kaiser Wilhelm II but a host of German royals were his close relations. By now the majority of Englishmen were firmly convinced that King Constantine had been, and was, passionately pro-German. Strong exception had already been taken to the fact that the English King had recently entertained two of his Greek cousins—King Constantine's brothers. And when Queen Alexandra offered open house to one of her Greek nieces—King Constantine's sister Marie, known as 'Greek Minny' to the family—there were more grumblings. Alexandra was furious. 'I will do my best not to be seen in public with the poor child,' she conceded, 'but will not give her up or [refuse to] see her in private here...'

Thus, when the Isle of Wight was suggested as a possible place of exile for King Constantine and Queen Sophie (a choice which would undoubtedly have had Queen Alexandra's enthusiastic approval) King George V was obliged to disapprove 'strongly' of the scheme. Instead, the Greek royal couple went to Switzerland.

2

A still more serious political furore in England followed the abdication of yet another of Queen Alexandra's nephews: Tsar Nicholas II.

After parting from the Dowager Empress (a parting which Dagmar described to her sister Alexandra as 'heart-crushing') Nicholas had returned as a prisoner to Tsarskoe Selo. King George V lost no time in commiserating with his fallen cousin. 'Events of last week have deeply distressed me,' he wired to Nicholas on 19 March 1917. 'My thoughts are constantly with you and I shall always remain your true and devoted friend, as you know I have been in the past.'

Nicholas never received the telegram. Russia's provisional government decided to withhold it. Sincere in their determination to safeguard the Tsar's life (a murder was hardly the best way of inaugurating a new and enlightened régime) the provisional government did not want to risk a misinterpretation of the British King's telegram. Despite its innocuous tone, it could be read as evidence of a family plot to rescue the Tsar. Any such suspicion would jeopardize Nicholas's position. The Soviet—a fiery assembly of soldiers' and workers' deputies sitting side by side with the more moderate Duma—was determined that the imperial family be kept imprisoned in Russia. They would be only too ready to believe that the royal cousins were hatching some scheme. Therefore the provisional government, who were anxious to get the Tsar away to safety, had to move cautiously. To send the Tsar out of the country would be impossible: the Soviet would simply instruct its workers to halt any train carrying the imperial party.

With King George V's telegram strengthening the provisional government's conviction that it must be in England that the Tsar sought asylum, the new

Russian Foreign Minister approached the British Ambassador, Sir George Buchanan. Would the Ambassador ask the British government to receive the imperial family? Buchanan wired the request. Somewhat reluctantly, the British government agreed.

Contrary to what might have been expected, the British offer of asylum disturbed King George V considerably. Queen Alexandra might have been in favour of it but he was not. His dealings with his Greek cousins having already landed him in hot water, King George was fully alive to the dangers of this latest proposal. In England, Nicholas II was hardly a hero. To many Englishmen, the Tsar was looked upon as a blood-stained tyrant, whose fall from power had been richly deserved. As for the Empress Alexandra, she was considered to be, not only unstable, but almost entirely responsible for the sorry situation in which the imperial family now found themselves; '...poor dear Alicky...' Queen Alexandra had once admitted, 'might have ruined the whole future of Russia through [Rasputin's] influence.'

In a letter to his government, King George explained his reservations. Might it not be better, he suggested, for the imperial family to take refuge in some neutral country, such as Switzerland or Denmark? His remarks were politely waved aside. The Prime minister, Lloyd George, had the highest regard for the new revolutionary government in Russia; it was because the request had come from them, and not from the Tsar himself, that he was willing to grant it.

Ten days later, in mid-April, the anxious King George wrote yet again. This time his warnings were more sympathetically received. For by now the proposal had raised a howl of protest from a certain section of the British public. Why, they demanded, should this reactionary autocrat be given asylum in freedom-loving Britain? Revolutionary Russia was still Britain's ally; might this granting of asylum to the rejected Tsar not alienate Russian left-wing opinion?

To this public clamour, Lloyd George's government began paying serious attention. From then on, the plan to receive the Tsar began to die a slow death. The British government could not risk offending the British public any more than the Russian provisional government could risk offending the powerful and valuable Soviet. The British were always to deny, however, that they had actually withdrawn the offer.

With one avenue of escape cut off, the Russian government was obliged to find another. Lenin had by now returned from exile and the provisional government's grip on affairs was becoming progressively shakier. The Tsar must be got out of St Petersburg while that grip still held. Nicholas was anxious to go to the Crimea; his mother had been living there ever since leaving Kiev, soon after his abdication. But the government considered the journey too hazardous. Instead, on 14 August 1917, the imperial family—the

Tsar, the Tsaritsa, the four grand duchesses and young Alexis—were packed off to Tobolsk, in western Siberia. Here they lived in comparative comfort for the next eight months.

In April 1918, not long after the signing of the peace treaty between Russia and Germany at Brest-Litovsk, they were moved yet again. This time they went to Ekaterinburg.

Throughout all these months of uncertainty, Queen Alexandra was in a state of extreme distress. Such news as reached her out of Russia was scanty, unreliable and always upsetting. She lived in dread of hearing that the entire family, including her beloved Dagmar, had been killed. In the summer of 1918 some of her worst fears were confirmed. Towards midnight on 19 July, Nicky, Alicky and their five children were executed in the cellar of the house in which they had been imprisoned in Ekaterinburg.

'The news were confirmed of poor Nicky of Russia having been shot by those brutes of Bolsheviks last week, on July 16th,' noted Queen Mary in her diary on 24 July 1918. 'It is too horrible and heartless—Mama and Toria came to tea, terribly upset at the news.'

But about the fate of her sister Dagmar and the rest of the family, Alexandra was still in complete, and anguished, ignorance. When last heard of, they were still in the Crimea. 'I can hear *nothing*', she wrote, 'and they are quite cut off from the world and alone in their misery and despair. God help them all.'

3

In fact, the Dowager Empress was not quite as miserable and despairing as her sister imagined. Dagmar's natural buoyancy had never stood her in better stead than during this confusing and agonizing period. The two years which she spent in the Crimea saw the Dowager Empress at her best: spirited, optimistic, uncomplaining, dignified.

At the beginning, things were not too bad. In their villas and palaces by the shores of the Black Sea were gathered a galaxy of Romanovs; the Dowager Empress, with her two daughters and their families, was at Ay Todor, the ornate white palace belonging to her son-in-law, Grand Duke Alexander. With the provisional government not knowing exactly what to do with them, they were left in peace. Except for constant anxiety about the Tsar and his family, the Dowager Empress could almost believe that nothing had changed. 'It was spring,' wrote her daughter Olga of that April of 1917, 'and the park rioted in blossom. Somehow there was hope.'

One of the most ardent hopes, of course, was that the Tsar and his family would be rescued. The air was thick with rumours of conspiracies to free the imperial family. Letters were smuggled in and out of the house at Tobolsk; the Tsar's confessor carried out a regular shuttle service between the captive Romanovs and Bishop Hermogene, who occupied the episcopal see of Tobolsk. It was to Bishop Hermogene that the Dowager Empress wrote, urging him to do everything possible to save her son. 'You bear the name of St Hermogene who struggled to liberate Russia,' ran one of her exhortations. 'It is a good omen. Now is your turn to save our motherland. All Russia knows you: plead, act, convince. May your name be glorified.'

But there was nothing that the Bishop could do. And by the time the leaves in the park at Ay Todor were falling, the Romanovs in the Crimea were beginning to fear for their own safety. The provisional government was becoming less effective by the day; all over Russia aggressive soviets were being established. When the Black Sea Fleet went over to the Bolsheviks, two soviets were established in the Crimea itself—at Sebastopol and at Yalta. With the provisional government too weak to restrain the militant members of these soviets, the position of the Romanovs became increasingly unsafe. They heard rumours of terrible massacres; they were at the mercy of marauding bands.

Once, on the pretext of investigating the Romanovs' 'anti-revolutionary activities', members of the Sebastopol Soviet ransacked Ay Todor. As the men searched the Dowager Empress's bedroom— ripping off wardrobe doors, tearing down curtains, scattering clothes and bayonetting chairs—so did the small, seventy-year-old but blazing-eyed Empress, who was still in bed, pour a stream of invective on to their heads. So effective, it seems, was her diatribe, that the raiders made off, leaving behind the most valuable object in the room: her huge jewel box. Realizing that she would not be so lucky a second time, Dagmar transferred all her magnificent pieces to small cocoa tins. In future, at the slightest sign of trouble, the tins were hidden in a hole in a rock by the seashore. When the Dowager Empress finally left Russia, the cocoa tins went with her.

With the fall of the provisional government and the triumph of the Bolshevik revolution in October 1917, things became worse still. The Dowager Empress and her family were first placed under arrest by the Sebastopol Soviet and then moved to a small, fortress-like house called Dulber. Here their imprisonment was more severe. Yet even now the Empress retained all the charm and dignity of her manner. At the sight of this tiny, erect and dignified old lady, even the surliest of her guards found themselves pulling off their caps. She seems, also, to have retained her childlike sense of humour. On one occasion a commission of Bolsheviks arrived at Dulber to check that all the prisoners were still there. Each member of the family, including 'Citizeness Marie Feodorovna Romanova', had to answer 'Here' to the role of names. When the inspection was over, the Empress lifted up her little dog. 'You have forgotten someone,' she cried out impishly, 'put his name down.'

Extremely providential, as far as these members of the imperial family were concerned, was the fact that they had fallen into the hands of the Sebastopol, as opposed to the Yalta, Soviet. Although both soviets were ready enough to execute their prisoners, the Yalta Soviet was anxious to do so immediately while the Sebastopol Soviet insisted on waiting for definite instructions from the new Bolshevik government.

By the beginning of 1918, no such instruction had been issued. On 3 March that year the Treaty of Brest-Litovsk was signed between Russia and Germany. By this treaty, the Germans were given the right to occupy the Crimea. This spurred the Yalta Soviet into action. Determined to kill off the family before the arrival of the Germans, they sent an armed party to Dulber. The representative of the Sebastopol Soviet, equally determined that the prisoners should not be captured by the rival soviet, decided to resist. Hardly had the Yalta attack been launched (no one, declared Dagmar in even this moment of supreme danger, 'would dare raise his hand against her') than an advance German column, acting on express orders from the Kaiser, arrived to rescue the Dowager Empress and her party. The family had escaped death, claims Grand Duchess Olga, 'by a hair's breadth'.

The family was free but it was also acutely embarrassed. 'I did not know whether to feel happy or sad,' admits Olga. 'Here we were, the Romanovs, being saved from our own people by our arch-enemy, the Kaiser! It seemed the ultimate degradation.'

Not only were the rescuing Germans bewildered at their lukewarm reception but they were astonished to hear the prisoners plead for the lives of their erstwhile captors—the members of the Sebastopol Soviet. The Prussian commanding officer was heard to mutter something about '*diese fantastische Russen*'. But what Grand Duchess Olga calls the most 'grotesque touch' of all came from the Dowager Empress. 'She, still holding that Germany was at war with Russia, refused to receive the German officer who had saved her from the Russian firing-squad.' Dagmar was still very much King Christian IX's daughter.

Free again, the Empress and her party moved to Harax, another of those sumptuous imperial villas overlooking the Black Sea. The occupying Germans treated her with great courtesy; a courtesy which she barely returned. When they offered to transport her to Denmark across Germany, she refused. But once more the family resumed its almost make-believe existence: of fishing, of picnics, of tennis parties, of walks along the wistaria-shaded paths above the shimmering sea. It was the sunset of a way of life that Dagmar had known for over fifty years.

But the tranquillity was a surface one only. The party was desperately worried about those members of the family who had not been fortunate enough to reach the Crimea. To the Tsar, the Dowager Empress wrote anguished letters. 'You know that my thoughts and prayers never leave you—I think of you day and night and sometimes feel so sick at heart that I believe I cannot bear it any longer. But God is merciful—He will give us strength for this terrible ordeal...

God bless you, send you strength and peace of mind, and may He not allow Russia to perish.'

Throughout the summer and autumn of 1918 frightening reports—of arrests and massacres—began to trickle south. For the Romanovs, this summer of 1918 was a Reign of Terror. More than seventy members of the family were brutally slaughtered by the Bolsheviks. In July 1918 Dagmar's son, 'darling Misha', was shot dead in a wood near Perm. Six days later Nicky and his family were executed at Ekaterinburg.

But the Dowager Empress refused to become either alarmed or depressed. She simply did not believe that her sons had been killed. The news of the murder at Ekaterinburg was just a rumour, she maintained. On the day that she was told of Nicholas's death there was to be a family tea party; when the others suggested that it be cancelled, she refused to hear of it. The Tsar and his family were still alive, she said; their friends had rescued them.

And she was to believe this, or to pretend to believe it, until the day she died.

In November 1918 came the Armistice. The German troops withdrew and an Allied fleet steamed into Sebastopol. Russia, by now, was in the grip of civil war, with the White armies fighting the Red. By February 1919 the Red Army had overrun the Ukraine and was advancing on the Crimea. None of the imperial party had any illusions about what would happen to them if they fell into Bolshevik hands. Yet the Dowager Empress refused to budge. Time and again British naval officers begged her to take refuge aboard their ships but she would not listen. It was her duty, she explained, to remain in Russia. An Empress did not flee in the face of danger. Her two sons might still be in the country; she could not desert them.

In April 1919 the French evacuated Odessa and the Red Army moved to within sight of the Crimea. Still Dagmar refused to move. Only on receiving a desperate letter from Queen Alexandra, urging her to get away while there was still time, did she give in. On 11 April she boarded the waiting H.M.S. *Marlborough*. Yet even now she gave evidence of both her kindheartedness and her stubbornness. When she heard that a mass of terrified refugees were gathered on the waterfront, she demanded that they, too, be evacuated. On being told that this would be contrary to Admiralty instructions, she threatened to return ashore unless they were taken aboard. The Admiralty acquiesced.

As H.M.S. *Marlborough* finally steamed out to sea, there took place one of those incidents of heart-rending poignancy. The British warship passed a troopship carrying members of the Imperial Guard on their way to join the ill-fated White Army. The men, suddenly recognizing the small, straight, black-clad figure on the deck of the warship, snapped to attention and broke into the old Russian National Anthem. As the first notes of that most solemn and stirring of anthems rang out across the churning water, Dagmar lifted her hand in greeting. 'The memory of those deep Russian voices, unaccompanied, but in perfect harmony which few but Russians can achieve, has surely never faded from the minds of those who were privileged witness to this touching scene,' wrote one of the British officers. 'Until long after the sloop had passed there was silence. No one approached the Empress…'

There she stood, this Danish princess, now a symbol of Imperial Russia, waving her hand until, through the blur of her tears, she could see the men no longer.

CHAPTER TWENTY-ONE

1

The Greek throne did not long outlast the Russian. By the year 1924 Greece, too, was a republic and the dynasty founded by King George I had taken the road to exile.

The decade following King George's assassination in Salonika in 1913 was one of indescribable confusion for the Greek royal family. Always mercurial, the Greeks proved never more so than during these ten tumultuous years. After King Constantine I had been forced off the throne by Venizelos in 1917, his second son, Alexander, had become King of the Hellenes. Alexander's reign lasted for just over three years. During this period, the dashing young King contracted a morganatic marriage with the daughter of one of his father's equerries. On 25 October 1920, having been bitten by his pet monkey, he died of blood poisoning, aged twenty-six.

His death, followed by the defeat of Venizelos at the polls, made possible the return of King Constantine. In a blaze of glory, the recently rejected Constantine came back to Athens. But the blaze quickly burnt itself out. Constantine, forced to continue a campaign against Turkey inaugurated by Venizelos, was soon floundering. The campaign was lost, the defeated Greek army revolted and once more Constantine was forced to give up the throne. In September 1922, he abdicated and left Greece. His eldest son succeeded him as King George II.

This second rejection finished Constantine. A few weeks later, in a hotel room in Palermo in Sicily, he died from a haemorrhage of the brain. In his hand was clutched a small leather pouch containing Greek soil.

The reign of his son, King George II, was even shorter. Convinced that the new King was in a plot to overthrow the government, extreme republican elements began agitating for his dethronement. New elections brought to power an even more unsympathetic National Assembly and, on 25 March 1924, it passed a resolution abolishing the monarchy and declaring Greece a republic. King George II went into exile.

It was just over sixty years since King Christian IX's son, the boyish King George I, had first come to Greece. His bags, he used to say in the early days of his reign, were kept ready packed in case his subjects ever rejected him. He had never needed them, but in the sixty years since his death, his successors have done a great deal of packing and unpacking.

2

The reunion with her sister Dagmar afforded Alexandra great joy and relief. But although the Dowager Empress spent the first few months in England and thereafter visited it several times, she chose to live permanently in Denmark. And Alexandra, by now, was too frail to journey abroad. In any case, the two women were no longer the skittish, insouciant pair they had once been. The days had long since gone when the two sisters, dressed alike, could charm the company with their beauty and their chic and their vivacity. They were both in their seventies now, querulous, unwell and unhappy. From having been so transcendentally smart, they suddenly appeared quaintly old-fashioned, almost bizarre. In a world of rapidly changing fashions, the two sisters clung resolutely to the styles of their hey-day: the towering toques, the spotted veils, the feather boas, the nipped-in waists and the floor-length skirts. Their talk was all of the past. Alexandra would bemoan her lost looks, her failing sight, her poor memory, her total deafness. Dagmar would complain of her arthritis, her reduced circumstances, the general lack of activity. Neither woman was equipped for the changed tempo of old age. Without mental resources, they could find few ways of amusing or interesting themselves. Their pleasures had always been the pleasures of youth; they had depended on good health, high spirits and constant diversion.

Both somewhat inconsiderate to those close to them, they became even more so. Poor, unmarried Princess Victoria, becoming more embittered and hypochondriacal by the year, remained firmly tied to her mother's apron-strings, as much of a 'glorified maid' as ever. Any attempt on Victoria's part to lead a life of her own would be bitterly resented by Queen Alexandra.

And the Dowager Empress treated her youngest daughter, Grand Duchess Olga, in exactly the same way. Olga complained that she was 'constantly at the beck and call of her mother, carrying out the varied duties of companion, nurse, lady's maid and secretary.' Olga's marriage to Colonel Koulikovsky—a commoner—was never really accepted by her mother; the Empress always regarded him as an intruder. If Dagmar had guests Olga, but never her husband, would be invited to join her. If the Empress were invited to some formal function, Olga alone would be expected to accompany her.

Both sisters remained as extravagant as ever. During the war, Queen Alexandra saw no reason whatsoever why she should make any economies. Not only did she refuse to run Marlborough House and Sandringham (where she retained the big house while King George, Queen Mary and their six children were crowded into the cottage) on even slightly less lavish lines, but she gave away vast sums to wartime charities. She could never understand that her parliamentary allowance was now taxed and that by the end of the war her income was less than half of what it had been before it. To any talk of cutting down expenses, Alexandra remained conveniently deaf.

The Dowager Empress was in a much worse financial plight. Other than her magnificent jewellery (out, now, of the cocoa tins and back in the jewel box) she had practically nothing. But as she would not dream of parting with a single trinket, Dagmar had to rely on the generosity of others. No sooner did she get her hands on any money, however, than she gave it away. Her generosity was reckless in the extreme. From all over the world, thousands of Russian *émigrés* wrote asking for help; she never refused it. And if she was not sending financial aid, she would be welcoming impoverished aristocrats to her little court; no one was turned away. 'It never occurred to my mother that there was hardly enough to support our own establishment,' complained Olga, 'but I cannot really blame her too much. She looked upon all the *émigrés*, whatever class they belonged to, as one family.'

And not only was Dagmar ready to give away whatever money she could lay her hands on, but she had no conception of saving others unnecessary expense. When she first returned to live in Denmark, her nephew, King Christian X, gave her a wing of the Amalienborg Palace. Here, to the King's mounting annoyance (for it was he who paid the bills) she made no effort to match her way of life to her reduced income. Eventually, his patience ran out. One evening as the Dowager Empress and her daughter Olga were sitting knitting in their drawing room, a footman of the King's household was ushered in. Sheepishly, he explained his mission. 'His Majesty has sent me over,' he stammered, 'to ask you to switch off all these lights. His Majesty said to mention to you that the electricity bill he had to pay recently was excessive.'

For a moment Dagmar sat quite still. Then she rang for one of her own servants. In front of the King's messenger, she gave her servant her instructions. He was to light up her entire palace, she commanded, from cellar to attic. And then, with every window in the palace ablaze, the Dowager Empress again took up her knitting.

It was another of her nephews, King George V, who came to her rescue. He first arranged that she leave the Amalienborg and make her home at Hvidore; obligingly, her sister Alexandra gave up her own interest in the house. King George V then settled an annual pension of £10,000 on his aunt. He none the less had the good sense to ensure that someone was appointed to manage her finances. To this yearly £10,000, Queen Alexandra blithely undertook to add another £850; somehow or other she never managed to pay it.

By this stage of their lives, Alexandra and Dagmar were not taking quite as much pleasure in each other's company as before. The younger Dagmar must have found her sister's vagueness, deafness and eccentricity increasingly irritating, while Alexandra found the Empress's long visits very tiring. In the spring of 1923, during one of her English holidays, Dagmar fell ill and Alexandra was obliged to remain at Marlborough House throughout the summer in order to keep her company. 'I have been too long here,' complained Alexandra to her daughter-in-law Queen Mary, 'and feel every day worse.' She could not have been sorry to see her sister return to Denmark at the end of August.

There is no doubt that Queen Alexandra was becoming daily more eccentric. Always rather distraite, her failing faculties made her more so. Unabashed, she would suddenly ask some startled guest if her wig were on straight, and a visitor to Marlborough House once discovered her walking about the room chanting *God save the King* over and over to herself. Some of these so-called eccentricities were simply manifestations of her kindness to strangers; it was a quality which she never lost. Once, on visiting a hospital, the Queen was told that a certain patient was feeling particularly depressed as he had just learned that he would be left with a permanently stiff leg. 'My dear, dear, man,' said Alexandra. 'I hear you have a stiff leg; so have I. Now just watch what I can do with it.' With that the Queen lifted up her skirt and flung her lame leg right over the top of his bedside table.

What Queen Alexandra perhaps regretted most of all was the loss of her celebrated looks. For year after year, for decade after decade, it seemed as though time would never touch her. The renowned Pierre Loti, seeing her at a ball at the French Embassy before the war, was astonished at her enduring youthfulness and beauty. She was then nearer seventy than sixty, but what he saw was 'a slender, youthful woman with a smile on her face. She was dressed entirely in black of some diaphanous material with a sort of pale fire, like the flame of alcohol, round the bottom of the skirt.' A 'cruel light,' he says, 'fell upon her. But she still looked young.'

Within ten years it had all gone. Queen Alexandra's beauty, like her amusements, had depended on youth, or at least, the illusion of youth. Unlike some women, she could not look both old and beautiful. And she knew it. For the last ten years of her life, she lived away from the public gaze—at Sandringham in the midst of her band of devoted servants. But always a brave and dutiful woman, Alexandra never gave in: whenever necessary, she would make the effort, and to the end she employed all the trappings of her once astonishing beauty.

It was during these sunset years that the Queen granted an audience to T. E. Lawrence, then at the height of his fame as Lawrence of Arabia. With the heartlessness that was yet another facet of his complex nature, Lawrence has described this meeting with Queen Alexandra at Marlborough House.

'We had to wait, of course: that is the prerogative of Queens,' he wrote in *The Mint*. 'When we reached the presence, and I saw the mummied thing, the bird-like head cocked on one side, not artfully but by disease, the red-rimmed eyes, the enamelled face, which the famous smile scissored across all angular and heart-rending...There were the ghosts of all her lovely airs, the little graces, the once-effective sway and movement of the figure which had been her consolation. Her bony fingers, clashing in the tunnel of their rings, fiddled with albums, penholders, photographs, toys upon the table: and the heart-rending appeal played on us like a hose, more and more terribly. She soon dismissed us.'

But to those who knew her better, and who had known her before, Queen Alexandra remained the 'Beloved Lady'; in many ways the same charming, decorative and scatter-brained creature she had always been. Nothing—not age, nor tragedy, nor the years of greatness—had ever quite obliterated that simple Danish princess; the 'Sea-King's daughter from over the sea.'

Queen Alexandra died, in her eighty-first year, on 20 November 1925.

3

Queen Alexandra's death dealt her seventy-eight-year-old sister Dagmar an irreparable blow. It caused her to retire even deeper into the almost make-believe world in which she had been living ever since her move to Hvidøre. Surrounded by all the souvenirs of her past life, the Dowager Empress refused to face the realities of the present. That her son Nicky was dead, she would not admit. To her, he was still the head of the Russian Empire. When various exiled Romanov grand dukes wrote to her, begging her to acknowledge their particular claim to the throne, she ignored their letters. Not even the arrival of a grisly collection of relics salvaged from the wood near Ekaterinburg in which the bodies of the imperial family had been burnt—charred buttons, singed scraps of cloth, blackened jewellery—could convince her of the truth. She made no cult of these remains; the box was simply sent to Paris to be buried in the Russian cemetery there.

The Dowager Empress was not, of course, the only one ready to believe that the Tsar and his family had escaped death. All Europe was alive with rumours about the reappearance of one or other or all of the members of the imperial family. But by the year 1925 one young woman's claim to be a member of the family was being taken more seriously than any other. A woman, since known as Anna Anderson, claimed that she was the Tsar's youngest daughter, Grand Duchess Anastasia.

Anna Tschaikovsky, as she was then called, had been dragged out of a Berlin canal in 1920, after an unsuccessful attempt to commit suicide. During her subsequent spell in hospital, the story was put about that this sad, sick and destitute young woman had survived the massacre of the imperial family at

Ekaterinburg. Merely wounded in the shooting, she had been rescued from the cellar and smuggled out of Russia.

Among those ready to believe the story was the Danish Ambassador and a number of Russian *émigrés*. As the conviction grew that the woman was indeed Anastasia, those who had been more intimate with the imperial family—relations, a tutor and a lady-in-waiting—came to Berlin in the hope of verifying the story. They found themselves unable to do so. But this did not discourage her champions. It was explained that the gravely ill Grand Duchess suffered from lapses of memory: this was why she could not recognize her visitors.

The Dowager Empress consistently refused to believe the young woman's claim. But some of her relations were not nearly so certain that Anna was a fraud. Dagmar's sister Thyra, Duchess of Cumberland, and her brother, Prince Waldemar, began interesting themselves in the affair. Prince Waldemar sent the impoverished woman money and Princess Thyra wrote to the Dowager Empress, urging her to investigate the affair. 'Just to clear up the case once and for all,' begged Thyra. Finally, against her mother's wishes, Grand Duchess Olga decided to go and see the woman for herself.

Olga, in contrast to most members of the Romanov family, had been fond of her sister-in-law the Tsaritsa and had always been welcome at Tsarskoe Selo. She had been very intimate with her brother's

children and Anastasia had been her especial favourite. If anyone should be able to recognize the Tsar's
daughter then that person would be Olga. And so,
in 1925, Grand Duchess Olga journeyed to Berlin to
spend four days by the bedside of the still sick and
distraught Anna.

She came away convinced that the woman was a
fraud. For this conviction, Olga had several reasons.
The woman did not look like Anastasia: 'the nose, the
mouth, the eyes were all different'. She could speak
only German; the one language which the young
grand duchesses could not speak. That Anastasia
might have forgotten the English or Russian or
French that she had previously spoken so well, Olga
was prepared to allow, but how was she now so fluent
in a language that she had never learnt? Then Anna
claimed that on reaching Bucharest after her flight
from Ekaterinburg, she had not sought protection
from her 'cousin Marie'—Queen Marie of Romania,
who was first cousin to both the Tsar and the Tsaritsa
and who knew the family well—because she was by
then pregnant and Queen Marie would have been
shocked. It is highly unlikely that the worldly Queen
of Romania would have been shocked by anything;
this, the real Anastasia would have appreciated. It
would have been the most natural thing in the world
for a desperate Anastasia, pregnant or not, to have
gone straight to the generous-hearted Queen Marie.

And there was another, less tangible reason for
Olga's conclusions. Anastasia, she afterwards said,

'was as dear to me as if she were my own daughter. As soon as I sat down by that bed in the Mommsen Nursing Home I knew I was looking at a stranger. The spiritual bond between my dear Anastasia and myself was so strong that neither time nor any ghastly experience could have interfered with it. I don't really know what name to give that feeling—but I do know that it was wholly absent. I had left Denmark with something of a hope in my heart. I left Berlin with all hope extinguished.'

Grand Duchess Olga's failure to credit Anna's story did not put an end to the young woman's claims. Not by any means. From then on, in season and out, for year after year and decade after decade, Anna Anderson maintained that she was the Grand Duchess Anastasia. She published her memoirs, she granted interviews, she appeared on television, she launched herself on a seemingly limitless sea of litigation to prove her identity. The world thrilled to her story but refused, in the main, to believe it.

What Dagmar's reaction to this incident was, one does not know. Perhaps, despite her disapproval of Olga's quest, she had nursed a secret hope that the young woman in Berlin might indeed be her granddaughter. Was it from this time that the Dowager Empress began to admit the possibility of her son's death? 'I am sure that deep in her heart,' said Olga afterwards, 'my mother had steeled herself to accept the truth some years before her death.'

Grand Duchess Olga always believed that Anna
had been put up to her imposture by someone anxious to get their hands on the rumoured Romanov
fortune. That any such fortune existed, Olga stoutly
denied. All foreign Romanov investments had been
withdrawn in 1914, she claimed, to help finance the
war. 'That is the reason why none of us, who managed
to escape, had funds to enable us to live comfortably
in exile. Most malicious rumours about that "fortune"
began floating about soon after Mrs Anderson's
appearance in Berlin in 1920. I heard that it ran into
astronomical figures. It was all fantastic and terribly
vulgar. Would my mother have accepted a pension
from King George V if we had any money in England?
It does not make sense.'

But if there was no Romanov gold in foreign
banks, there was a fortune under the Dowager
Empress's bed at Hvidore; for this is where Dagmar
kept her huge jewel box. Here, to something like the
value of half a million pounds sterling, was all that
spectacular jewellery that the once young and beautiful Empress had worn to such brilliant effect in the
great days of the Russian Empire: flashing tiaras, glittering diamond necklaces, 'ropes of the most wonderful pearls...all graduated, the largest being the
size of a big cherry, Cabochon emeralds and large
rubies and sapphires...' To this magnificent collection had been added several pieces bequeathed to
Dagmar by her sister Alexandra. Sometimes, the sad-
eyed old Empress would open the velvet-lined cases

and run her arthritic fingers over these dazzling treasures. But she would never consider selling even one piece. Her jewels were a tangible link with her imperial past; and they were the only safeguard for the future of her two surviving children: her daughters Xenia and Olga.

There were other relations, however, who were anxious for a share of this treasure trove. Dagmar's nephew, King Christian X, felt that he was entitled to some of the proceeds from any proposed sale; her daughter Xenia, who now lived in France, was anxious for the immediate sale of her share; her son-in-law, Xenia's husband Sandro, was forever urging the Empress to pawn the jewellery so that the family could start a paper factory; her English nephew, King George V, suggested that the box be deposited in an English bank.

But Dagmar ignored them all. The box remained under her bed.

Her determination to hang on to the jewels seems to have been fully justified. For after the Empress's death, her jewel box was to become the cause of a bitter family conflict. The details are confused but what seems crystal clear is that her daughters did not get their full share of the treasure.

No sooner had the Dowager Empress been buried than King George V sent an emissary to fetch the jewel box. In the presence of Grand Duchess Xenia only, the box was sealed and then taken to England. To her bemused sister Olga, Xenia explained that as Olga had married a commoner, she could not hope to be as closely involved with the arrangements. Xenia then hurried over to England. The slighted Olga did have the satisfaction, however, of telling her cousin King Christian X, when he came hurrying to Hvidore in search of the precious box, that it had already left the country.

In England the sealed box was opened in the presence of Queen Mary and Grand Duchess Xenia. For Queen Mary, who adored jewels ('I think she could cover herself from head to foot with them and yet never look overladen' enthused one of King George V's Greek cousins) the sight of these imperial treasures must have been exciting indeed. The firm of Hennell and Sons was given instructions to price and sell the jewels. Their sale, says Frederick Ponsonby, who was present at the opening of the box, fetched £350,000. The King, he claims, put this 'large sum in trust for the Grand Duchesses'.

Yet Xenia and Olga received nothing like this. According to what Sir Edward Peacock, the Director of the Bank of England, told Ian Vorres, Grand Duchess Olga's biographer, Xenia received £60,000 and Olga £40,000. What had happened to the other £250,000 or at least the jewellery that should have realized that sum?

In her penniless old age, Grand Duchess Olga commented 'that May [Queen Mary] was passionately fond of fine jewellery. I remember how in 1925 the Soviet government, being badly in need of foreign currency, sent a lot of Romanov jewels to be sold in England,

and I heard that May had bought quite a few—including a collection of Fabergé's Easter eggs. I also know that at least one item of my own property, looted from the palace in Petrograd, was among the lot shipped to England, but its price proved too high even for May...'

On 13 October 1928, just three years after her sister Alexandra, Dagmar died. She too, was in her eight-first year. Her body was taken from Hvidore to the Amalienborg Palace and given a state funeral. She was buried, amongst the members of her family, including King Christian IX and Queen Louise, in Roskilde Cathedral. All the royal houses of Europe were represented, and a host of Russian *émigrés*, headed by a galaxy of Romanov grand dukes, came to pay tribute to the little Danish princess who had lived through such splendid, such tumultuous and such tragic times.

4

Some five years later, on 26 February 1933, the third sister, Princess Thyra, Duchess of Cumberland, died at her home in Gmunden. She was seventy-nine.

Never as close to her sisters Alexandra and Dagmar as they had been to each other, Thyra had drifted still further away during the last years of her life. A barely perceptible chill had developed between them. The marriage of Thyra's son, Ernest Augustus, to Kaiser Wilhelm II's daughter, must have seemed like a betrayal to her violently anti-Prussian sisters. And the fact that Thyra had been on the opposite side during the war had considerably widened the estrangement between them. In that surge of wartime anti-German feeling in England, an act of parliament had removed the Duke of Cumberland from the Order of the Garter and deprived him of his British peerages.

The end of the war had done little towards bringing the three sisters closer together. Thyra could hardly have been expected to share Alexandra's delight at the collapse of Wilhelm II's Germany. The Duke of Cumberland, having finally renounced his stubbornly-held claim to the throne of Hanover, died in 1923, at the age of seventy-seven. Princess Thyra lived on into a world vastly different from that of her youth. She did not live long enough to see the marriage of her granddaughter Frederika (granddaughter, also, of Kaiser Wilhelm II) to Prince Paul of Greece, grandson of Thyra's brother King George, and a future King of the Hellenes. But, in the month before her death, Adolf Hitler became the new German Chancellor.

Princess Thyra was buried in the family vault, built by her father-in-law to house the bodies of the sovereigns of Hanover.

5

Of that generation, the only one left was Prince Waldemar. In the year of his sister Thyra's death,

Waldemar turned seventy-five. By now this amiable and popular Prince was one of the most respected royal figures in Europe. Although three of his four sons had renounced their rights to the Danish throne in order to marry commoners, Waldemar had enough nephews and grand-nephews on various European thrones to be known as 'The Uncle of the Kings'. He still lived in the Yellow Palace in which he had grown up, and at Bernsdorff which, in the half-century before the First World War, had been the scene of so many of those vast family gatherings. Of that concourse of royalty, very few were left now; one of Waldemar's closest companions was Prince George of Greece, that one-time rumbustious Greek Georgie, now himself grown old and staid. Right up until his last illness, early in 1939, Prince Waldemar would stroll with Prince George about the streets of Copenhagen, as cheerful, as unaffected and as approachable as ever.

He died, after a ten-day illness, on 14 January 1939. Like his sisters Alexandra and Dagmar at the time of their deaths, Waldemar was in his eighty-first year. He was buried in Roskilde Cathedral.

It was as well, perhaps, that he died when he did. Had he lived for another eighteen months, he would have seen Denmark invaded and occupied by the Germans; the Germans against whom his family, and particularly his energetic and long-dead wife, Princess Marie of Orléans, had campaigned so tirelessly and so long.

EPILOGUE

EPILOGUE

Although King Christian IX's family enjoyed its most spectacular flowering in the years before the First World War, it by no means withered away during the years that came after. Indeed, the growth proved as vigorous as ever. To the thrones still occupied by the old King's descendants at the end of the war—the British, the Norwegian and the Danish—were added no less than five others.

In 1934 King Christian IX's great-grand-daughter, Astrid, whose mother had married a Swedish prince, became Queen of the Belgians, the wife of King Leopold III. This radiant and popular Queen was killed in a motor accident in the second year of her husband's reign. Their eldest son—King Christian IX's great-great-grandson—is the present King Baudouin I of the Belgians.

In 1936 the Greek throne was restored. King George II, the eldest son of King Constantine I, returned to Athens. One of his first moves was to arrange for the return from exile of the bodies of his father and mother, King Constantine and Queen

Sophie, and of his grandmother, Queen Olga, to Greek soil. They now lie buried, beside King George I, on that pine-covered hill-top at Tatoi, overlooking the dusty plain of Attica. This restoration lasted for almost forty years, until the declaration of yet another republic in 1973. Ex-King Constantine II of the Hellenes, now living in exile, is the great-great-grandson of King Christian IX of Denmark.

It was this Greek branch of the Danish royal house that provided yet three more crowned heads. King Constantine I's daughter Helen, who married the feckless King Carol II of Romania, is the mother of the last King of Romania: Carol's son Michael, who was forced out by the Communists soon after the Second World War. King Constantine I's second son, Alexander, who for a short while replaced his father as King and who died as the result of a monkey bite, was the father of the last Queen of Yugoslavia: Princess Alexandra, who in 1944 married King Peter II of Yugoslavia. His throne, too, fell before the Communists after the Second World War. And finally, Princess Sophie of Greece—sister of ex-King Constantine—is the wife of Prince Juan Carlos, already sworn in as the future King of Spain. All three, of course, are the great-great-grand-children of King Christian IX.

In Great Britain, both Queen Elizabeth II and her husband, Prince Philip of Greece, are the old King's descendants: she is his great-great-grand-daughter and he his great-grandson. In Norway, King Olav is his great-grandson. In Denmark, Queen Margrethe is his great-great-grand-daughter.

Thus, of the seven monarchies in Europe today— Great Britain, Belgium, the Netherlands, Norway, Sweden, Denmark and that kingdom without a king, Spain—the ruling families of five are directly descended from King Christian IX. Only in Sweden and the Netherlands are the dynasties not directly descended from the Danish King.

It would be idle to pretend, however, that the characteristics of the old King and his children are still evident in these ruling families today. Yet in many royal households the reputation of King Christian's family for this or that trait persisted deep into the twentieth century. When, for instance, King George V's son, the Duke of Kent, married Princess Marina of Greece (grand-daughter of King George I of the Hellenes) Queen Mary expressed her delight; 'the women of the Danish family,' she explained to Lady Airlie, 'have the art of marriage.' How else could those three Danish sisters, Alexandra, Dagmar and Thyra, have coped with their extremely difficult husbands?

More absurd still would be the claim that this common ancestry in any way affects relationships between the various states in which the members of the family now happen to reign. Most present-day European monarchs are descended from either Queen Victoria or King Christian IX (and, in many cases, from both) but this close relationship brings no advantage whatsoever to the remaining kingdoms of Europe. To a greater or a lesser degree, present-day monarchs have been stripped of all personal power, or even influence in affairs of state. The benefits of being the second cousin once removed to the monarch of a neighbouring country are negligible. Personal advantages there may well be, but politically it is of very little consequence.

But the spread of King Christian IX's family remains, for all this, an extraordinary phenomenon. That Queen Victoria's descendants should have filled the thrones of nineteenth- and twentieth-century Europe is understandable; but that the family of the poor, unambitious and unimportant King of Denmark should have done the same is remarkable. And perhaps, after all, these Danish princes and princesses did introduce something more than just their good looks and their gaiety and their talent for harmonious family life into the various courts of Europe. They were in no small measure responsible for injecting the approachability and the sense of identification with one's subjects that made it easier for the various monarchies of Europe to adjust to changing circumstances and so survive. King Haakon's decision to ride on trams stood him in better stead than Kaiser Wilhelm II's insistence on being referred to as the All-Highest. The reasons for the fall of some thrones and the survival of others are complex but, by and large, it is the kings who have willingly yielded their powers and moved freely amongst their people who have kept their thrones. The simplicity and domesticity which made King Christian's family so exceptional a century ago are the royal rule today.

And if nothing else, for half a century—from the accession of King Christian IX in 1863 until the outbreak of the First World War in 1914—the members of the old King's family enlivened the European scene with their decorativeness, their panache, their cosmopolitanism, their cheerfulness, their grace and their generosity. To often pompous, reactionary and joyless courts they brought a breath of fresh air. There have been royals with worse records.

NOTES ON SOURCES
AND
BIBLIOGRAPHY

Notes on Sources

Prologue

Decorations ('a vista of...') London *Times*. Christian IX's reply, *Illustrated London News*. Crown Prince's banquet ("of brilliant...") London *Times*. Golden Wedding ('the celebration of...') Nicholas of Greece, *My Fifty Years*. Christian ('but a mediocre...') Madol, *Christian IX*. Queen Victoria ('are wonderfully united...') Royal Archives, Windsor Castle. Queen Louise ('gentle expression...') Nicholas, *My Fifty Years*. Queen Victoria on Louise, Pope-Hennessy, *Queen Mary*. Nicholas of Greece, ('Apapa and Amama...) *My Fifty Years*. Jamborees ('the entire family...') Christopher of Greece, *Memoirs*. Reunions ('seventh heaven...') Frederick Ponsonby, *Recollections of Three Reigns*.

Chapter One

Victoria on German element, Victoria, *Dearest Mama*. Victoria on Danish family ('it would be too horrid...') Magnus, *Edward VII*. Victoria ('good looks, health...') Victoria, *Dearest Child*. Vicky ('without some attractions…') Royal Archives, Windsor Castle. Victoria ('Princess Alexandra is indeed…') Victoria, *Dearest Child*. Vicky ('most men fire and flames…') *Dearest Child*. Albert ('You must not…') Magnus, *Edward VII*. Victoria ('I feel daily…') Magnus, *Edward VII*. British princess ('In those days…') Marie of Romania, *The Story of My Life*. Leopold on Alexandra's qualities, Royal Archives, Windsor Castle. Christian on Alexandra, Queen Victoria's Journal, Royal Archives, Windsor Castle. Bertie on Christian's delight, Magnus, *Edward VII*. Field ('taken the fancy…') *More Uncensored Recollections*. Willie and Commander, Christmas, *King George of Greece*. Christian's depression ('Do whatever…') Madol, *Christian IX*. Athenian Newspaper, Christmas, *King George*. Leopold to Victoria, Gould-Lee, *The Royal House of Greece*. Brigands ('Too bad for him…') *Punch*.

Chapter Two

French Minister on Christian, Madol, *Christian IX*. Victoria ('What is…') Longford, *Victoria R.I.* Victoria on Dagmar, *Letters*. Alexander ('was essentially a man…') Poliakoff, *The Empress Marie*. American Naval Secretary on Dagmar, Poliakoff, *The Empress Marie*. Princess Radziwill on Dagmar's entry, *Recollections*. Wedding banquet, Poliakoff, *Empress Marie*. Crown Prince ('Freddie with the pretty…') Battiscombe, *Queen Alexandra*. Frederick's education, *Illustrated London News*. French Minister on Frederick, Madol, *Christian IX*. Victoria ('Kindly but in a manner…')

Paget, *Embassies of Other Days*. Reception of bridal couple, *Illustrated London News*. Style of life ('the young couple...') Michael, *Haakon, King of Norway*. Freddie and Bertie ('Miss Hannah...') Rigsarkivet, Copenhagen.

Chapter Three
Victoria on Alix, Royal Archives, Windsor Castle. Victoria on Bertie ('a very confidential...') Magnus, *Edward VII*. Victoria to Louise and Alix on Bertie, Royal Archives, Windsor Castle. Alix and Danish butter, Trowbridge, *Queen Alexandra*. Alix in Denmark ('much more than...') Ponsonby, *Recollections*. Alix at Kiel, and with Kaiser Wilhelm I, Trowbridge, *Queen Alexandra*. Victoria on Alix ('If only she understood...') Royal Archives, Windsor Castle. Vicky on Bertie's speech, Victoria, *Letters*. All quotes from Rumbold, British Minister, *Recollections of a Diplomatist*. King George and stolen watch, Griscom, *Diplomatically Speaking*. Cold in palace ('the wind...') Christopher, *Memoirs*. Decor ('ancient Greek...') Nicholas, *My Fifty Years*. Olga's arrival and family home life, Christopher, *Memoirs*. Tatoi ('Tatoi was a refuge...') Nicholas, *My Fifty Years*. Home farm, Christmas, *King George*. Constantinople ('For every Greek...') Nicholas, *My Fifty Years*.

Chapter Four
Sir Frederic Hamilton, *The Vanished World of Yesterday*. Pobedonostsev ('The massive build...') Lowe,

Alexander III of Russia. Radziwill ('Adore her...') *Behind the Veil at the Russian Court.* Poliakoff, *The Empress Marie.* Fredensborg ('evokes all the best years...') Nicholas of Greece, *My Fifty Years.* Languages ('Tower of Babel' and 'This gift...') Christopher of Greece, *Memoirs.* *Øllebrød,* Nicholas, *My Fifty Years.* Boisterousness ('The noise...') Victoria of Germany, *Letters of the Empress Frederick.* Dagmar's hat ('Uncontrollable mirth...') Nicholas, *My Fifty Years.* Dinner ('heavy, not to say...') Ponsonby, *Recollections.* Loo ('very small points...') Nicholas, *My Fifty Years.* Thyra's looks ('most beautiful large...') Trowbridge, *Queen Alexandra.* Thyra's nature ('gentleness...') Nicholas, *My Fifty Years.* Gypsy's prediction, Trowbridge, *Queen Alexandra.* Ernest's looks ('practically...') Christopher, *Memoirs,* and ('poor, dear Ernest...') Pope-Hennessy, *Queen Mary.* Alexandra ('the robber...') Royal Archives, Windsor Castle. Henry Ponsonby, Arthur Ponsonby, *Henry Ponsonby.* Victoria ('a very plain...') Royal Archives, Windsor Castle. (The Author is indebted to Georgina Battiscombe's *Queen Alexandra* for much of the information on Princess Thyra's marriage.)

Chapter Five

Alexander ('His unaccountable...') Lowe, *Alexander III.* Disraeli ('I did something...') and Bertie ('I shall, of course...') Magnus, *Edward VII.* Edward VII ('the triumph...') Lord Hardinge, *Old Diplomacy.* Almedingen, *Alexander II.* Tsar to Dagmar ('Come, my dear...') Poliakoff, *The Empress Marie.* Manifesto ('crowning touch...') Almedingen, *Alexander II*. Alexander III's proclamation, Lowe, *Alexander III*. Garter ceremony, Hamilton, *The Vanished World*.

Chapter Six

Gladstone, Morley, *The Life of W. E. Gladstone*. Victoria ('The King and Queen...') Corti, *The English Empress*. Roma Lister, *Reminiscences*. Algernon West, *Recollections*. Alexandra and Tennyson ('one could...') West, *Recollections*. Tennyson and Dagmar, Tennyson, *Alfred Lord Tennyson*. Gladstone, Morley, *Gladstone*. Sarah Bernhardt ('yes to, France...') Skinner, *Madame Sarah*. Bernhardt and Alexandra ('her beloved...') Woon, *The Real Sarah Bernhardt*. Tsarevich ('having a thorough...') West, *Recollections*. Gladstone ('the unrestrained...') Morley, *Gladstone*. Tutor on Eddy, Magnus, *Edward VII*. Alexandra on Eddy ('*dreadfully* distressed...') and ('dawdly...') Royal Archives, Windsor Castle. King George in Denmark ('When I am there...' and 'The old King's...') Paoli, *My Royal Clients*. Mechanical piano, Christopher, *Memoirs*. King and grandchildren ('not only encouraged...') Nicholas, *My Fifty Years*. German Crown Princess to Victoria, Victoria, *Letters of the Empress Frederick*. Crown Prince Frederick ('rather pedantic...') and Crown Princess Louise ('austere...') Nicholas, *My Fifty Years*. French Minister on Louise, Ponsonby, *Recollections*. Louise ('She is a good soul...') Pope-Hennessy, *Queen Mary*. Tsarevich on Louise, Nicholas II, *Letters of Tsar Nicholas and Empress*

Marie. Olga and Christopher, Christopher, *Memoirs.*
Tsar on train ('through a line...') and marginal com-
ments, Lowe, *Alexander III.* Tsar ('the busiest man...')
Vorres, *The Last Grand Duchess.* Tsar's stupidity, Lowe,
Alexander III. Tsar's will, Poliakoff, *The Empress Marie.*
Olga and dentist, Christopher, *Memoirs.* Tsarevich
and True Cross, Vorres, *The Last Grand Duchess.*
Coronation ('The blaze...') Lowe, *Alexander III*
('The Empress stands...') Ponsonby, *Mary Ponsonby*
('At that moment...') Radziwill, *Behind the Veil.* Tsar
in Denmark ('He loved getting...') Vorres, *The Last
Grand Duchess.* Nicholas, *My Fifty Years.* Christopher,
Memoirs. Olga ('It was freedom...'), and dinner
('splendid sight...') Vorres, *The Last Grand Duchess.*
Tearful farewell, Royal Archives, Windsor Castle.

Chapter Seven
George and Kaiser's speech, Christmas, *King George.*
Conversation-making and cabby at court ball,
Christopher, *Memoirs.* American matron, audiences
with King, informality, Alexandra's hat, toy kingdom,
Evzoni and runaway horse, E. F. Benson, *As We Were.*
Dancing at Tatoi, Nicholas, *My Fifty Years.* Corfu
('which even the want...') Hardinge, *Old Diplomacy.*
Paoli, *My Royal Clients.* George and laundresses,
Christmas, *King George.* George ('I am my own...')
Nicholas, *My Fifty Years.* German Crown Princess
on Constantine, Corti, *The English Empress.* Empress
Frederick, Victoria, *Letters of the Empress Frederick.*
Wedding ('none of the gorgeous...') Nicholas, *My*

Fifty Years. Tsarevich on excessive heat, Nicholas II, *Letters of Tsar Nicholas and Empress Marie.* Reception by people ('There arose from all...') Nicholas, *My Fifty Years.*

Chapter Eight
Private secretary ('the great beauties...') Ponsonby, *Recollections.* Eddy's military career ('simply a waste...') Pope-Hennessy, *Queen Mary.* Alexandra on May ('*right bride...*' and 'and the fact...') Royal Archives, Windsor Castle. Alexandra to parents ('I still see him...') Rigsarkivet, Copenhagen. Prince George's chaff, Pope-Hennessy, *Queen Mary.* Alexandra on George ('Fancy my Georgie boy...') Nicolson, *King George V.* Alexandra on Heidelberg ('that old *sauerkraut...*') Royal Archives, Windsor Castle. Missy ('*Entre nous...*') Pope-Hennessy, *Queen Mary.* Weather in Athens, Pope-Hennessy, *Queen Mary.* Tsarevich on Alexandra, Nicholas II, *Letters of Tsar Nicholas and Empress Marie.*

Chapter Nine
George and Nicholas ('I was immediately...') Lowe, *Alexander III.* Dagmar's endearments, and advice to Nicholas, Nicholas II, *Letters of Tsar Nicholas and Empress Marie.* Tsarevich and Tsar ('You can imagine...') Lowe, *Alexander III.* Tsarevich at Sandringham, Nicholas II, *Letters of Tsar Nicholas and Empress Marie.* Bertie on Tsarevich, Magnus, *Edward VII.* Nicky on Hélène, Nicholas II, *Journal.*

Nicky's looks ('gentle charm…') Marie of Romania, *Story of My Life*. Nicky ('My dream…') Nicholas II, *Journal*. Samson-Himmelstierna on Dagmar, Tisdall, *The Dowager Empress*. Lady Randolph Churchill, *Reminiscences*. Greek relations, Vorres, *The Last Grand Duchess*. Floating ballet, Christopher, *Memoirs*. Dagmar ('To us boys…'), and marriage and death of Grand Duchess Alexandra, Nicholas, *My Fifty Years*. Dagmar on George ('It really is too sad…') Nicholas II, *Letters of Tsar Nicholas and Empress Marie*. Dagmar and court life, and Palace balls, Vorres, *The Last Grand Duchess*. Dagmar ('I danced…') Nicholas II, *Letters of Tsar Nicholas and Empress Marie*. Drummer ('too frightened…' and 'Well, I suppose…') Vorres, *The Last Grand Duchess*.

Chapter Ten

Son of French Minister ('The comings and…') Madol, *Christian IX*. King and sentry, and stranger and three royals, Christopher, *Memoirs*. Marie and offer of throne, Madol, *Christian IX*. France kissing Russia, Lowe, *Alexander III*. Tsar ('most alluring…' and 'Why don't you hurry up…') Madol, *Christian IX*. Crash ('For weeks…') Tisdall, *Dowager Empress*. Nicky's engagement, Nicholas II, *Letters of Tsar Nicholas and Empress Marie*. Alicky ('Be firm and make…') Nicholas II, *Journal*. Tsar's death ('I feel the end…') Radziwill, *Behind the Veil*. Olga ('Everything seemed…') Vorres, *The Last Grand Duchess*, Nicky ('My god…') Nicholas II, *Journal*. Prince of Wales

('Alix is everything...') Magnus, *Edward VII*. Christian comforts Dagmar, Radziwill, *Behind the Veil*. Alicky on Nicky, Buxhoeveden, *Alexandra Feodorovna*.

Chapter Eleven

Charles on slow promotion, Michael, *Haakon*. Nicholas and Maud's engagement, and Maud ('delightfully wild...') Nicholas, *My Fifty Years*. Duchess of Teck on Maud, Pope-Hennessy, *Queen Mary*. Alexandra ('on *no* account...') Royal Archives, Windsor Castle. Dagmar ('Poor Uncle Willie...') Nicholas II, *Letters of Tsar Nicholas and Empress Marie*. Greek enthusiasm, Christmas, *King George*. Dagmar to Nicky ('to *insist*...') Nicholas II, *Letters of Tsar Nicholas and Empress Marie*. Prince of Wales to Salisbury, Arthur, *Queen Alexandra*. Marie Mallet, *Life with Queen Victoria*. Princess of Wales and Olga (Aunt Olga...'), and Grand Duchess ('Her feeling...') Pope-Hennessy, *Queen Mary*. Story about dog and ('My grandmother was just...') Nicholas, *My Fifty Years*. Princess May ('In some ways...') Pope-Hennessy, *Queen Mary*. Grandson ('The return to Bernsdorff...') Nicholas, *My Fifty Years*.

Chapter Twelve

Alexandra ('I know better...') Esher, *Journals and Letters*. Dagmar ('I have no words...') Nicholas II, *Letters of Tsar Nicholas and Empress Marie*. Prince George ('Mamma, as I have always...') and Alexandra ('All my happiness...') Royal Archives, Windsor Castle. Alexandra ('Keep him waiting...') Airlie, *Thatched with Gold.* Princess Victoria ('was just like a...') Vorres, *The Last Grand Duchess.* Dagmar in wheelchair, Christopher, *Memoirs.* Secretary at Legation ('Queen Alexandra descended...') Baring, *The Puppet Show of Memory.* All quotations on Alexandra's chiding of children about visiting Denmark, James Pope-Hennessy, *Queen Mary.* Nicky and reliance on Dagmar, Poliakoff, *The Empress Marie.* Olga ('She was absolutely...') Vorres, *The Last Grand Duchess.* Dagmar's advice on pregnancy, Nicholas II, *Letters of Tsar Nicholas and Empress Marie.* Olga ('I remember the tall...') Vorres, *The Last Grand Duchess.* Vachot ('You will someday...') Massie, *Nicholas and Alexandra.* Nicky ('A great...') Nicholas II, *Journal.*

Chapter Thirteen
All quotations in this chapter are from Maurice Michael, *Haakon, King of Norway.*

Chapter Fourteen
Nicholas ('That is for...') Radziwill, *Behind the Veil.* Olga ('I shared his roof...') Vorres, *The Last Grand Duchess.* Nicholas ('I think no matter...') Nicholas II, *Letters of Tsar Nicholas and Empress Marie.* May ('For a wonder...') Royal Archives, Windsor Castle. Dagmar ('No *patriotism*...') Nicholas II, *Letters of Tsar Nicholas and Empress Marie.* Opening of Duma ('extremely moved and...') Radziwill, *Behind the Veil.* Alexandra ('I fear the Constitution...') Royal Archives, Windsor Castle. Dreary court ('Queen Alexandra...' and

'The Danish suite...') Ponsonby, *Recollections*. Baring *Puppet Show*. Jusserand, *What Me Befell*. Kaiser Wilhelm II ('Just leaving...') Nicholas II, *Letters of Tsar Nicholas and Empress Marie*. Alexandra and Kaiser, Pless, *From My Private Diary*. Tsar on Kaiser's telegram, Nicholas II, *Letters of Tsar Nicholas and Empress Marie*. Christian IX's last day, Madol, *Christian IX*.

Chapter Fifteen

Court ('We had to undergo...') Hardinge, *Old Diplomacy*. Accession. speech, *Illustrated London News*. Frederick and popularity, Ponsonby, *Recollections*. Iceland visit, Stefannsson, *Denmark and Sweden*. Hvidore, Eulalia, *Court Life from Within*. Royal party on Corfu, Pope-Hennessy, *Queen Mary*. Ponsonby at Athens, in carriage with King George, Edward VII's opinion of George, Ponsonby, *Recollections*. Prince George on Crete, Battiscombe, *Queen Alexandra*. Greek visit ('Frankly speaking...') Hardinge, *Old Diplomacy*. Haakon and trams, Ponsonby, *Recollections*. Oslo visit ('A family rather...') Hardinge, *Old Diplomacy*. Gmunden ('were always asking the mother...') Arthur, *Queen Alexandra*, and ('Gmunden is beautiful...') Nicholas, *My Fifty Years*. Guest ('an unbelievable...') and Thyra's necklace, Varè, *Laughing Diplomat*. French Minister on Marie, Jusserand, *What Me Befell*.

Chapter Sixteen

Alexandra ('So my Geòrgie boy...') Royal Archives, Windsor Castle. Alexandra's and Fisher's telegrams,

Fisher Papers. Edward VII and Kaiser ('there was always a feeling...') Ponsonby, *Recollections*. Alexandra ('dragged there...' and 'The Queen was secretly...') Hardinge, *Old Diplomacy*. Nicky to Dagmar ('Thank God the German visit...') Nicholas II, *Letters of Tsar Nicholas and Empress Marie*. Ponsonby, *Recollections*. Dagmar in Italy ('You cannot imagine...') Nicholas II, *Letters of Tsar Nicholas and Empress Marie*. Alexandra ('Willy dear...') Battiscombe, *Queen Alexandra*. Grand Duchess ('may the pernicious...') Royal Archives, Windsor Castle.

Chapter Seventeen

Kaiser on Frederick ('a friend with whom...') *Illustrated London News*. Dagmar ('The daughter of...') Poliakoff, *The Empress Marie*. Olga's marriage ('Own dignity and...') Vorres, *The Last Grand Duchess*. Dagmar on divorce, and Alexis's illness ('The days between...') Nicholas II, *Letters of Tsar Nicholas and Empress Marie*. Telegram ('God has seen...') Viroubova, *Memoirs*. Olga on cure ('Within an hour...') Vorres, *The Last Grand Duchess*. All quotations on Dagmar and intervention with Nicholas, Massie, *Nicholas and Alexandra*. Poliakoff, *Empress Marie*.

Chapter Eighteen

All quotations in this chapter are from Walter Christmas, *King George of Greece*, except Alexandra ('Hawkins...') Battiscombe, *Queen Alexandra*.

Chapter Nineteen

Tsaritsa ('Its much better...') Alexandra, *The Letters of the Tsaritsa to the Tsar.* Olga's marriage ('exceedingly modest...') Alexander, *Once a Grand Duke.* Dagmar ('May God give her...') Nicholas II, *Letters of Tsar Nicholas and Empress Marie.* Olga ('I was shocked...') Vorres, *The Last Grand Duchess.* Nicholas to Alexandra, Nicholas II, *Letters to the Tsaritsa.* Grand Duke Alexander ('We presented...') Alexander, *Once a Grand Duke.* Dagmar ('My thoughts never...') Nicholas II, *Letters of Tsar Nicholas and Empress Marie.* Dagmar's views on revolution, Eulalia, *Memoirs.* Olga ('We still imagined...' and 'The news of...') Vorres, *The Last Grand Duchess.* Sandro ('Nicky must have...') and Dagmar ('My unfortunate Nicky...') and Dagmar at Mogilev, Alexander, *Once a Grand Duke.* Olga on Dagmar, Vorres, *The Last Grand Duchess.*

Chapter Twenty

Alexandra ('clutches') Rigsarkivet, Copenhagen. Alexandra ('We must thrash...') and ('poor, excellent...') Royal Archives, Windsor Castle. George V ('justified in...') Hourmouzius, *No Ordinary Crown.* George V ('I simply cannot...') Battiscombe, *Queen Alexandra.* Alexandra ('I will do my best...') Royal Archives Windsor Castle. Dagmar ('heart-crushing') Battiscombe, *Queen Alexandra.* George V's telegram, Nicolson, *King George V.* Alexandra ('poor dear Alicky...') Royal Archives, Windsor Castle. Queen Mary ('The news...') Pope-Hennessy, *Queen Mary.*

Alexandra ('I can hear *nothing...*') Royal Archives, Windsor Castle. Olga, Vorres, *The Last Grand Duchess.* Dagmar to Bishop, Alexandrov, *The End of the Romanovs.* Dagmar and dog, and ('would dare raise...') Poliakoff, *The Empress Marie.* Dagmar to Nicky, Nicholas II, *Letters of Tsar Nicholas and Empress Marie.* Dagmar and national anthem, Pridham, *Close of a Dynasty.*

Chapter Twenty-one
Unless otherwise indicated, all quotations from Olga are from Ian Vorres, *The Last Grand Duchess.* Alexandra ('I have been too long...') Royal Archives, Windsor Castle. Alexandra ('My dear, dear, man...') Battiscombe, *Queen Alexandra.* Loti, Trowbridge, *Queen Alexandra.* Lawrence, *The Mint.* Dagmar's jewels ('ropes of the most...') Ponsonby, *Recollections.* Queen Mary ('I think she could cover...') Christopher of Greece, *Memoirs.* Ponsonby, *Recollections.*

Epilogue
Queen Mary on Marina, Airlie, *Thatched with Gold.*

BIBLIOGRAPHY

Alexander, Grand Duke of Russia: *Once a Grand Duke*. Cassell, London, 1932.

Alexander, Grand Duke of Russia: *Always a Grand Duke*. Cassell, London, 1933.

Alexandra, Empress of Russia: *Letters of the Tsaritsa to the Tsar, 1914–1916*. Duckworth, London, 1923.

Alexandrov, Victor: *The End of the Romanovs*. Hutchinson, London, 1966.

Airlie, Mabelle, Countess of: *Thatched with Gold*. Hutchinson, London, 1962.

Almedingen, E. M.: *The Empress Alexandra, 1872–1918*. Hutchinson, London, 1961.

Almedingen, E. M.: *The Emperor Alexander II*. The Bodley Head, London, 1962.

Anon (One of His Majesty's Servants): *The Private life of the King*. C. Arthur Pearson, London, 1901.

Anon: *The Royal Family of Greece*. Warwick Bros, and Rutter, Toronto, 1914.

Arthur, Sir George: *Queen Alexandra*. Chapman and Hall, London, 1934.

Baring, Maurice: *The Puppet Show of Memory*. Heinemann, London, 1922.

Battiscombe, Georgina: *Queen Alexandra*. Constable, London, 1969.

Benson, E. F.: *As We Were*. Longmans, London, 1930.

Benson, E. F.: *The Kaiser and His English Relations*. Longmans, London, 1936.

Bröchner, Jessie: *Danish Life in Town and Country*. George Newnes, London, 1903.

Buchanan, Sir George: *My Mission to Russia*. Cassell, London, 1923. Buchanan, Meriel: *Recollections of Imperial Russia*. Hutchinson, London, 1923.

Bulygin, Paul: *The Murder of the Romanovs*. Hutchinson, London, 1935.

Buxhoeveden, Baroness Sophie: *The Life and Tragedy of Alexandra Feodorovna*. Longmans, London, 1928.

Christmas, Walter: *King George of Greece*. Eveleigh Nash, London, 1914.

Christopher, Prince of Greece: *Memoirs*. The Right Book Club, London, 1938.

Churchill, Lady Randolph: *Reminiscences*. Edward Arnold, London, 1908.

Corti, Egon, Count: *The English Empress*. Cassell, London, 1957.

Cust, Sir Lionel: *King Edward VII and his Court: Some Reminiscences*. John Murray, London, 1930.

Disraeli, Benjamin: *The Letters of Disraeli to Lady Bradford and Lady Chesterfield*. (2 vols) Ernest Benn, London, 1929.

Dubourg, Alain-Yves: *Royal Haemophilia*. (Abbottempo, Book 2). Abbott Universal, Amsterdam, 1967.

Esher, Lord: *Journals and Letters*. (Vol. I) Ivor Nicholson and Watson, 1934.

Eulalia, Infanta of Spain: *Court Life from Within*. Cassell, London, 1915.

Eulalia, Infanta of Spain: *Courts and Countries after the War*. Hutchinson, London, 1925.

Eulalia, Infanta of Spain: *Memoirs*. Hutchinson, London, 1936.

Fabritius, Dr Albert: *Genealogy of the Danish Royal Family*. Ministry of Foreign Affairs, Copenhagen, N.D.

Field, W. O.: *More Uncensored Recollections*. Eveleigh Nash, London, 1926.

Fisher, Lord: *Fear God and Dread Nought: Correspondence of Admiral of the Fleet Lord Fisher* (ed. A. J. Marder). Jonathan Cape, 1952–9.

Fülöp-Miller, René: *Rasputin: The Holy Devil*. G. P. Putman's Sons, New York, 1928.

Gilliard, Pierre: *Thirteen Years at the Russian Court*. Hutchinson, London, 1920.

Glyn Jones, W.: *Denmark*. Ernest Benn, London, 1970.

Gore, John: *King George V*. John Murray, London, 1941.

Gould Lee, Arthur S.: *The Royal House of Greece*. Ward Lock, London, 1948.

Grant, N. F. (ed.): *The Kaiser's Letters to the Tsar*. Hodder and Stoughton, London, 1920.

Grey, Hon. Mrs W.: *Journal of a Visit*. Smith, Elder and Co., London, 1869.

Griscom, Lloyd C.: *Diplomatically Speaking.* John Murray, London, 1941.

Hamilton, Lord Frederic: *The Vanished World of Yesterday.* Hodder and Stoughton, London, 1950.

Hardinge, Lord: *Old Diplomacy.* John Murray, London, 1947.

Hibben, Paxton: *Constantine I and the Greek People.* The Century Company, New York, 1920.

Hourmouzius, Stelio: *No Ordinary Crown.* Weidenfeld and Nicolson, London, 1972.

Jullian, Philippe: *Edward and the Edwardians.* Sidgwick and Jackson, London, 1967.

Jusserand, J. J.: *What Me Befall.* Constable, London, 1933.

Kerensky, Alexander: *The Kerensky Memoirs.* Cassell, London, 1965.

Kurenberg, Joachim von: *The Kaiser.* Cassell, London, 1954.

Lawrence, T. E.: *The Mint.* Jonathan Cape, London, 1955.

Lee, Sir Sydney: *King Edward VII.* (2 vols) Macmillan, London, 1927.

Leslie, Seymour: *The Jerome Connection.* John Murray, London, 1964.

Lister, Roma: *Reminiscences.* Hutchinson, London, N.D.

Longford, Elizabeth: *Victoria R.I.* Weidenfeld and Nicolson, London, 1964.

Lowe, Charles: *Alexander III of Russia.* Heinemann, London, 1895.

Ludwig, Emil: *Kaiser Wilhelm II.* Putnam, London, 1926.

Ludwig, Emil: *Bismarck.* George Allen and Unwin, London, 1926.

Lyall, Sir Alfred: *The Life of the Marquis of Dufferin and Ava.* (2 vols) John Murray, London, 1905.

Madol, Hans Roger: *Christian IX.* Collins, London, 1939.

Magnus, Sir Philip: *King Edward the Seventh.* John Murray, London, 1964.

Mallet, Marie: *Life with Queen Victoria.* John Murray, London, 1968.

Marie, Queen of Romania: *The Story of My Life.* (3 vols) Cassell, London, 1934.

Marie, Grand Duchess of Russia: *Things I Remember.* Cassell, London, 1930.

Massie, Robert: *Nicholas and Alexandra.* Gollancz, London, 1968.

Melba, Nellie: *Melodies and Memories.* Thornton Butterworth, London, 1925.

Michael, Maurice: *Haakon, King of Norway.* George Allen and Unwin, London, 1958.

Morley, John: *The Life of William Ewart Gladstone.* (2 vols) Macmillan, London, 1907.

Münz, Sigmund: *King Edward VII at Marienbad.* Hutchinson, London, 1934.

Mussolov, A. A.: *At the Court of the Last Tsar.* Methuen, London, 1935.

Nicholas II, Tsar of Russia: *Journal Intime de Nicolas II* (Trans. A. Pierre). Payot, Paris, 1925.

Nicholas II, Tsar of Russia: *The Letters of the Tsar to the Tsaritsa, 1914–1917*. Bodley Head, London, 1929.

Nicholas II, Tsar of Russia: *The Letters of Tsar Nicholas and Empress Marie* (ed. E. J. Bing). Ivor Nicholson and Watson, London, 1937.

Nicholas, Prince of Greece: *My Fifty Years*. Hutchinson, London, 1926.

Nicolson, Harold: *King George the Fifth*. Constable, London, 1952.

Paget, Walburga: *Scenes and Memories*. Smith, Elder and Co., London, 1912.

Paget, Walburga: *Embassies of Other Days*. (2 vols) Hutchinson, London, 1923.

Paléologue, Maurice: *An Ambassador's Memoirs*. (3 vols) Hutchinson, London, 1923.

Paoli, Xavier: *My Royal Clients*. Hodder and Stoughton, London, N.D.

Pares, Sir Bernard: *The Fall of the Russian Monarchy*. Jonathan Cape, London, 1939.

Pless, Daisy, Princess of: *From My Private Diary*. John Murray, London, 1931.

Poliakoff, Vladimir: *The Empress Marie of Russia and her Times*. Thornton Butterworth, London, 1926.

Ponsonby, Arthur: *Henry Ponsonby*. Macmillan, London, 1943.

Ponsonby, Sir Frederick: *Recollections of Three Reigns*. Eyre and Spottiswoode, London, 1951.

Ponsonby, Mary: *A Memoir, Some Letters and a Journal*. John Murray, London, 1927.

Pope-Hennessy, James: *Queen Mary, 1867–1953.* George Allen and Unwin, London, 1959.

Pridham, Sir Francis: *Close of a Dynasty.* Allan Wingate, London, 1956.

Radziwill, Princess Catherine: *My Recollections.* Isbister, London, 1904.

Radziwill, Princess Catherine (pseud. Count Paul Vassili): *Behind the Veil at the Russian Court.* Cassell, London, 1913.

Radziwill, Princess Catherine: *The Intimate Life of the Last Tsarina.* Cassell, London, 1929.

Rodzianko, M. V.: *The Reign of Rasputin.* A. M. Philpot, London, 1927.

Rumbold, Sir Horace: *Recollections of a Diplomatist.* (2 vols) Edward Arnold, London, 1902.

Skinner, Cornelia Otis: *Madame Sarah.* Michael Joseph, London, 1967.

Sokolov, Nicholas A.: *The Sokolov Investigation.* Souvenir Press, London, 1972.

Stefannsson, Jon: *Denmark and Sweden.* T. Fisher Unwin, London, 1916.

Tennyson, Hallam: *Alfred Lord Tennyson.* Macmillan, London, 1897.

Tisdall, E. E. P.: *The Dowager Empress.* Stanley Paul, London, 1957.

Tooley, Sarah A.: *The Life of Queen Alexandra.* Hodder and Stoughton, London, 1902.

Trowbridge, W. R. H.: *Queen Alexandra.* T. Fisher Unwin, London, 1921.

Varè, Daniele: *Laughing Diplomat.* John Murray, London, 1938.

Vassili, Count Paul: *see* Radziwill, Princess Catherine.

Victoria, German Empress: *Letters of the Empress Frederick* (ed. Sir Frederick Ponsonby). Macmillan, London, 1928.

Victoria, German Empress: *The Empress Frederick writes to Sophie* (ed. A. Gould Lee). Faber and Faber, London, 1955.

Victoria, Queen of Great Britain: *Letters of Queen Victoria.* (9 vols) John Murray, London, 1907–32.

Victoria, Queen of Great Britain: *Dearest Child: Letters between Queen Victoria and the Princess Royal* (ed. Roger Fulford). Evans Bros., London, 1964.

Victoria, Queen of Great Britain: *Dearest Mamma: Letters between Queen Victoria and the Crown Princess of Prussia* (ed. Roger Fulford). Evans Bros., London, 1968.

Victoria, Queen of Great Britain: *Your Dear Letter: Private Correspondence of Queen Victoria and the Crown Princess of Prussia* (ed. Roger Fulford). Evans Bros., London, 1971.

Viroubova, Anna: *Memoirs of the Russian Court.* Macmillan, London, 1923.

Vorres, Ian: *The Last Grand Duchess.* Hutchinson, London, 1964.

West, Sir Algernon: *Recollections, 1832–1886.* (2 vols) Smith, Elder and Co., London, 1899.

Witte, Count Sergius: *Memoirs.* Heinemann, London, 1921.

Wolff, Sir Henry Drummond: *Rambling Recollections.* (2 vols) Macmillan, London, 1908.

Woodham-Smith, Cecil: *Queen Victoria: Her Life and Times.* Hamish Hamilton, London, 1972.

Woon, Basil: *The Real Sarah Bernhardt.* Boni and Liveright, New York, 1924.

Youssoupoff, Prince Felix: *Lost Splendour.* Jonathan Cape, London, 1953.

Newspapers and Periodicals
The Times, Daily Mail, Graphic, Illustrated London News, Annual Register, Dictionary of National Biography, Almanach de Gotha, Royalties of the World.

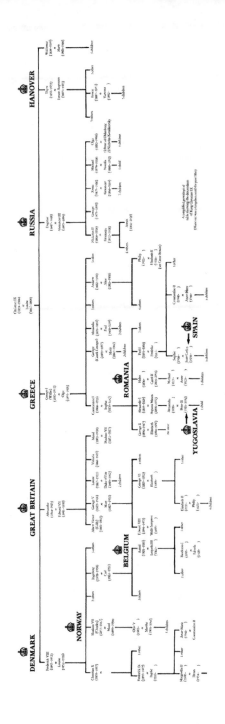

A simplified genealogical table showing the descendants of King Christian IX
(However, this is a bogwhat, until the year bits)